THE INVISIBLE GHETTO

THE INVISIBLE GHETTO

LESBIAN & GAY WRITING FROM SOUTH AFRICA

edited by
matthew krouse
assisted by
kim berman

THE GAY MEN'S PRESS

First published in South Africa by COSAW Publishing (Pty) Ltd
(Congress of South African Writers), P O Box 421007,
Fordsburg 2033, Johannesburg, South Africa.

World copyright © 1993 The Contributors

International edition published 1995 by GMP Publishers Ltd,
P O Box 247, London N6 4BW.

*A CIP catalogue record for this book is available
from the British Library.*

ISBN 0 85449 204 6

Distributed in North America by Inbook,
140 Commerce St, East Haven, CT 06512, USA.

Distributed in Australia by Bulldog Books,
P O Box 155, Broadway, NSW 2007.

Printed and bound in the EU by Nørhaven A/S, Viborg, Denmark.

Acknowledgements

'Summer Holiday' by Johannes Meintjes first published in *New South African Writing*, Purnell & Sons, 1966. 'Discussions in the Canaan Women's Group' by Wendy Annecke first published in *Agenda* Number 11, 1991. 'The Creation' by Marcellus J. Muthien first published in *Take Any Train* edited by Peter Daniels, The Oscars Press, 1990. 'Bring Out Your Dead' by Stephen Gray first published in *Season of Violence*, Dangaroo Press, 1992. 'The Historical Moment' by Stephen Gray first published in *Apollo Café and Other Poems*, David Philip, 1989. 'Richard Rive: A Memoir' by Stephen Gray first published in *Staffrider* Volume 9 Number 1, Ravan Press, 1990. 'Riva' by Richard Rive first published in *Staffrider* Volume 2 Number 1, Ravan Press, 1979. 'Bye Bye, Forget Me Not' by Welma Odendaal first published in *Lip* edited by Isabel Hofmeyr and Susan Rosenberg, Ravan Press, 1983. 'Confessions of a Failed Lesbian Separatist' by Dee Radcliffe first published in *Exit* Number 51, 1991. 'On Despondency Square' by Hennie Aucamp translated by Ian Ferguson first published in *House Visits*, Tafelberg, 1983.

Contents

INTRODUCTION

Matthew Krouse	About the Contents	xi
Kim Berman	Lesbians in South Africa: Challenging the Invisibility	xvii

ACCOUNTS, BIOGRAPHIES, EPISODES

Mamaki	Two Episodes:	
	I. Corner of Insults	1
	II. The Gathering	2
Simon Nkoli	This Strange Feeling	19
Wendy Annecke	Discussions in the Canaan Women's Group	36
Stephen Gray	Richard Rive: A Memoir	79
Two Sex-Workers:		
I. Joaquim	In a Dark Corner	106
II. Bester	Life is Hard	112
Tanya Chan Sam	Coloured School Days	155
Dee Radcliffe	Confessions of a Failed Lesbian Separatist	192

INTERVIEWS

Love on the Mines:		44
Vivienne Ndatshe	Two Miners:	
	I. 'Daniel'	45
	II. 'Themba'	49
Mpande wa Sibuyi	Tinkoncana Etimayinini: 'The Wives of the Mines' An Interview with 'Philemon'	52

POETRY

Graeme Reid	We Are Too Young To Contemplate Our Death	17
	Y'Know?	18
Rosalee Telela	Unbroken Silence	35
Marcellus J. Muthien	The Creation	40
	Brother	42
Stephen Gray	Bring Out Your Dead	76
	The Historical Moment	77
Gerry Davidson	Knife	105
	Blood	105
David Lan	Above the Bridge	141
	The Siege	142
Lucas Malan	Welcoming	175
	Veterans	176
Johann de Lange	Soldier	177
	Two Sailors Pissing	178
	Imago	179
	Tongue-Fuck	180
Shona Elder	Four Poems	181
Tanya Chan Sam	Tropical Juice	183
Joan Hambidge	Octet	196
	Departure	197
Ernst van Heerden	Rain	198
	Dance of Death	199

SHORT STORIES

Jerome Morrison	Tomorrow	4
Adrian van den Berg	Wild Trade	9
Johannes Meintjes	Summer Holiday	27
Mikki van Zyl	Pathway to the Moon	31
Stephen Gray	The Building-Site	65
Richard Rive	Riva	95
Alan Reynolds	Our Rent	116
Jay Pather	Red Wine	120
Matthew Krouse	The Barracks Are Crying	123
Koos Prinsloo	'Border Story'	134
Brent Meersman	A Fear Comes to the Door	143
Karen Williams	They Came at Dawn	151
Shaun de Waal	Stalwart	164
Welma Odendaal	Bye Bye, Forget Me Not	184
Hennie Aucamp	On Despondency Square	200

GLOSSARY 205

NOTES ON CONTRIBUTORS 209

The 'Cape Carnival', a New Year tradition dating back to the reign of Queen Victoria, has often sported parading drags. This portrait from the popular *Drum* magazine of the 1950s carried the caption: '...they even brought out that marvellous *moffee*, Denise Darcelle, to trip the light fantastic too. Flashing a smile she says, "Just call me Madam." '

Photograph by Barney Desai

Introduction

About the Contents

This book is the first of its kind to have emerged from South Africa. Recent cultural advances have encouraged its coming out.

The major advance has been the emergence over the past decade of organized groups of lesbians and gays in South African life, a process which has made this long-standing invisible community more apparent. These groups have encouraged cultural exploration through the production of newsletters, plays and literary readings, and by organizing small film festivals and so forth. In this new climate a hitherto forbidden area of our lives is being opened out, and this book has been able to grow.

At the same time progressive organizations have committed themselves to countering gender-divisions. The Congress of South African Writers, the originator of this book, is one such organization. It forms part of the network of cultural and educational groups who regard the development of human self-realization as a crucial means of overcoming the imbalances created by apartheid.

It was under the auspices of the Congress of South African Writers that the editors collected new writing, as well as existing texts. Our task has been to constitute a book containing a broad range of themes and genres, descriptive of contemporary South African lesbian and gay life, viewed from as many perspectives as possible.

These works deal with virtually all of the themes discussed in the 'ghetto': youth, urban life and the effects on people of migrating to the city, militarism, South African politics in relation to lesbian and gay politics, love and the erotic, ageing and death. These were the dominant themes that manifested themselves in the course of our reading. And it is these themes that have become the running order of the writing anthologized here.

This book comprises accounts, biographies and episodes, interviews, poetry and short stories. There are two categories of material — work produced by writers in the traditional way, and oral testimony appearing in the form of interviews and accounts.

The non-fiction and documentation have been taken from existing published and unpublished material, and have also been gathered through the process of interviewing a small sample of people who have interesting stories to tell. 'Two Episodes' by Mamaki is the combination of an interview with this township youth and an extract from a true account written by her. 'This Strange Feeling' and 'Coloured School Days' are edited transcripts of lengthy interviews with the activists Simon Nkoli and Tanya Chan Sam. Further interviews were conducted with sex-workers in Johannesburg, and the two that were chosen show street-life from both sides of the apartheid divide.

Research also brought to light existent interviews with veteran Pondo mineworkers conducted by Vivienne Ndatshe in 1982, and with a migrant Mozambican mineworker conducted by Mpande wa Sibuyi in 1987. These interviews describe the system of love found on the South African mines where, over the last fifty years, single-sex hostels have given rise to a widely-practised homosexual subculture. The two studies for which the interviews were conducted deserve special mention. 'Migrancy and Male Sexuality on the South African Gold Mines' by T. Dunbar Moodie (with Vivienne Ndatshe and Mpande wa Sibuyi) was first published in the *Journal of Southern African Studies* (1988); and appeared again in the comprehensive Penguin collection of lesbian and gay histories, *Hidden from History* (1989). 'Symbols and Sexuality: Culture and Identity on the Early Witwatersrand Gold Mines' by Patrick Harries was published in the journal *Gender and History* (1990).

The interviews describe the ravages of the South African labour system. Yet, according to Patrick Harries the love manifested in this harsh context 'reflected a forceful rejection of employers' demands that miners invest their libidinal energies in their work and that they value the virtues of sexual restraint. The homosexual relationship contradicted the imposed morality of industrialism and established an alternative propriety. These gender relationships provided workers with their own sense of hierarchy and status and with their own indices of prestige, power and pride. *Bukhontxana* gave men a sense of security, upward mobility and self-worth in the constrained world of the colonist.'[1]

Other essays that have been published previously are 'Discussions in the Canaan Women's Group' by Wendy Annecke, a version of which first appeared in the local journal on women's issues, *Agenda* (1991) and Dee Radcliffe's 'Confessions of a Failed Lesbian Separatist' which first appeared in South Africa's oldest commercially-based gay newspaper, *Exit* (1991). These essays explore ideas about the integration of lesbians and gays into the broader community.

INTRODUCTION

The poetry selected presents the work of twelve poets. No attempt has been made to represent a comprehensive history of lesbian and gay poetry; rather, works were chosen that illuminate the themes mentioned before.

The common thread that binds the poems is that they deal with sexuality. Whether or not this brands them all 'love poems' is open to question. In many instances love is used as a point of entry into other subjects.

Poems that speak of a country undergoing painful political change are frequent. 'Y'Know' by Graeme Reid concerns the emotional fluctuations that occur when we experience love in the throes of war. Similarly, 'The Historical Moment' from *Apollo Café* (1989) by Stephen Gray has the poet abandoning love and living in 'a moment of history' with 'news only of massacres'. Graeme Reid's 'We Are Too Young To Contemplate Our Death' and Stephen Gray's 'Bring Out Your Dead' from *Season of Violence* (1992) both deal with the politics of Aids in South Africa. While Reid compares the blood spilt in war with the pus spilt in illness, Gray observes that, 'An epidemic virus makes us kin/as nothing more humane has done'.

Staying with the political, Gerry Davidson's new poems 'Knife' and 'Blood' focus on the different life experiences of white and black women in the cities.

African forms of expression have been incorporated into lesbian poetry. Take these stanzas of the poem 'Unbroken Silence' by Rosalee Telela:

> Africa goddess of all
> Yours is a soul
> that has been smashed
> by the chains
> of male religion
>
> Names given to you
> labels of intolerance
> bitch, witch;
> but you were
> mother of revolutionaries
> sister to all
> Lesbian!

Here the traditional African oral idiom is used, but given a lesbian context. The poem creates a form that is familiar to African women in protesting their designated roles.

White male writers, on the other hand, have tended to use poetry to show their ambivalence towards militarism and all-male environments. This is one way of arbitrating between the erotic image of the soldier and what is known about the South African Defence Force's role as oppressor. This is evident in the new poems 'The Siege' and 'Above the Bridge' by David Lan, as well as 'Soldier' by Johann de Lange from *Nagsweet* (1990).

Some of the best-known Afrikaans poets are also included in this selection. The translation of Afrikaans poetry provides English readers with a brief overview of developments in lesbian and gay themes, and shows that within the dominant body of Afrikaans literature there have been writers who, to varying degrees, have been outspoken. Over the years lesbian and gay themes in Afrikaans poetry have evolved from mere suggestions of love to explicit portrayals of the erotic.

Ernst van Heerden, whose career began in the late 1940s, is a noted critic, travel writer, autobiographer and poet. The two poems of his selected here are 'Dance of Death' from *Anderkant besit* (1966) and 'Rain' from *Amulet teen die vuur* (1987).

Prominent Afrikaans writers who have emerged in the previous decade belong to the movement now known as the 'Tagtigers' ('Writers of the Eighties'). Concerning the works of this period, the poet Joan Hambidge has said:

> The poetry is highly intellectual and technical. It deconstructs a social and political order. ...Gay literature is far more open and daring.[2]

This new openness takes writers to the cutting edge of complex emotional conflicts. In Lucas Malan's 'Welcoming' from *Tydspoor* (1985) and 'Veterans' from *Edenboom* (1987) questions of survival occur in the context of social alienation. Similarly, Joan Hambidge's poems 'Departure' from *Kriptonemie* (1989) and 'Octet' from *Donker labirint* (1989) deal with estrangement in the context of gender relations.

In contrast, the affirmation of the erotic adds a political dimension to personal expression. These qualities are evident in the four poems of Johann de Lange taken from *Nagsweet*. De Lange's poetry is void of the gentle metaphors that have provided a safety barrier between the gay poet and the straight audience. 'The Creation' by Marcellus J. Muthien from the recent British anthology *Take Any Train* (1990), as well as the hitherto unpublished 'Four Poems' by Shona Elder and 'Tropical Juice' by Tanya Chan Sam, discard shames and guilts in favour of a new language of affirmation. Here the reader, and not the poet, is the outsider. Positive portrayals of the love act turn out to be inoffensive and contest the held belief that the erotic belongs under the censor's knife.

The short stories form the main body of the book and, as a collection, deal with all the pertinent themes.

INTRODUCTION

The previously unpublished stories 'Wild Trade' by Adrian van den Berg and 'Pathway to the Moon' by Mikki van Zyl focus on the difficult paths chosen in youth. In these stories, set in the city and in the rural lands respectively, the common point of reference is the effect of a growing lesbian and gay morality upon traditional adult society.

'Summer Holiday', by the late Johannes Meintjes, shows the alienation experienced by an adult when he meets his childhood fancy now 'pot-bellied and bald, a father of five children'. 'Summer Holiday' was first published in the P.E.N. anthology, *New South African Writing* (1966).

The inclusion of Meintjes's work is significant. In 1990, the Afrikaans writer Hennie Aucamp edited an anthology titled *Wisselstroom*, subtitled (in English translation) *Homo-eroticism in the Afrikaans Short Story*. In his introduction to *Wisselstroom*, Aucamp refers to Meintjes's early collection of short stories, *Kamerade* (1947) as being a true starting point of the gay tradition in Afrikaans story-telling. He suggests that the Second World War might have contributed towards the erosion of sexual taboos. This era saw the rise of writers like Genet and Isherwood, and this climate must have influenced some Afrikaans writing. But Aucamp also points out that the early works of Meintjes, like those of the poet I. D. du Plessis, remain isolated in their time. It is fitting that these early works begin to find themselves in good company at last in volumes like this.

An important contemporary development in South African writing is the *grensverhaal* or 'border story'. The term has become synonymous with writing about the conscription of white male youths into the South African Defence Force. Koos Prinsloo's 'Border Story' is one of the best known of this genre, and is taken from his book *Die hemel help ons* (1987). It also appeared in the anthology of anti-war stories *Forces Favourites* (1987).

Two new stories that deal with military themes are Matthew Krouse's 'The Barracks Are Crying' and Brent Meersman's 'A Fear Comes to the Door'. In general, the stories of the war deal with the barracks, military prisons, sanatoriums and queer platoons, where gay men experience ostracism and isolation. The content of the military theme adds a new voice to the existing outcry against conscription and ultimately places these writers in solidarity with those whom they are conscripted to oppress.

Other new short stories are 'They Came at Dawn' by Karen Williams and 'Tomorrow' by Jerome Morrison. These stories, along with Stephen Gray's 'The Building-Site', which was first published in the British journal of new writing *Passport* (1991) and then in the British anthology *More Like Minds* (1991), show the development of a new consciousness. Set in the urban context, they take into account the country's racism, its politics of oppression and problems of sexual otherness. They show the difficulties encountered when people gesture towards a world, beyond apartheid, in which all may interact freely.

This broadened awareness is reflected too in the stories 'Our Rent' by Alan Reynolds and 'Red Wine' by Jay Pather. 'Our Rent' describes the transaction between a white rent and his potential client, with the author concluding that both are equal victims. 'Red Wine', on the other hand, describes a night in the life of a black man who is taken for a prostitute in a night-club. The white man soliciting him seems unable to break with the harmful stereotypes that are often projected onto black men.

The inclusion of work by the late Richard Rive is controversial, since nowhere in his published work does he mention his own sexuality. His story 'Riva', first published in the arts magazine *Staffrider* (1979), introduces the very camp Dame Riva Lipschitz, whose emotions get the better of her when she meets a young black man. And when she tries to seduce him, she fails. Or does he? The story is a masterpiece of ambiguity and understatement.

Stephen Gray's 'Richard Rive: A Memoir', which first appeared in *Staffrider* (1990), depicts the social world of some of South Africa's literary greats, a world in which Rive occupied a prominent place. But even fame and success, with all its satisfactions, seems to have placed him in a situation where, because of scrutiny, he could express his Blackness in his writing more openly than his sexuality. About Richard Rive's death, Stephen Gray concludes:

> Whether Richard's terrible end is reducible to yet another instance of the attrition of South Africa's constitutional racism, or was merely the verdict of poverty delivered by two aggrieved rent-boys, is uncertain. But the former interpretation is likely to enter the mythology. Like so many others in South Africa, Richard was killed because he wished his spirit out of bondage.

Shaun de Waal's award-winning 'Stalwart' extends the exploration of South African politics in relation to sexual politics. Here we meet the veteran communist Russell Blair, recently returned from exile, a misplaced old man who, in his own words, 'failed in love'.

In moving thematically from youth to old age, it can be observed that the problems encountered in youth are not always resolved in maturity. The story 'Bye Bye, Forget Me Not' by Welma Odendaal was first published in the women's anthology, *Lip* (1983). It emphasizes the cyclical nature of experience — how the innocent games played in youth become less innocent as time wears on.

Lastly, Hennie Aucamp's story 'On Despondency Square', first published in Afrikaans in *Volmink* (1981) and later in translation in *House Visits* (1983), draws attention to the problems of social integration that some single men find in old age. Aucamp's story is about an old man in Athens, 'discarded by life', who spends much of his time in pursuit of meaningful social contact.

It has been important for this selection to include sympathetic expressions of what it means to be 'old and gay'.

For their valuable assistance in compiling this book, thanks are due to: Stephen Gray for his guidance, Tanya Chan Sam with whom we discussed criteria for selection, Khethiwe Marais who assisted with the Tsonga translation, Kobus Opperman for his knowledge of the works of Johannes Meintjes, photographers Juhan Kuus, Vanessa Wilson and Sharifa, and Ivan Vladislavić who did the copy-edit.

In conclusion, we hope that *The Invisible Ghetto* will be seen to embody the wish that all South Africans, including lesbians and gays, will soon be afforded the right to live with dignity. Surely this can only be achieved by ensuring that we all enjoy equal constitutional rights, and that the society we live in is respectful of what is ours.

Matthew Krouse

Lesbians in South Africa: Challenging the Invisibility

The lesbian writing in *The Invisible Ghetto* addresses questions of marginalization that exist within the confines of underexposure, censorship and patriarchal control. The lack of identifiable lesbian iconography has brought about a precarious set of circumstances causing lesbians to be marginalized within the broader definition of marginalized sexuality. And very often it is lesbians who have maintained our own isolation.

In our society white gay male culture has often been marketed and encouraged, and has dominated the lesbian and gay community.

Activism has, however, begun to replace apathy as an antidote to chauvinism and homophobia. The process is long and arduous, but, as the following essay reveals, the abundance of lesbian and gay organizations indicates a new openness and a willingness to deal with the real gender issues.

Kim Berman

Photograph by Vanessa Wilson

In 1990 hundreds of lesbians and gays of all colours marched through the streets of Johannesburg. It was the first time an event of this kind had taken place in Africa. From there campaigns by lesbian and gay activists were launched to include our liberational issues in a draft Bill of Rights that could form part of the new constitution of a non-racial and democratic South Africa.

The march was the first step towards expressing our existence, and the publication of creative writing is a further step towards integrating and sharing our lives with the communities in which we live.

The existing network of formal and informal lesbian groups supports a vibrant subculture pocketed around the country. Yet the common perception is that no lesbian groups exist in the townships or among the black community, as do male groups. While a few urban women do attend gay shebeens and parties, most lesbians remain invisible in the townships. There are sports clubs such as the Soweto Women's Soccer Club — popularly called the 'Gloria Team' — with a predominantly lesbian membership. But, in the words of a team-member, 'it is just so difficult to expose yourself that even there it is not always safe to come out to women you suspect are also gay'.

Another woman, when asked what it is like to be lesbian in Umtata in the Transkei, says, 'It is so hard to have no safe places to meet and I know very few black lesbians. That's why I came to Johannesburg to join the Women's Forum here.'

Outside of the cities, women *have* created clandestine enclaves. A skeletal survey conducted among lesbian activists in various parts of the country indicates that lesbians and gays are, to some degree, organized almost everywhere. This has happened fragmentedly, with instances of visibility. (While most visible flames burn out quickly, they often light the way for more groups to follow.) Today, most notably, the women of GLOW (Gays and Lesbians of the Witwatersrand) have formed a non-racial lesbian forum. The GLOW lesbian forum was started in 1990, and by 1992 black women made up about seventy percent of its membership. A Johannesburg-based lesbian magazine called *Quarterly* was started in late 1992 for national distribution.

Durban's lesbian community has formed Sunday's Women, which has supported discussion groups as well as the publication of a newsletter. Among the groups started in this region, some more successful than others, are GAIN (Gay Association of Inland Natal), as well as a group of senior citizens called A Company of Friends which hopes to begin a retirement village and a lesbian and gay holiday resort.

The Orange Free State is one of the most conservative and racially divided provinces in South Africa. Here there is a small organization called GOGS (Gays of the Goldfields) operating from the town of Welkom. It is primarily a white gay men's social group but women do attend their events. A woman who grew up in Bloemfontein recalls the recent formation there of a small women's group called OBS (Old Bags Society). According to her there are many underground groups in the Orange Free State.

In Cape Town the most visible and active group is called OLGA (Organization for Lesbian and Gay Activists). OLGA produces a newsletter, and has also been a prime mover in the active lobbying for the gay and lesbian clause in the ANC's proposed Bill of Rights. Another Cape Town group called ABIGALE (Association of Bisexuals, Gays and Lesbians) was formed in 1992 to support township citizens in the Cape Province. Its membership is made up primarily of men. ABIGALE is involved in social networking and in the education of people around Aids issues.

Many smaller groups function in the Cape region. An active Women's Centre existed in 1991, and, at the same time, a group called Lilacs was formed for the gathering of lesbian stories.

Women's reading and discussion groups have also found popularity among the lesbians living in the city centres. The group Wildfire in Cape Town is not exclusively a lesbian forum but it does take up lesbian issues such as gender rights and constitutional representation. They have also commissioned projects concerned with the collation of lesbian stories, and have begun producing a video about 'body politics'. Often, though, such initiatives suffer from lack of funds, the need for wider representation and more cohesive networking.

A social lesbian-only venture that appears to be successful in the Cape Town area is the Gateway Club. It tends to attract white suburban women whose identities are protected by closed elitism. Popularly called Brenda's Bash, it has become a gathering held in a hall once a month. When asked why she thought there were no sustainable women's venues in Cape Town, the organizer of Brenda's Bash reiterated the fear most women have of being 'out'.

Exclusive clubs like Brenda's Bash also exist in Johannesburg where the group PAWS holds parties on a monthly basis, tucked away discreetly on a remote farm. These parties tend to be predominantly white and male.

Many other groups exist in the country. The existence of predominantly white groups, coupled with the lack of facilities in black communities, indicates that we still have a long way to go in networking and in organizing people towards reconciliation in a post-apartheid South Africa.

Apartheid, and the privileges of whites in South Africa, have given disproportionate exposure to the presence of the white gay and lesbian community. This has contributed to the belief held by many black South Africans that homosexuality is an un-African, white, Western phenomenon. At the same time, the scarcity of documentation is not evidence that same-sex relationships do not exist in traditional African cultures. In compiling a lesbian history of South Africa this is an area that requires much exposure.

There are examples of African matriarchal societies in which same-sex relationships do occur. A notable exception to the lack of documentation is found in the study by Judith Gay called ' "Mummies and Babies" and Friends and Lovers in Lesotho', first published in the journal *Cambridge Anthropology* (1979), and then in the book edited by Evelyn Blackwood called *Anthropology and Homosexual Behaviour* (1986). This study examines a form of institutionalized friendship among adolescent girls and young women in Lesotho. Young girls develop close relationships they call 'Mummy-baby' with slightly older girls in which sexual intimacy is known to play an important role. These relationships provide emotional support prior to marriage, but they also provide a network of support for married and unmarried women in new towns or schools, either replacing or accompanying heterosexual bonds. In her essay Judith Gay suggests that, for these women of Lesotho, certain roles in traditional matriarchal society have provided a context in which same-sex relationships take place. Gay writes, 'wherever initiation is practised, small girls spend an intense period of time in the company of agemates and are prepared for adult sexual lives by female teachers who are not their own mothers'.[3]

'Mummy-baby' relationships are, however, shrouded in a certain degree of secrecy. As Gay has noted, she only became aware of such intimate relationships after a year of living in the Lesotho village where she conducted her fieldwork. She had never heard anybody mention them — 'But my oversight can be attributed to the privacy that is an essential aspect of these relations, and points out the women's fear of condemnation by an outsider.'[4]

Taking into account women's fears, it is not surprising that lesbian writing forms such a small part of cultural production. Our writing remains hidden, often disguised in brown paper bags at the bottom of cupboards. One needs to keep questioning whether this is born out of inertia, self-censorship, the taboos on women's creativity, or a male-dominated mainstream. The danger, always, is that women's contributions are patronized, problematized or moulded by ideological institutions.

These were some of the problems we encountered in compiling this book.

Because of these complexities this book is loaded with significance. *The Invisible Ghetto* introduces the idea, in literature, that there can be positive lesbian role models for African women. Much of the feminist debate is taken up with the need to separate from the main body of Western literature and to resist the assimilation of lesbian writing into a canonical tradition that has inhibited those who have been otherized. In our racist and homophobic society it is essential that we begin to confront and decipher difference. *The Invisible Ghetto* is our belated beginning.

Kim Berman

Notes

1. Harries, P. (1990) 'Symbols and Sexuality: Culture and Identity on the Early Witwatersrand Gold Mines' in *Gender and History*, Volume 2 Number 3, Oxford: Blackwell, p.333.
2. Brown, D. & Van Dyk, B. (1991) *Exchanges*, Pietermaritzburg: University of Natal Press, p.35.
3. Gay, J., ' "Mummies and Babies" and Friends and Lovers in Lesotho' in Blackwood, E. (Ed.) (1986) *Anthropology and Homosexual Behaviour*, New York, London: The Haworth Press, p.101.
4. Ibid.

Mamaki

Two Episodes

I. Corner of Insults

Being a girl in Soweto you play safe, find safe streets to use, and I had mine just like most girls. On my way to school and from school I turned a corner where most gangs hanged out, but for me it was still safe 'cause I knew some of the guys and it was near my place.

But a time came when it was the most dangerous corner for me to turn and that was after one of the guys proposed to me, and after a long argument I told him I was gay. I knew I shouldn't have said it, but the whole thing was getting scary. The following day my lover and myself turned that corner just to hear our names and immediately they laid eyes on us it sounded as if a cassette of insults was being played. Some were promising to rape us and others were promising to beat us up. We knew the guys too well and we knew they weren't making empty threats. We had to find some protection, but the question was from where? We had homophobic parents and we knew nobody who felt the way we do. We ran home and started praying that the following day mustn't come, but it came, and as we passed that corner the same things happened.

It was not very long afterwards that I was on my way home from school and I saw six boys I knew holding sticks. And somehow I knew they were coming for both of us. But I was alone, my lover was still at school playing chess. They came and made a ring around me and started using the sticks they were holding, and they were swearing. I didn't cry for help 'cause I knew that nobody was there for a 'sinner' and an 'Aids-bringer', as we were called. I didn't even try to fight or run. I just stood in the circle with tears running down from my eyes.

After they were through with their motion I picked up my bag and ran back to school. I had to tell her what had happened. I couldn't let it happen to her too. I knew they would wait for her also, and I was scared that maybe they'd do more.

As I was running back to school I heard some of the spectators saying how I deserved it.

I waited for her at the gate. I was trembling, scared the whole thing was going too far, and we had no way of stopping it. She ran as she saw me standing there and held me close trying to comfort me. I didn't have to tell her, she knew. We stood at the school gate holding onto each other, not knowing what to do.

We decided to go home.

As we were about to turn, at the corner of insults, they greeted us. And my lover did the most surprising thing. She told them that if they were real men, then they would fight us.

One of the guys came over. I tried pulling her hand, and running, because I didn't want her to feel the pain. I knew she felt it from everyday insults, and from when I was beaten, but she had her mind made up and was going to fight.

Everybody watched as she broke the guy. And as things got bad some of the guys came to help their friend and we ran.

A few days later I arrived home from school to find my mother holding my diary.

She told me that she didn't want evil people in her house. She instructed me to stop loving or to go. I stood there and gave up hope.

I went to my bedroom and started to pack.

II. The Gathering

My parents were wild. I never had their love, because they fought, and I was always being beaten up and sweared at. Every Friday night they'd go out in Soweto, to a gathering where they'd drink, and then it would happen.

So my grandparents took me when I was little. They were very ancient. Because I am a woman, I started doing household work from the age of seven. My older sister, Prudence, used to wash for the whole family. She started when she was nine. We were brought up that way. Prudence said she actually found it to be the right way. Our parents prepared us for the future — to be a woman and a housewife.

I was treated like a woman at home. But usually, when I went out to play, I was always wild, beating up other kids and being a guy. I used to enjoy hanging around with guys 'cause they never cared, they took you for what you were.

In this way, I grew up feeling like a man. But it was just a joke. We did play with other ladies as well. And when we played, if we were short of guys, I'd be the father. I had my dreams while playing, and I started kissing women.

Now this gathering, which my parents used to go to, was something like a stokvel. Every Friday. And it had gay people in it. In fact, it was dominated by gay people, the gathering. They would pool their money and go to a bottle store to buy liquor, and then they'd go to somebody's house to drink. Every week I would see these men, when it was my parents' stokvel. They wore make-up and walked like ladies. And I used to enjoy their company. I started asking questions, 'But what's wrong with these guys?'

And there was another guy, he wasn't gay, he was straight. He was a homophobic guy, and he told me, 'Let me tell you a secret — your mom doesn't want you to know of this — but gays have two genitals, and that's why they act like this.'

He meant that gays have bisexual organs, that they are ladies and guys at the same time. At first I thought I was one of them. But afterwards I thought, 'I can't be gay because I have to have two things, and I don't have two things.'

My best friend was called Notando, and I had to look after her one weekend. She was going to be left alone at her place because her brothers, who were her guardians, had to travel to Sun City, where they would sell African pots and curios.

We were left alone in the house, and we decided, 'How about a blue movie, guys?'

We sat there, in Notando's lounge, watching a blue movie. And ultimately we ended up doing what was being done on the television.

The next day we waked up somehow embarrassed, until she mentioned it, 'Mamaki, but are you aware that we are the same as those guys at the stokvel?

'We are gay!'

Jerome Morrison

Tomorrow

Dion's mother, Mama May, came out of her bedroom, her face youthful and revived. She gave Dion a warm smile and he responded awkwardly, as her boyfriend, Tyrone, also made his way out of the room. May seemed like a lioness that had just been fed. Tyrone too seemed light-hearted and drained.

A little earlier that morning the door to Mama's bedroom had been slightly ajar, and Dion had tiptoed past, full of excitement and confusion. The boy's dark eyes rested comprehensively on the two bodies moving as one, with absolute connivance and rhythm, until their breath became heavier, their movements wilder.

Dion had felt left out, yet strangely exhilarated and satisfied.

'Don't forget to buy gas when you come from school this afternoon, Dion,' said May, her voice calm and controlled.

But all Dion could hear was the sound of Tyrone's piss falling hard down the pot.

'Captain Space-cadet...are you there?' asked May mockingly, breaking through her son's dark thoughts.

'I heard what you said, Mama.'

May left for work an hour later. Her flat belly and curvy thighs were draped in one of the many designer garments she had sewn herself. A whirl of black curls was splashed around her tiny shoulders. Her olive skin had been slightly darkened by the sun that was now awakening on the vast Cape Flats. She was respected and admired, despite her boyfriend's habits, and this overpowered common envy and silenced the lizard-tongues of many a woman from Bonteheuwel and beyond. That was May. She gave herself a hard, critical look in the rear-view mirror of her Fiat, and left for Derma Fashions in Woodstock.

Being alone in the house with Tyrone always made Dion want to bunk school. But he went, and sat in class at Bonteheuwel High School that morning with the scene between May and Tyrone constantly in his mind. It was like a movie being played over and over, yet each time it had a strange and different ending.

It so happened that Mosheen, his bosom friend (they had grown up together in old Jakkalsvlei Avenue, in an area infested with gangsters), was having a fiery discussion this morning with Sedick and Graham. He was determined to convince his class-mates that arse-fucking is prime time in jail. 'So many *ouens* I know fucked arse, or were fucked in there,' Mosheen said. He was street-wise, very skollie-orientated, and very against the rigidity of the social system. His brothers were old '*pandiete*'. Dion wondered about Tyrone, who came back from jail looking rusty, earthy, very brown and wholesome. With a slight sense of guilt, he contemplated the persistent possibility of Tyrone's hard male flesh against his own.

After school, Dion rushed home to their sub-economic house in Seventh Avenue, where he found the amber-eyed, wide-shouldered Tyrone in the yard seeing to his pigeons. Tyrone held a bottleneck stuffed with 'herbs' in his one hand, while he fed the birds with the other. These racing pigeons had been tended by Dion and May, year after year, while Tyrone did his time at Victor Verster Prison, or the 'Holiday Inn' as he sometimes called it mockingly.

Stray bricks and used matchsticks were scattered all over the raw Cape Flats sand of the yard. These bricks and matchsticks were the signs of dagga-smokers...this was their haunt. Yet the yard was fairly clean, and fully enclosed in corrugated iron. The only way in was through the back door of the house. This was Tyrone's domain, where he played it safe from the *lastige boere* and the neighbours — fanatically converted Christians who seemed to have lost the true meaning of daily life in all its forms. Their rigid way of life urged Tyrone to defy them, as he took another pull of his bottleneck and bellowed the light-grey smoke high until it disappeared into the fine coastal air.

'So you'll be seventeen tomorrow, hah?' greeted Tyrone with intense eyes fixed on Dion. 'What do you want for your birthday?'

The boy broke out in hopeless, nervous laughter, and a strange light was brought to his eyes at the thought of what he really wanted. This he transformed into something more immediate. 'Could I have...a puff of your smoke?'

'Sure,' said Tyrone, caught slightly off guard, and feeling sheepish just for a moment. It was the first time he was giving in to the boy's temptation. For Dion it spelled a small victory.

Dion took the neck, their flesh met briefly, causing his heart to beat vigorously and he prayed that Tyrone wouldn't be able to hear it. He sat down on two bricks that already posed as a seat, put his mouth to the bottleneck and slowly inhaled the smoke, letting it emerge swiftly through his nostrils. Once he had smoked a highly secretive pipe with Mosheen, and it was glorious...but this!

He passed the neck back to Tyrone. Once again their hands met, but this time for a fraction longer, until Tyrone's coarse, hairy hand brushed over and away — into his pocket.

Dion was familiar with this kind of torture. 'I'll change and go and get the gas,' he said, and went inside.

In the lounge Dion switched on the hi-fi, and then made his way to his bedroom where he slipped off his school trousers and shirt. Now in his underpants and socks he ran back to the lounge where he irritably switched off the tape-deck, throwing Mosheen's cassette to one side while searching for another. His turbulent body, now slightly calmed by the dagga, yearned for deepdown music. He slipped Tyrone's soul cassette into the deck, turning it on to a warm, mellow volume which filled the small living-room.

Tyrone wandered in with red, stoned eyes fixed on Dion. There was a silent comprehension between the two of them. Tyrone recognized in Dion the agony of youth, and at the same time realized that he himself was the cause of the boy's lust. But nothing else mattered now, because the last of Dion's will-power cracked.

'Is it true that men fuck each other in jail, like Mosheen says?' Dion asked.

Tyrone studied the innocent face, sculpted in high cheek-bones with a broad, pouty mouth. His lean, nimble, almost girlish body was developing into something smooth, taut, athletic. There was much more boy than there had been nine years ago, before he went to prison.

'It happens, yes.' He wasn't going to take on the role of sex-instructor, but Dion's naive attitude enticed him. 'When I was in jail I had this young guy as my "laura". We got on well. He turned to me for protection and paid me back in his own way. You get a hell of a hunger for *naai* in there.'

It was the first time Tyrone had said anything about his life in jail.

'But what happens in there is different from the life outside...If a boy happens to be a handsome rosebud, he'd be a prime target for men who break the fine line. It's loneliness and want. Even for rapists and murderers, like Ougat and Lucky. I developed the same feeling for Rufus, he was nineteen, inside for selling Mandrax. He was getting rich the tough way. But between those walls he was just a kid. I wanted to protect him, so I made him my laaitie. That was my first experience of *holnaai*. It was four walls, remember. It happens.'

Dion understood Tyrone, a man normally without words, and he was glad to feel, not only sexually, towards him. He had missed Tyrone as much as Mama did. Even these days he felt an aura around himself when laaities discussed Tyrone at school, when they called him 'a big number, outside and inside jail'.

Tyrone moved among gangsters and the moneyed alike. The biggest gangsters in the whole of the violent Cape Flats knew Tyrone, one who could take on a whole rap by himself. But when he got out of jail his cut wasn't waiting for him. The gangsters kept it neatly intact for themselves. And so Tyrone was left with May and Dion only.

Yet May was a warm, vivid, wondèrful woman who scrambled along for years as a seamstress for Derma Fashions, the home of the Cape's continental wear, until she herself became a skilled designer. And all the time Tyrone urged her from behind bars to continue with her career. For those nine years she waited for him with unshakeable loyalty, while he was sleeping with other men. He thought that it was all over now. But he realized with shock that this inexperienced boy could overpower him, even though they faced none of the demands and obligations normally found behind bars — the place where men sometimes have to love other men.

Tyrone stood silently thinking of May, blaming his feelings on sexual deprivation, doing time in that hole called Victor Verster. But he felt that what was happening here was much bigger than anything he had done inside. Now he was trying to be a father to a son he never had. A nerve in his cheek twitched violently. He wanted to give the boy a hug, to crush him, to do more than just shake hands, the way they always did, 'like *ouens*'. Dion certainly stirred something in him. Oh, this feeling for arse.

'Arses are meant for shitting,' Tyrone fended absently.

'In the case of two males, I think they're meant for fucking.'

A slight shuffle. Another shuffle. It was getting hot in the lounge.

'Relax. Don't rush it,' Tyrone said coarsely. 'Your birthday is only tomorrow, remember.'

'Tomorrow...when Mama goes to work....'

'When Mama goes to work,' echoed Tyrone.

Dion felt powerful at the thought of having both Mama and Tyrone. He didn't feel as though he was cheating Mama. It was a feeling of sharing; he wanted something from both of their worlds.

'Hey, the gas!' He put on a T-shirt and jeans, got onto his bicycle and whistled all the way to Parker's, feeling satisfied.

Tomorrow...when Mama goes to work....

Adrian van den Berg

Wild Trade

His empire would have been incomplete without a Johannesburg residence, so John 'Cullin' Rhodes 'captured the hill' and bought a mansion off Monroe Drive, coiling down into Lower Houghton.

It was apt, for Rhodes was a sly side-winder. He was kingpin of the wild game and animal trade, where legal loopholes were always too small to haul the sack of profits, or the sack of carrion, through.

Yes, he was a smuggler. But a discreet, efficient and influential man who had never ever touched raw meat, despite the brutal implications of his nickname.

Besides providing animals for zoos (which seemed to have inherent mechanisms guaranteeing vacant cages), Rhodes's international network also catered for the Eastern palate's love of rare flesh, and its fetish for selected organs. Vivisectionists could secure shipments, ranging from donkeys to cats, through his office. And if you were not satisfied with an indigenous specimen as a pet, well, your slight fixation with Polynesian tree-worms needn't have stayed at just that.

Other distinguished clients of Rhodes's were the genetic engineering chaps, over in the U.S.A. — those creators of master-predators and game for connoisseurs. No animal was too big or too small for Mister Rhodes.

Despite his reputation as a cruel poacher, Rhodes's family was sublime, timid, and vegetarian too. Sensitive people, the mother and son. Although the latter, Edward or 'Kayo', was a wee bit flustered, and some thought that, even if he had inherited his father's pale Germanic features, he lacked the mentality to become such a man.

Back in their abode, no pets were allowed. But Kayo had a porcelain Dalmatian which he kept in his room, diplomatically, because his mother was of the opinion that the piece was a trifle gauche, while his father was wary of the mere depiction of an animal. If he had to encounter one outside of business he became filled with anxiety and fear.

Adrian van den Berg

On his ranges, animals were numbers to be caged, wrapped or potted. And any stray that dared to cross his Houghton turf was solemnly 'put to sleep' by the butler. Kayo, of course, never saw any of the victims.

Tonight John Rhodes would have haemorrhaged through his pores, and issued all the servants with guns to make a Custerish stand, had he known that there was a queer trespasser in his garden. It was nature's utter contempt for his dignity, for there was a baboon by the mansion's swimming-pool, a baboon in Houghton, a huge battle-worn sentry. Yellow dagger-fangs, bloody eyes, fingers with scabs, ticks circling, jumping from its anus, festering folds in its muzzle from too many wide snarls. The creature was powerful and mean-looking. A perfect complement to the moon, a silver virile old male. A psychopomp, not conventionally real, it inferred seemingly irrational consequences from another world, and concluded itself in ours.

It was a magical entity, and sexual contact was its means of communicative interaction. The baboon thus stank of sex, a crude hormonal scent.

This being the case, the Rhodes household was about to encounter a foul bugger-up. But pin-striped 'Cullin' John was not due back until the next day and, anyway, everybody was oblivious to the visitation outside.

From its favourable vantage point at the pool the hairy thing scanned the dwelling. It could see Kayo, transparently clear, asleep in bed in his blue room with the larger-than-life Dalmatian and posters of sperm whales thrashing playfully about, wallowing in the ocean off a pinetum coast.

The next day Kayo came home from school, after cricket practice, with a distinguished Aryan sunburn, and one of their maids met him half-way up the drive to carry his books. She was old, and just another subject in one of 'Cullin' Rhodes's raw deals. She started to lag behind Kayo, after only a few steps, and suddenly he heard something being flung down. He turned to take his books from her, and she was smiling, but a huge African had come to her aid, giving Kayo a callous, scornful look. He felt dismissed, as if the man had seen his lack of compassion, his ignorance. Kayo knew him, he had seen the man thrive on his own vicious incompetence. He was still doing just that, as in a dream. The African was eating the weakest part of his white soul, assimilating it and growing. And then the African's skin darkened.

A startling, chilling bark. The trance was shattered — the triangle of the smiling maid, the African who was the pinnacle, and Kayo.

There were no animals near, no dogs, both Kayo and the maid knew it. Perhaps a stray had made the sound? But even the diminishing, waning presence of the African was still too compelling for either of them to look away.

The man took each of them by an elbow and directed them to the open front door. Kayo was still too stunned to consider the African's behaviour patronizing. His hand was warm and it felt alien, incongruous with the beckoning, dim interior of the house.

John Rhodes would have appreciated a severe reprimanding response from his son to counter the new gardener's 'disregard'. And Kayo's face did get flushed with anger, but certainly not on cue. Only once he had gotten to his room and heard the African at work by the pool (the dull sound of a garden fork stabbing the soil, roots tearing as the prongs were lifted), only then did Kayo exhibit signs of being a true Rhodes. He kicked the Dalmatian to pieces, violently enough to make his mother enter to inquire about the noise. She left and Kayo started peeling the sweaty cricket uniform off his sore red body.

His shorts were drenched with his own urine, he remembered vaguely that it had happened when he heard the bark in the garden. It stung and irritated his cock, but he found his rage and his discomfort inexplicably arousing. He pulled his foreskin back and used the sleeve of his white shirt to wipe dry the exposed crown. Despite his resistance his crotch surged upwards. He jumped up and decided to go for a swim. And maybe to teach that big black a lesson. He shut his eyes tight as he pulled his blue briefs, with white stars, over the sensitive bulge. Then he went outside.

The African was working with his back to Kayo, who applied a dignified look, in vain.

Okay, thought Kayo. He dropped the towel from around his waist and leaped into the pool, intending to wet the man's back. But when he surfaced, the man greeted him with a smile. Astounded, he smiled bashfully back. The man turned, went down on his haunches, the fork resting on his thick thighs with his arms dangling over it.

'God he is so black, shiny black.'

Kayo tried his best to look like 'our young master in the pool'. He started swimming with graceful strokes, correct rhythm, executing a subtle somersault at the end of each length. After twenty-five lengths he stopped to see what the gardener was doing. The whole flower-bed was done, the air was smelling of the dark exposed soil and pregnant with something else —

the unmistakable scent of male testicles, alien balls these. Perhaps the gardener had pierced a larva or a worm with his fork. But he seemed oblivious to the strange smell, just smiling and squatting.

The gardener smiled, a smile like a wry contraction, no admiration or envy in his look, or the longing that Kayo had expected. The man seemed to be swimming along, sensing the water around him in spirit. Like another vessel, a seal, a teasing torpedo darting through the archway of Kayo's spread legs.

He had a huge ganja spliff hanging from the corner of his mouth.

In the shallow end Kayo went down on his knees, to capture the cause of this sudden ripple between his thighs, but all he felt was the motion of swirling water. Exhaustion pulled him forward and he propelled himself, looking downwards into the water, raising his head only for a deep breath. His buttocks were exposed above the water, he was still being watched and there was none of the shame, as earlier that afternoon. Now he was being appreciated, being played with, his penis stretching over the rim of the briefs reaching its full length to touch his muscles at the abdomen. After a while he opened his eyes underwater to watch the white strands escaping from his cock's tip, like gob in the water. He lifted his head to give the African another smile, sincerely, and the man's eyes were soft.

The Rhodes mansion glimmered in the late afternoon sun, but the pool area was already overrun by shadows. Kayo lay on the marble paving flanking the swimming-pool, with one hand hanging in the water and the other cuddled to his chest. He shivered and then relaxed, while the African proceeded to complete his chores rhythmically.

Then Kayo woke up immersed in light. The African had pruned a neat hiatus into the hedge surrounding the pool and the last rays of the day were shining down onto the exact spot where he lay. In a reverie he thought of the day's happenings. He thought of how snotty the boys at school got with each other when actually they were only seeking out each other's company; how their petty jealousies were only an expression of need, and they desired friendship with those at whom the jealousy was directed. He thought of how intimate that magical triangle had been, earlier, during his disdainful contact with the African. And he came to the conclusion that a mutual attraction was motivating his and the African's absurd behaviour towards each other.

Then Kayo stirred, distracted by the familiar sound of a gardening implement being thrown down...the African stretched and sighed while he looked at Kayo. They still hadn't spoken, and the gaze lasted for several moments until the African turned abruptly and started walking away. Kayo imagined that he detected pity and sympathy in the man's eyes, forcing him to turn his back. This thought ripped the boy from his immersion in his own smug happiness, making him acutely aware and causing the hot glow on his skin to revert to fiery sunburn.

'There goes the over-compensating gardener,' he thought, tempted to dismiss the man in the same way that he himself had been 'sent off' earlier. But instead he ran into the house to seek out the maid. From a window in the bunkerish house watched Mrs Rhodes.

No. The big gardener had been given a trial run this afternoon, and would not be staying in the servants' quarters, was what the suspicious maid told the curious Kayo.

So he rushed back to his room to put on track-suit pants, a T-shirt and sneakers, before hurrying outside. There, he saw faintly the man's tall frame in the dusk, disappearing down the driveway.

At the same moment, a Mercedes turned into the grounds and approached the house. The car drove past a pillar, where the passenger in the rear saw his son speaking to the new gardener. Rhodes noted the man's muscular arms, wrapped around his son. He screamed at the couple, but a trickle of spit against the vehicle's dark windows was all he accomplished. The black chauffeur smiled before asking, in his soothing docile way, whether the master would perhaps have the window let down? But Rhodes had already attempted to open both doors, unsuccessfully, and now he was feeling like one of his trapped animals.

The car pulled up in front of the house before he could utter further instructions. First, he saw a cat running from inside the house, dashing out, past his wife's legs, and then he noticed her. And then her strange tale followed of how the new gardener had watched Kayo the whole day long, and how the boy seemed forced, how he dressed in a rush and left without a word, without permission, in the gardener's company.

'John, somebody is trying to get back at us — those unreliable, blackmailing, crooked ex-colleagues of yours or perhaps rivals! Oh God forbid if that black man is a vindictive poacher...they stole our student prince!'

It took John Rhodes thirty minutes to initiate a search for his kidnapped son. He got a famous tracker — a big-game hunter and colonel in the South African police, an old friend of his — to take charge. The operation received the blessing and cooperation of all the echelons in the police hierarchy, and several big names in the fight against crime and anarchy were preparing to join the search, within hours. All they wanted in return were several favours, and all for a great man like old 'Cullin'. Meanwhile, an exterminator, the SPCA, and a municipal delegation arrived at the Rhodes mansion to address a reported plague. Cats apparently. They knocked on the door, on which was a small pottery plaque inscribed with the words: 'THIS HOUSE IS PROTECTED BY PSALM 23 — The Lord is my shepherd....'

'Where are we going?'

'Illbrow.'

Kayo and the African had already disappeared into the flatlands by the time a police helicopter swept the area between Houghton and Hillbrow. He had been in Hillbrow numerous times, but was always shielded by a car window and his parents, their droning voices dismissing the despair, the celebration, vendors, whores, workers, beggars and flat-dwellers alike. But now he was happy to be among them, to be one of them.

He felt anonymous, but intensely aware of the crowds. Hillbrow's inhabitants were pristine, average. Some were exaggerated and decorative, and some tarts and junkies were compelling creatures staring up from a Rhodes Inc. brochure. Kayo realized that even sympathy could be a commodity. The African laughed at the boy's enchantment, tugging him along to their destiny — a small flat in the corner of a monolithic building inhabited by three Mozambicans and the African. Everybody spoke Portuguese and English, and it soon became apparent that the African was a newcomer.

Kayo's hosts offered him a warm beer and the use of their telephone. Telephone? His parents, and that house...school tomorrow? He declined the telephone call without giving the issue any further thought.

Each one of the flat's inhabitants had a corner where their beds were neatly made. The African's corner had a colourful cloth on the wall and pictures of formidable, stern-looking men, among whom Kayo recognized Fidel Castro and Mao.

Kayo sat next to the African on his mattress, while the latter asked him questions about his father. But when Kayo inquired about the man's own parents, he merely replied that he never had any. Surely it must be a sensitive issue, was Kayo's conclusion. Meanwhile the African had taken Kayo's right hand. He compared sizes and sniffed his palms. Kayo dared to lean forward and slide his hand under the man's shirt, a fascinating, hairless, satin skin. His body odour alarmed Kayo, that same provocative smell that he first sensed beside the pool (carrion and cinnamon). The man seemed to know and gave a chuckle. And Kayo made a sincere effort to move his hand inconspicuously down to the African's groin, despite the presence of the three other people deep in conversation in a stew of Portuguese and English. But the big man's hand took his own firmly and squeezed it hard.

Outside, the low rumble of cars receded as a helicopter swept past the building. The African shook his head and started rolling a spliff, in contempt. And Kayo then took it for granted that most blacks smoked, wine to the Bible...spliff to Africa. Yes, he supposed he would have some — despite his skin colour. He watched intensely as the man dropped the leaves onto newspaper.

The African led them up the fire-escape onto the building's asphalt roof. Kayo watched him bend slightly forward, at the edge of the roof, to look down into the street. He kept this posture for several moments, as if he was scanning the bustling crowds for somebody familiar, with the spliff's burning tip sending smoke into his face. He turned, and looking Kayo squarely in the eyes took long sucks on the joint and started circling him. Then he came up behind Kayo and placed his arms over his shoulders, holding the spliff for him to suck. A deep explosion, Kayo's soul coming right out of his body into the night air.... Visceral abandonment. He wanted to scream because he, or something belonging to him, began moving to the building's edge and then he saw the people in the street, among them were monkey children, everywhere. And Kayo saw tiger-whores, and old bird-women. Surrounded by howls and chirps, and the barely audible sound of helicopter blades cutting the air...swaying in the black man's arms. That smell was there again, and so was the smell of manure, animal copulation, dogs, deer, birds, and Kayo felt a transformation in the man's hands, on his chest. Now they were waning, hairier, scabs, a muzzle over his shoulder, and the same soft eyes, only more curious and smaller, straining to meet his.

And without taking his eyes off the creature's, Kayo knew that the helicopter had appeared at the building's edge, hovering among shouts and animal sounds. Hands in his pants, small fingers circling his penis, up, until it became unbearable.

'That's them! That's my son!'

Rhodes's sweaty hand had shot out to refer the spectacle on the roof to the pilot, and the craft lunged forward, coming dangerously close to the building....

'Shoot that bastard! Why are you waiting?'

A sniper leaning out spraying the dark roof with fire, Rhodes jumping up and down as much as the interior would permit. Chaos in the cockpit.

The air was empty. No more sounds. There wasn't a helicopter any more, no animals, only the small fingers making a strange rustle in his hair. Kayo felt a reclining motion through his body, a tug, short and urgent. The similarity between the African guiding him through the streets and the short pulls that he felt now was comforting...far off, a hint of an animal sound, and he decided to follow it.

The baboon seemed to be wrestling with Kayo's body and he finally pulled what seemed to be an identical second corpse from Kayo's and started dragging it towards a silver hole like a shiny areola expanding in the air inches above the roof behind him.

Graeme Reid

We Are Too Young To Contemplate Our Death

You have pushed me into the
future; dealing with your death
I now live thirty years ahead
as I contemplate your dying.

You have told me you are
dying; and still we smile
on long-distance calls when we speak
of your days at the beach:

We are too young to
contemplate our death at
such close distance. And we watch
the sun set deep into the sea.

Now tell me it's a lie
and that you'll live.
We are too young to watch a death
at such close distance.

Yes I have watched
the Sebokeng bodies on TV
but they did not bleed pus onto my sheets as you
will surely do

and they did not say:
Wash my dressings
as I know when you are sick and dying you
will surely do.

Graeme Reid

I have never contemplated
death as I now wonder at your
dying; and I cannot comprehend a life
in which you are dying.

One day you said: I will inevitably die
and I said try AZT
because as the sun sets
I cannot comprehend your death.

So, I will pick daisies
and put them on your grave
because as the sun sets
I will not comprehend your death.

Y'Know?

'Do y'know that
in your sleep,'
I said to him one morning
over breakfast
a month to the day after
he had returned
(a month in which the war began
a month of iron fists and curfews
a month in which the jasmine I planted
bloomed and winter passed one night
to summer), 'I watch
your body ripple
when you breathe?'

Simon Nkoli

This Strange Feeling

Born in Soweto in 1957, and schooled in the rural areas, today Simon Nkoli is the country's major gay activist as well as an Aids educator.

In 1976 he became involved in the struggle for students' rights, and this led to his imprisonment. He was held for three months that year, for suspected 'terrorism'. He was imprisoned for the same reason for several months in 1977; and again in 1978, for five months, under the Internal Security Act. He was detained for a further seven months in 1979, and a further three months in 1981.

In 1984, along with other prominent township activists, he was tried for treason in the notorious Delmas Treason Trial. He was finally acquitted in 1988 after being detained for a year. While on bail that same year he helped establish GLOW (Gays and Lesbians of the Witwatersrand), and became its chairperson and first co-ordinator.

Since his acquittal, he has travelled extensively as a gay political activist. He currently works for TAP (Township Aids Project) as a counsellor.

In this account, recorded by Matthew Krouse in late 1991, Simon Nkoli tells of his childhood and youth.

I.

I was born thirty-three years ago in Soweto, in the township of Phiri. My parents separated when I was very young and my mother decided to take me to my grandparents, for them to bring me up. They lived on a farm in the Orange Free State. And that's where I grew up, from the age of two or three, until I was thirteen.

I started school a year early, because I looked older than other children. Every day I had to walk to and from school, fourteen kilometres a day.

We were living on a white man's farm, and he was a nuisance. My grandpapa used to get one rand a month. And we lived in houses that our grandparents built for themselves. They were mud houses with roofs made of grass or zinc, and there were big rocks on top of the houses to hold the roofs down.

Each farm-hand had his own cows. They could have no more than three cows each. If you had three cows and one gave birth, then the farmer would be entitled to possess the calf.

They used to have fields where mealies were ploughed, and everyone would be given a certain amount of acres.

I remember that one winter my grandfather got about fifty-six bags of meal and he was very happy. They used to sell one mealie-bag for about five rand. The farmers would buy it from our fathers.

The farmers never really thought of the black children's education at all. When the children were nine years old, the farmers would contract them. The boys had to look after the sheep and cows, or would become child labourers, picking up dried mealies and putting them into bags. I was on that farm and I had to do the same as other kids did. I used to work with mealies and look after sheep.

But I was very clever. When I was in Standard Two, at nine years old, I used to dodge this work. I would leave the work and run to school, and then I would quickly return to the farm at playtime, because my grandfather would smack me if he heard that I had been to school. I would do this for the whole of winter. I used to reap the mealies, which was quite a heavy thing for a child. I couldn't even carry the bag, because it had to be carried on one's back, and I was the same size as the bag. So, in the end, all I could do was to stack the mealies before they were put into the bags.

Once a child had completed ten bags, it would get ten cents. So if you did a hundred bags, you would get one rand. And if you hadn't done anything by a certain time, then you would get flogged. My grandmother used to help me to make up my bags, because she didn't want me to be beaten. The farmer used to chase us on his horse, and then we would get flogged with his whip.

At the end of Standard Three the farmer said I should leave school, because I am educated now, I can read and write, and I can say, '*Ja baas,*' and '*Nee baas.*' ('Yes boss,' and 'No boss.') And my grandpapa agreed with him.

I wasn't happy about this, and luckily, I happened to know where my parents lived, in Bophelong in Vanderbijlpark. I'd never been there before, but I had heard people talking about how to get there. I had the address, and one morning I just decided to leave. I left my grandparents. Everybody on the farm knew that I had gone to my mother's, because I had left a note.

I managed to get a lift to the local station, and then I took a train. But I could only pay for the train as far as Wolwehoek, and so I asked around and got a lift to Sasolburg. Eventually, somehow I arrived at Bophelong. And it was dark that evening, I didn't know where anything was. But people know their townships, and I just showed someone the address and I got home. My mother was very upset at what I did, but I just told them that I wanted to go to school.

And that's how I arrived in Bophelong.

I couldn't go to school that same year, because I arrived at my parents very late. I had to wait until the following year while my parents obtained the correct papers, permitting me to be there. They were squatting in a shack at the back of a woman's house.

While I was living there, the township residents were constantly being arrested by the police. The police were called 'blackjacks', and they were the ones who would come and check people's permits. If you didn't have a permit, if you were a squatter, then they would arrest you, and they would fine you. The fine was ten rand. If you didn't have the ten rand, then they would take you to the police station and charge you.

And that reminds me of what happened one day, when I had already returned from the farm, to my mother, and had started school.

I was living with my mother, stepfather and my younger sisters. One was about three years old, and the other was just a baby.

On this particular day, I came back from school and the baby was crying. No one was at home. My three-year-old sister was also crying, and the only word she was saying was 'blackjacks'. And I knew, of course, that my parents had been arrested. There was no money in the house. I didn't have ten rand to go and bail my mother and my stepfather.

Both of my parents had been arrested, because if they arrested a woman then they would go to where her husband was working, and they would take them both.

This is what happened, and what I hated most about it was that the baby had been left behind. They left the baby with a little girl, who was hardly more than a baby herself.

I arrived back from school at one o'clock in the afternoon, and my parents had been arrested at about eleven o'clock in the morning. The baby hadn't been breast-fed. So I picked up the baby and took it to where my mother was. But the baby couldn't stay in the jail, and so I had to return home with it and ask people for money. I asked my uncles. I asked everybody, and eventually I made up the ten rand.

When they were arrested, the people of the townships knew that they would be released. But they also knew that the next time they had nowhere to go, they would get arrested again. This happened mostly at the end of every month. And so the whole story would have to repeat itself, over and over.

In the townships, people have had to survive from one month to another. They have had to survive. They have always had to keep another ten rand, just in case the blackjacks come today.

II.

In the townships, people use the Sesotho word *sitabane* to describe gay people. It means a person who has got two organs — sexual organs — a vagina and a penis. Whether you're gay or transvestite, or if you are transsexual, to them it's the same thing.

We never really saw people with two organs. But if you are a feminine man, many will say you are a *sitabane*. And if you happen to be over twenty years old, and you don't have a girlfriend, many will presume you are gay.

So, if you discover that you are absolutely attracted to men, you'd better keep quiet in the township. Don't ever tell somebody he's beautiful, because he will tell you, 'Why are you saying this? Don't think I am a *sitabane*. Go away!'

In the black community, people don't know what a gay is. They don't talk about it. I didn't know myself until I discovered the word 'gay' in the library.

I was in high school when I told my parents. It was at my eighteenth birthday party, and it really did upset my mother. She was very hysterical. She was crying, she was pushing everything around. She threatened to kick all of my friends out of the house. The children were crying. My stepfather was just quiet and shocked. And I was confused. But I was lucky. Many parents in the black community reject their children when they tell them.

They chase them out of the house. They take them out of school. My parents didn't do that.

My stepfather said, 'I thought you are normal, you've got only one organ!'

They told me to keep quiet about it. They told my sisters and brothers to keep quiet.

People in the townships are very religious. We are Catholic. And my parents said, 'The only person you can tell is Father Edward. Because you've got to confess. You're lucky you haven't done anything yet. You're still pure.'

I went to the priest. I told the priest that I love other men, and that the best thing would be for me to live with it, to accept it. Of course, the priest said that there is no way I could live with it. It was the first time that the anti-gay quotations from the Bible were quoted to me. I spent four hours in the chapel. And the priest was coming to me to pray with me. He would go out and then come back with a new chapter. Those four hours really didn't do any good for me, because I wouldn't read what was quoted. I would go on reading what other chapters were saying. And I discovered other things that people do and are not supposed to be doing. And they're not condemned for these other things.

I told my priest that there are lots of other issues that priests have to deal with before they can tell us about these little quotations. Then I left.

Of course, I was chased out of church because I was possessed by evil.

My parents took me to the witchdoctor. He said I'd been bewitched. I didn't believe the witchdoctor and I told him so. And he said that it was not him saying so, but his tokoloshe — it's helping him to talk.

I said, 'You're lying.'

And he said, 'You see! The bad spirit is in you!'

I said, 'Go, bad spirit!' And everybody was crying.

So, in my family I was a little bit outcast. I tried to argue with my mother and my stepfather. I told them that I'm not bewitched. I said that I don't think God has forsaken me.

At that time I was secretary of the students' organization in the Vaal Triangle. I had a friend who happened to be the chairperson. I said, 'You know, I've got this strange feeling towards other men. I think I'm gay.'

And I was surprised when he said, that if it's so, then I've got to live with it. And he helped me to tell other students. And, of course, there was some war. In the Executive Committee of our branch, people said I should be struck off the records. Others said I should be demoted from my post.

I then left the organization, because they had to discuss me. They had to decide whether they wanted me to leave permanently. This was a bad principle, because people were making decisions on behalf of others. Then, within two weeks, I was called in and I was told that I am still a member. And lots of students agreed that I should remain as secretary. There were students who felt that I was really honest to come out.

But it never ended there.

The word went around in Sebokeng township that I am not a normal person. One of my uncles decided to stop me seeing my young cousins, in fact he banned me. He said, 'I don't want to see you near my children at all, you'll be a bad example to our family.' And I stopped going.

People gossiped behind me. And soon, the whole township knew. I lived my life fearing to be victimized, assaulted.

People would pass remarks. They would say, 'Hey, lick a butt, lady!' Or, 'Look at that queer.... Is that the guy they said is queer?'

They would go to my brothers and sisters, and say, 'Is it true that your brother has got two sexual organs?'

When I was in the school toilet, then students would come in and be curious. They would say, 'We want to see you.'

I left school and I became a worker. I became a machine operator at African Cable. Out of a hundred and fifty people, I was chosen for training, to deal with machines and other tools. I really topped.

I was quite happy to be employed. I went for further training, and within a week I was appointed a shop-floor leader. I had to see to it that workers came to work. If their machines were broken I was able to help them, because I mastered the fixing of cable machines. And then people started gossiping about me.

And all of a sudden people started hating me. They said that they could not be led by me, because they had heard from other people that I am gay. But out of thirty of them, I had one good friend who was absolutely willing to listen to me. My foreman was also reserved, he didn't want to talk to me.

At the end of that time I found my first lover, who was working and earning good money, and wanted me to come and live with him.

He was a white guy. We had been writing to each other as pen-friends from late in 1979. I found his address in *Hit* Magazine, a magazine for teenagers. He was twenty-two, I was nineteen. We became good friends, and then along the line he proposed to me. We met for the first time, after writing for seven months, and we really knew that it was love at first sight.

He was a bus-driver and his name was André. He wanted to meet me and he invited me to drive with him down to Durban. He was transporting schoolchildren from the township to the coast for seven days.

I told him that I was working, but he insisted that I come. I knew I was going to lose my job, but I didn't really care because nobody wanted me at work. So I travelled alone from Sebokeng to Meadowlands, where we were to meet, in Zone 9.

Three buses arrived in Meadowlands. The first two were driven by black drivers, and André drove the third. When he arrived he was wearing clothes the same as the ones I had on. Black corduroys and a white T-shirt. It was as if we had phoned each other and discussed what to wear.

At first, I refused to drive in his bus, because I was too shy to speak to a white person. In fact, he was going to be my first white person as a friend. So I refused, and in the end all the schoolchildren were screaming at me out of their buses, that I should drive with him. And I did.

We drove, and I was shy. I couldn't face the children and so I looked at my feet, the whole way. The children were singing and were very happy. But André and I never talked to each other along the road because we couldn't communicate very well, we were both shy.

I had to stay in Umgababa township, in a hotel, and he had to stay in town, at the Blue Waters Hotel. Because of apartheid, that was the deal during those times. When we arrived at the coast, it was after midnight, too late for him to drive back into town. And so he dropped us at Umgababa, where he had booked me into a room along with the other drivers. And he decided to sleep in the bus.

As I was sitting in the hotel, these other drivers mentioned that it was dangerous for André to sleep in the bus, he might be killed. At this thought, I just took my sleeping-bag and went to sleep in the bus as well.

I entered the bus, and we started talking. We talked until four o'clock in the morning. We talked about everything, and we both invented girlfriends.

The following day, he was allowed on the black beach because he was a driver. He had a camera and was taking lots of pictures. A teacher came to us and asked us if we were lovers, and we just laughed. We went to the dolphins, we went everywhere. He showed me everything. We walked along the beach holding hands. We became close to each other, and then we had to leave. I was so sad.

When we arrived back in Johannesburg it was late at night, and so I booked into a little hotel for black people in the city. And the following day I went back to my parents' house.

During this time, a strange thing occurred.

Somebody had suggested to my mother that I see a psychologist. And coincidentally, the psychologist my mother sent me to turned out to be the same psychologist André's mother sent *him* to.

We visited the same man. And it was through talking that the man, a nice Jewish man, explained that there was nothing wrong. He said that he was dealing with lots of gay people.

Through this man, André's mother came to know of me, and I discovered that she was anti-me, anti-him, anti-black, and anti-everything. We realized that our relationship was not going to work. Even if my mother accepted me, his mother would not accept me. I phoned him, and his mother said to me, 'One day I want to meet you, and shoot you to death.'

Both of our families were upset. We had accepted ourselves, but there was no community that was supporting us. He suggested that we should commit suicide, and I agreed with him.

But we didn't, because my mother found a letter we had written together, stating what we were going to do. And she spoilt everything.

She used to search my clothing, and she found this letter. In it she read that we had set a date to kill ourselves. We had decided to drive to Durban once again, to go back to the first place where we met. Then we were going to come back to Johannesburg and do it.

We didn't kill ourselves. Instead, we did whatever we could to be together.

André moved away from his parents, into his own flat in town. And, at the same time, I also moved away from home. I got a little room, also in town, because I had decided to go to a college in Johannesburg, to improve my education.

Johannes Meintjes

Summer Holiday

They had gone on a visit to relatives at a small seaside village called Waenhuiskrans in the Western Cape. His aunt spent most of the day sitting on the stoep, her eyes gazing out over the ocean, leaving Marc, as usual, to amuse himself. He shared a room with the son of the house, a boy of eighteen with a club-foot. To Marc it was an ordeal to share a room, for he was unused to it and obsessive about his privacy. Then too, he was nauseated by any form of physical deformity. So he spent all day and evening out in the open, on the water, on the rocks, on the sand.

Although he did not go out of his way to make friends, he soon found himself part of the leading group of youngsters of the place, something which astonished him. A certain strangeness and wildness about him attracted others, and it was a further revelation to him that he had the ability to amuse. Boys normally fight shy of the extraordinary, or the eccentric, and try to conform to an accepted code — feats of daring are a different matter — but they accepted Marc, odd as he was at times, for the simple reason that he was so likeable, so good-looking and at times hilariously funny. Hiding away somewhere he heard voices calling: 'Marc! Marc!' They were searching for him, and this made him leap away in exuberant escape.

The arrival of a new family next door brought Marc closer home. There were four sons, one of Marc's own age, and from the moment their eyes met over the low white wall separating the two cottages, the sun burning down on sand and rock, they drew together with shy broken speech, to spring forward in a wild sprint and fling themselves into the water, swimming furiously, hearts beating in their throats. They fell on the sand and looked at each other, the sun on their bodies, laughing without speech, their eyes exploring each other with the candour made possible after their joint exertion. That was Marten, shorter, muscular, with brown hair and hazel eyes, dark of skin, his good teeth glittering in pink-tongued laughter.

The smell of Marten was to linger for years, the very texture of his faded blue shorts was remembered, his khaki shirt heated by the sun to an exquisite sweetness. His body — every hair glinting on his legs with their definition of muscle, his chest as smooth and hard as a sea-washed stone, his stomach rising and falling in speech and laughter, his strong young neck strangely vulnerable.

Every detail had clarity: the sand on which they lay, its soft moistness or dry looseness, white with a sheen of pale yellow; shells tiny as grains of sand, finely indenting palms and arms and clinging to the skin; smooth granite boulders washing slimy green and glittering open to the sun, as familiar as Marten's skin fresh out of the water, now faintly sour in smell, gleaming in its saltiness like the fish flopping out of the baskets of the fishermen. The blue of the bluebottles with their thin lines of fiery sting along the edge of the surf, and Marten's frayed blue rugby shorts — usually all he wore; the odour of sea bamboo curling in rotting streamers from a hand-like head, or the smell of bonfires made of driftwood at Christmas, with their woolly smoke burning the nostrils; the taste of salt water on the tongue, or after it had dried on the skin, on the lips, mixed with sweat to a sour-sweetness. Hands and shells, limbs and driftwood, the cry of a bird and the heart soaring with it, the touch of bodies and the brush of sand and spray, stinging and tingling, and the sweet breath when heads knocked together. They wrestled sometimes, and hurt each other, the pain and the pressure of limbs, agonizing and disturbing in breath held, was similar to the hush when the moon rises over the sea. Footsteps in the sand. 'Race you!' The swirl and skidding into the turmoil of water, cutting a foot on a rock, blood rising purple through the blue, the red dripping into the softness of sand where Marten examined the injury. Their toes linked up with the sour-figs they collected; a perfect shell — and Marten's eyes, the shine of them in sudden laughter, flecks of amber in the brown.

Marten was a quiet one, and to him Marc talked as he had never talked to anyone save his animals, but never without reserve. Marten wanted to be amused, and Marc saw to it that he was. Day after day, together in crowds, Marc's love grew — a love which was never spoken or expressed beyond a hug. Living in the sun, their bodies darkened, glints of gold appearing in the fine hairs of arms and legs. Marten's fine head of hair was lightening too, his eyes appearing softer and gentler. He would talk of rugby and cricket, and sometimes of girls. In the presence of girls he went all stiff and walked with an odd sort of angular movement, laughing too loudly, slapping Marc, even hitting him painfully. And Marc would dash away in a wild bound of inexplicable flight. Later they would find each other again, and then Marc would tease Marten, even cruelly, playing up to the girls who responded at once. Marten looked sick, and that filled Marc with exuberance — until Marten disappeared. After a fruitless search Marc went to bed and wished to die.

Marten was no more than an ordinary boy with average intelligence and average good looks, although he was indeed beautifully built. His reserve, which Marc found so impressive and interesting, was partly shyness and partly lack of imagination. He was genuinely fond of Marc, of whom he had no understanding whatever, and was loyal to him. In later years when he grew pot-bellied and bald, a father of five children, in a steady position and a mass-produced house, he might have thought back on the pal of a boyhood holiday. He met Marc again at that stage and greeted him with real pleasure — 'Christ, how good to see you! How are you, old boy!' — only to find that Marc was formally polite and went his way as soon as it was decently possible to do so. Marten, who had immediately hoped to introduce Marc to 'the wife' and to show him his children, had found this bewildering and smarting, and even more so when Marc passed him in the street a few days later without a sign of recognition.

It was impossible ever to bring the person he had just seen into any relationship with the boy he had known, with the long tramps they had enjoyed along the coast, the games with others at night, the fun in rowing-boats, on surf-boards, on a stoep somewhere with the rain beating down on sand and sea. Apart from being a first love, Marten had fulfilled the function of freeing him of the oppression of his lonely boyhood. He was a bridge to a new life, and this Marc realized the day of Marten's departure after six weeks of close intimacy. Marc was not there when the family left, but hiding in a hollow behind a sand-dune. 'Goodbye, Marten,' he wrote with a shell in the sand, wondering if Marten was searching for him, or worried about him. He could see his eyes as the car drove away, looking back, a familiar frown on his forehead on which the skin had begun to peel. Marten was gone, and the holiday was over.

'You'll miss Marten,' his aunt said unnecessarily on their way back. 'He was such a nice boy. I hope you meet again.'

Marc said nothing, regarding her with some contempt. What could she know of someone like Marten? Marten putting on shoes, the texture of his socks, the crease in the shoes, the way he tied the laces, the way he stood — and suddenly his smile. He studied the thin features of the woman and, although he did love her, pitied her.

'Why weren't you there to say goodbye?'

'I don't know,' he said truthfully.

His aunt, who understood him better than he knew, did not pursue the subject. She also knew that Marc had changed in those weeks, and glancing at his sunburnt face she could not resist an impulse to put her hand on his knee. She withdrew it at once, for she sensed that Marc did not like her to touch him — unless he touched her of his own accord, or in sleep when she tucked him in, blinded by the tears she never showed. It was now ten years since she had lost her daughter, her only child. And that was the source of her endless grief — a grief which Marc despised. His aunt was surrounded by mementoes of this daughter, things she had made, her books, everything she had left.

'Lettie had such a friend, too,' his aunt began in a tone of voice which reminded him of marshmallows, 'when we went to the sea when she was about your age, no, younger. They corresponded for years —'

Marc saw and smelt Marten again, his clothes, the black swimming-trunks with the small tear; saw his knees, the turn of his calf, the smooth hardness of his chest — and all the rest of him, every hair, mole and freckle. He closed his eyes and felt the tears sting under his lashes.

'I'll never see Marten again,' he said slowly.

'Why on earth not? His mother told me they'll probably come again next summer. Anyway, you can write, keep in touch, like Lettie —'

'I am not Lettie.' He blinked at the flitting landscape, fighting his grief, for he never cried in front of anyone. 'I always lose everything I love.'

'Don't say that!' His aunt grabbed his hand fiercely. 'What a terrible thing to say — a mere boy, a child!' Marc freed his hand.

'I know,' he said quietly.

They were silent and sat with heads averted watching the changing landscape.

Mikki van Zyl

Pathway to the Moon

With a final heave, Zimanga slipped into the world from between her mother's strong thighs. Her enthusiasm for life could be discerned from the first moment. According to the wise midwife and her mother — who by this, her sixth child, was already quite experienced in the matter of birthing — Zimanga should have waited another hour. But impatience was her essence, and so she was aptly named. She was always hurrying somewhere, if not on her feet at least in her head. Where her eyes went, her imagination followed.

At four-and-a-half she delighted in playing with the braids her older sister had put in her hair. Zimanga looped them and peered through the windows they made. She loved the softly curved patterns they etched in the air. Maybe they inspired her herring-bone designs on the stone walls of her buildings...but that is getting ahead of our story.

In this early part of her life, Zimanga tottered around freely on her strong little legs. She played with the rich, warm mud at the river when the women were washing or fetching water. At other times she ran for hours teasing the birds around the kraal. She also became aware of her mother's belly ripening like a melon. And when her little brother entered the world screaming, on a cold winter's night, it was she who draped the kaross around her mother's shoulders. Little did she realize that she was destined to walk on a much rockier path from now on.

Her mother was the biggest of her father's wives, strong and fat like the sun. She would bask in her power as she watched her pound the mealies into powdery flour underneath the heavy stone. She marvelled at the glistening forearms rolling the rock forward and back, forward and back. She felt protected and safe when those hands lifted her high in the air so she could soar like a bird.

But the coming of her little brother soon tethered her freedom. She could no longer dash off with her girl-friends to play in the mud by the river because he was always strapped to her back. Sometimes she would sneak away from him, leaving him gurgling under a small shrub while she shaped and patted the red mud. She loved creating this world of sinuous shapes almost as much as eating newly-made mealie bread.

Then one day — it was hot and muggy — her brother's sniffling and crying attracted her mother's attention. With her voice dangerously low, and her finger raised against the sun, her mother warned, 'You are responsible for this boy, and if anything happens to him it will be your fault!'

The enormous injustice of this statement struck her five-year-old chest like a granite boulder toppling off a koppie. Why should she take care of him? She vowed to keep her life for herself, even if she had to hide it. Seething with anger she strode back to the homestead where the women had already lit the evening fires. The flames fuelled her resentment, and in a fit of fury she flung a granite stone at a nearby water pitcher. As the calabash toppled, its cold water hissed over the hot stone and shattered it into several oblong shards.

The cracking stone sobered her. She quickly filled the empty pitcher with scoops of water from several others and hid the pieces of stone in her treasure-trove in the corner of the kraal. If anyone had witnessed her temper tantrum, they wisely ignored it, knowing the spirit of life ran strong within her.

The years passed.

One clear night she lay singing under the heavens, tunefully tracing patterns around the moon and the stars. The mottled face of the moon reminded her of the granite hills of her earth, and she yearned to make a strong stone womb for herself and the moon. Slowly, her secret hiding-place in the corner of the kraal came to mind. She went there to look at the symbols of her vow of independence. Lovingly she pulled out the neat pieces of stone. Then came her other treasures — a copper-wire bangle, some birds she'd carved from soapstone, and a little ivory box. (Six hundred years later, archaeologists would puzzle over how a third-dynasty Chinese box had found its way into the heart of Africa; but let's not digress.)

She idly played with her treasures, building a small enclosure out of the rocks. Then she noticed a slanted shadow etched by the moonlight, and her imagination started rolling. She could see the stones rising, stacked layer upon layer, making a pathway to the moon. That night as she nodded to sleep on her straw mat she saw the moon wink and confirm her plan. She would sculpt a bed for the moon, right there among the rolling hills of her own valley.

When the morning came, she started carrying boulders to the river. She made fires, heated the stones, then dumped them in cool water where they shattered. Her legs and back grew strong as she hauled wood for the fires, and her arms bulged under the boulders that she carried down to the river. Every free moment she had, she worked — watching the stone piles grow into walls.

Of course, this kind of activity couldn't go unnoticed for long, and soon Zimanga had a following of other children who would help her from time to time. The adults were relieved that there was something to preoccupy the youngsters, and they only complained when the building interfered with the execution of chores around the homestead. The main culprits were Zimanga and her best friend Khoteka. In spite of the occasional disagreement, both were so fired by their vision of this path to the moon that they inevitably laughed and hugged and kissed, to show that they really liked each other.

As time went by, they became inseparable — laughing together, eating from the same bowl, and more than often sleeping on the same mat. Often, their secret giggles had to be stifled for fear of waking the others. Besides the pathway to the moon, the greatest secret they shared was a vow never to fall in love with a man. They were women who wanted to walk with their own shadows.

But they were approaching a dangerous age. At eleven or twelve, girls like them were being promised in marriage, to young men who could afford a generous lobola. Both were plump and strong, lively and sharp, competent but unfortunately too independent. This could, of course, bring the bride-price down. Both young women started looking at each other as men would, trying to see what womanly attractions should be avoided. The only problem was that they liked what they saw: Zimanga wanted to hold Khoteka's firm buttocks tight against her hips; and Khoteka couldn't stop her eyes from searching out the rhythm in the sway of Zimanga's walk.

One dark night, as they huddled together in front of the fire, they overheard the grown-ups talking about some people who were coming to speak to Khoteka's family. The voices caused a cloud of fear which made them dive for protection in each other's arms. With Zimanga's strong arms around her back, Khoteka sobbed softly into her shoulder. The stroking, which was meant to pacify, soon transformed to passion. Khoteka turned her big round eyes to look up in Zimanga's face, but was silenced by a warm tongue licking away her tears. Zimanga's lips moved down over Khoteka's mouth to stifle the sobs that still erupted intermittently. That night they proved their love for each other with a passion which confirmed that their vow would hold, no matter what happened.

Glowing in the languorous aftermath of lovemaking, they planned to escape their fate. They realized that the only escape was madness, so they contrived to do something so outrageous that no man would have them. Then it struck them that they should fuel whisperings about a pathway to the moon — it would be the ideal subterfuge. On purpose they let small details of their secret slip, and the manic building started in earnest.

The two fell to the task with an intensity that brooked no reproval. Complaints about the neglect of their duties fell on deaf ears — they merely laughed in scorn at the various attempts to redeem them. At first they were insulted, then scorned, and finally ignored. Their infamy coursed through the valley, into the next, and across the mountains. And meanwhile, the stone edifices arose. People came to admire them, sometimes helped to stack a few layers of stone — always under strict supervision.

Finally they completed a great enclosure — a womb of stone. By now there were many who wanted to live there because it looked inviting and safe. Zimanga and Khoteka were strict: people had to help build the walls if they wanted their protection. So they did. And all the time Khoteka and Zimanga made furrows, for the pathway to the moon.

They lived together in the valley, and later in their lives, when the moon's nest was ready, they started to construct the finger that would beckon the moon down. At the bottom, they made a space for their tomb, from where they would depart for the world of the ancestors, together.

Today, the city still stands.

But why is it that none of the history books mentions the entwined skeletons of two women, which were found at the bottom of the conical tower in the great enclosure?

And why is nobody allowed in the ruins after dark?

I have heard that a drama of the spirits still plays itself out in the moonlight. A man stands at the foot of the tower, entranced, and calls on the two strong women to testify to his virility. The two women, knowing him to be mistaken, start laughing and laughing until the moon joins in and, rolling with laughter, it comes tumbling down the pathway built by Zimanga and Khoteka.

The present government, afraid that these happenings will harm the lucrative tourist market, closes the gates early every evening, before sunset.

Rosalee Telela

Unbroken Silence

Seeking to violate
all that you
were
is like needing
to destroy part
of your soul

Africa goddess of all
Yours is a soul
that has been smashed
by the chains
of male religion

Names given to you
labels of intolerance
bitch, witch;
but you were
mother of revolutionaries
sister to all
Lesbian!

Spirit of the goddess
now you're in me
charging me to
relive all my
lives

Giving me the courage
to be what you were
and I am
as I have always
been
your lover

Wendy Annecke

Discussions in the Canaan Women's Group

Canaan is an informal settlement that was established on the unstable slopes of a vacant hill adjacent to the N2 highway in Durban. Facing the threat of eviction, the residents sought the assistance of the Black Sash. It was as a member of the latter that I became involved in Canaan and in particular with the women's group, which was formed to facilitate the expression of women's needs and interests. The group met once a week and discussions covered a wide range of topics: the frustrations of motherhood, traditional weddings, feeding children, relationships with men, and gossip. Interestingly, gossip was identified by the women as providing the opportunity to learn about other people's social practices. On the occasion recorded here the discussion centred around sexual behaviour with a focus on homosexuality and lesbianism. The group, only one of whom had schooled further than Standard Four and was in paid employment, exchanged information and opinions which revealed an openness and curiosity uncommon in the dominant discourse of our homophobic society. This challenges the notion that the underclasses are either ill-informed or inherently conservative.

The women in the Canaan Women's Group met once a week at Sis Mkhize's shack. On this particular afternoon I arrived at the shack to find a lively discussion in progress and was privileged to share the women's understanding of the role of gossip in their lives for the transmission of information and the exploration of different ideas and attitudes. On this occasion homosexual and lesbian anecdotes were swapped and an admirable openness and tolerance were revealed. Once our greetings had been completed I asked what I had interrupted and the conversation that followed went like this:

'Nothing really, we were just gossiping.'

'Do you like gossiping?'

Sis Mkhize explained to me. Her voice was honey-coloured, warm and thick. 'Do we like gossiping? It's our l-o-v-e. More especially in the evenings when everyone has had supper. Women come to my shack almost every evening and we sit gossiping until eleven o'clock.... What do we gossip about? A-l-l things, even sex. We learn a lot from each other talking about sex. Only last evening I shared a special story with the other women about this friend of mine called Ben.

'Ben was married. He had a peaceful and stable marriage. But one day he had this adventure which changed things in his life. It was a Friday and we met after work for a few drinks at a local hotel. I was expected home but Ben and some others went on to a party.'

Her tone changed to one of excitement. 'The people at the party were very glad to see him. They said, "Hmm, we've run out of things to drink. Could you please help us with your car? Could you go to another shebeen and get some beer and spirits?" Ben was happy to oblige because by supplying the transport he could drink for free for the evening.

'Now apart from having a car, Ben was big and tall and handsome. Just as he was pulling off, a young man jumped into the passenger seat next to him. The road to the shebeen wasn't quite smooth or straight. As he went around the corner, Ben leaned against this young man who immediately started holding him and stroking his leg. Straight away it rang a bell with Ben that this young man must be homosexual. And he thought, "All right, today's my day — I'm going to learn all about homosexuality." Then, as if it were a mistake, he brushed his cheek against the young man's. The boy just turned around and kissed him once.

' "Heh!" I said, "Ben, how could you do this?"

' "Hmm," he replied, "you know I am very much adventurous. I just wanted to know what happens between men." They got the booze and went back to the other party.

'After a while Ben approached this young man and said [Sis demonstrated in a conspiratorial whisper], "Excuse me, would you like to come with me?" Then Ben and the young man went to another friend of ours who is good at entertaining people. We all used to go there; if you were down or frustrated you could go there and be sure you would cheer up because you'd meet all sorts of people there. All classes of people went there from graduates to nobodies, and we'd all blend so well. Now when they got there, Ben spoke to the owner of the house who offered them a room. There he experienced what he had never experienced before — being intimate with another man.'

A communal sigh rose and fell in the shack. Sis continued:

'Ben told me that homosexual love is much better than having a woman. When I asked him why, he said, "Sis, listen to me. A woman is so adamant. A woman is just bad; you tell her not to do something and she'll do it. A woman is just cheeky; outright very cheeky. These men who are homosexual, they respect you, they are so loving. When you have sex with one you have no fear that he's going to fall pregnant. You have no fear that whenever you have missed him, he's going to tell you he's unwell, that he's got his monthly periods — there's nothing like that. He'll always buy the best food when you are coming, unlike your wife. When she cooks, it's fish and putu. She'll tell you, 'Eh! There's putu and fish, take it or leave it.' A man will bring you the best food, and the sex is much more adventurous."

'When Ben discovered homosexuality he forgot about his wife for three months. I had to talk to him very seriously so he wouldn't let these new experiences affect his marriage....'

She leaned back satisfied. It was the turn of the other women to tell of their encounters with homosexuals.

Memi and Dora said they knew a lot about homosexuals. They even knew areas which were restricted to homosexuals. Memi knew of an area in Durban North and Dora knew another in Greyville. Nozi said Musgrave was where homosexuals stay together and if, after eight o'clock, they see you as a woman walking alone, if there is no one coming they will get hold of you. They'll hit you and stab you because as a female you are a rival.

Lindiwe told of a certain teacher called Mr K in Claremont. The story was that he was homosexual and always used to have many boys around him. One of these boys was forced by his parents to get married. But when it came to bedtime this boy would dodge going to sleep because he didn't want to share a bed with his wife. He would go to the bathroom and lock himself inside. This was because he was missing Mr K.

The women's laughter and clucks were both derisive and sympathetic.

A question as to whether there was general hostility towards homosexuals elicited different responses. One woman said she thought there was widespread hostility and personally she was afraid of the whole subject because it was strange to her. Another explained how she had been afraid of homosexuality but she had to accept it 'because I have learned to know more about it. I feel it's something people cannot change. I came to accept it because it so happened that two of my very close male friends are homosexual. I watched them closely and I could see that there was absolutely nothing that could be done to change the way they behaved. In fact one was a priest, my priest, and the whole congregation rejected him and attacked him openly. Even academic people, people who are supposed to know or look at things with a broader frame of mind — they seemed to attack from the church side of the thing. I felt very bad about it. At the time he had no shoulder to cry on; I just had to stand by him all the time....'

A question about lesbianism drew a largely positive response, and one woman explained: 'Three of us here have never been acquainted with lesbians, but I would very much like to be friends with a lesbian. I'm very adventurous — I like to be extraordinary and try different things.' Another woman told of her experience of 'two married women whose husbands went to Johannesburg to the gold mines. These two women were attracted to each other, fell in love and had a lesbian relationship. This went on and on until their families and the in-laws' families all knew about it, and someone had to tell their spouses in Johannesburg. One of the husbands came back. He beat his wife severely and said to her, "It would have been better if you had had a private affair with another male so as not to disgrace and embarrass me so much by having an affair with another woman." ' All the women jeered at this.

Thoko said her friend, Vini, had worked for two white women who stayed together. Vini had asked them, 'Why do you choose to have this kind of arrangement, where I have to make only one bed for two ladies?' They answered that two women loving each other is f-f-f-a-a-r-r better. When the house was dirty either one of them cleaned it; they were not going to fall pregnant sleeping with each other; they were not going to catch any diseases from each other, and it was just convenient. It's just much better. To which a woman added, 'So although the three of us aren't quite familiar with this, we have learned what others tell us and are happy.'

Considering the uniformly heterosexual standards and values taught by the society, the ease with which most of the women embraced notions of variable sexual practices may be considered remarkable. The implications of each account are for each reader to unpack for herself; keeping in mind that the women were either working class or unemployed, came from relatively conservative backgrounds and had little or no schooling. None would call herself a feminist. Yet their attitudes challenge the notion that the status quo is maintained by the unconscientized. The criticism levelled by one woman specifically at academics for their hypocrisy, and the enthusiasm of another to have a 'lesbian friend', are perhaps the most telling moments of the discussion.

Marcellus J. Muthien

The Creation

I have first seen you
in a magazine
my eyes rolling like pearls of sweat
down the dark contours
of your body — taut as a bow

I have searched for you
everywhere
but when I got there
you were gone

have you ever been there

where I could look
I have
but

have you ever been

dreamed up
tonight I will
blow you to life
and my fingers will frantically feel
the ebony wood sculpture
muscle to life

and will it be true
I would need to know

have you ever

like wood burnt black and polished to perfection
glowed with a light of your own
I will ignite you
and let your dark nipples nestle
in the round softness of my lips
and you will come into me
with your halo of pubic hair
to make music like magic
from rhythm into rhyme

have you

lavaed into me
then come watch
my beautiful brown body
move glisteningly in the mirror
before the morning sun
would make me search for you

I will have you know
that I have made me
for you and you for me to come

have

Marcellus J. Muthien

Brother

Because you used to say
you'd take me for a ride
I used to wait for you
'til shadows grew long
and my longing for you
was overcome by mummy's food
drowsying my gooseflesh arms
to come inside the warm kitchen
where chicken casserole cackled
around everyone and sizzling lamps and candles

wash your hands mummy says
and I will wash my hands
slowly
looking through the window
for the long blue car
come eat now and I would eat
slowly
thinking how I will get up and
out in the frosty morning tomorrow
to help soap your beautiful body
in the cold shower of the outhouse
feeling the smoothness of your muscles
under my small bubble-purring hands
excited that I should not
get wet
or I will get a cold you know
mom said
but watch out don't shake your hair
so much
the candle will go out
and your big shadow
would not look able
to break through

MARCELLUS J. MUTHIEN

the concrete walls of the small toilet
and I would smell the soap
that filmed us together
when you kissed me goodbye
and nuzzled my neck
before you went to big school
and I could sleep for two hours more
mum said stop lying awake in the early
hours of the morning aah isn't he
sweet
mwha mwha   help

so many shadows have passed
and another monster from my mind
made me remember

that I am still waiting

Vivienne Ndatshe & Mpande wa Sibuyi

Love on the Mines

The following interviews, by Vivienne Ndatshe and Mpande wa Sibuyi, were part of the background research for the study 'Migrancy and Male Sexuality on the South African Gold Mines' by T. Dunbar Moodie.

They were recorded separately by the interviewers, who travelled to the rural areas to speak to elderly men who had spent many years working on the South African mines. The interviews contain recollections of mine life dating from the 1930s, 1940s and 1950s.

The interviewer Vivienne Ndatshe and the anthropologist T. Dunbar Moodie have collaborated on a number of research projects about the lives of township residents, people's resistance during historical strikes, and various topics about aspects of miners' lives, including sexuality.

In Pondoland in August of 1982, Vivienne Ndatshe collected life-histories from old men in the countryside. She was particularly interested in miners' lives because her father had been a mineworker. Two of these interviews, with 'Daniel' and 'Themba', are included here.

In February of 1987, Mpande wa Sibuyi travelled to the Bushbuckridge area to interview the Tsonga man 'Philemon', who, as a youth, had migrated to South Africa from Mozambique to work on the mines. Mpande wa Sibuyi was assisting the historian Patrick Harries who later authored 'Symbols and Sexuality: Culture and Identity on the Early Witwatersrand Gold Mines'. 'Philemon' had worked on the mines with one of Sibuyi's relatives.

These three interviews contain accounts of the system of homosexual love that has been widely practised in the single-sex compounds of the South African mines.

Vivienne Ndatshe

Two Miners
*Interviews with 'Daniel' and 'Themba'
conducted in August 1982*

I. Daniel

Daniel went to the mines. He wanted to work so that he could eventually pay lobola, the price by which he could marry his betrothed. He wanted a household, like married men had.

He left for the mines with two older men who were already working there. The trader, for whom he had worked as a youth, gave him three pounds, two of which were his provision; the third he gave to his mother.

His father had been a miner, and when he was very young his father would talk about the mines. He remembered that one day, on his return from the mines, his father brought back boots and a yellow raincoat called the *umgwaja*. This was the clothing used underground. And when Daniel tended the cattle he would wear the raincoat, and the boots, which were too big for him.

He left for the mines with his friends. His ambition was to go to Springs, the place his father always talked of. But the men with whom he went left for City Deep. On the train to Jo'burg, they happily sang songs. Miners on the train said to the new ones, 'Where are you going to? You will think of your mothers when umlungu will be kicking you!' When the new ones heard this, they took no notice.

'When we arrived at Mzilikazi there were policemen from different mines who came to meet people. Our policeman took us to a waiting bus. We arrived at City Deep and we were given food, and we slept on sacks in a hall. On the following day all the new miners went to see the doctor, and then we were taken to the compound rooms. Afterwards we went to have our lunch, and then we had to rest.

'While in the hall we were told *umthetho* of the compound by a policeman, together with the manager. Then the compound manager talked

Vivienne Ndatshe

Fanakalo language which every miner knew. We were told not to go to the township, because the mine wouldn't be responsible for one's death or injury if one went outside of the mine.'

'I took eight days in the mine school, underground. There was nothing difficult about it and it went quickly. Then, having learnt about mining, I was transferred underground to work there. I was *layisha* for nine months.

'The new miners were fearful of the white staff. We were afraid and worked very hard. The boots we wore were heavy and the heat was terrible.

'After a few months I was used to the hard job. But I wasn't sending money home nor writing letters. I was used to the mine life, staying in the compound, paying visits to other homeboys on the other mines. Together we were drinking beer, and eating compound meat.

'We obeyed and respected the law. No one ever went to the township in those days, especially Pondos, unless one had a Basotho friend who took you with him, to the township, to visit his friends. The person with whom you went had to ask for a permit, from the clerk of the mine, to go to the township.

'While I was in Crown Mines there was a faction fight between Bomvanas and Basothos. I don't know what year that was because I didn't go to school. But the Pondos helped the Bomvanas while they fought. I don't know the reason for the fight, but I do remember that Basothos and Bomvanas often quarrelled. In this fight many Basothos were killed. Soldiers were called in, and only then were the miners afraid.

'Faction fights, like this, would happen over weekends, when miners participated in traditional dancing competitions. While they did *indlamu* and other dances the fighting would break out. Sometimes, when this fighting broke out, miners from other mines would get involved.

'In the compound each tribe lives separately to others, and so compounds housed only Pondos or Xhosas, etc. People only mixed at work.'

'Eventually I went back home to where my parents still lived and bought some cattle.

'Then I went back to Crown Mines. I worked there for nine months as a driver of the *ingolovane*. For this I was paid 23 cents a day. Then, without going home, I went to Simmer and Jack where I worked as a boss boy.

'After some time, I went back home from Simmer and Jack; in fact, I went home from this mine three times, and each time I returned to the same job. As a boss boy it was very difficult to look after the miners. They were

New recruits await their medical examinations.
Photograph courtesy of the Africana Museum

cheeky, and some preferred to be ordered by a white man than by myself. And there was no chance of that because the boss boys were in charge.'

'There were boss boys who liked boys. Don't tell anyone but I had done that once myself. There were boys who looked like women, fat and pretty, handsome. My girlfriend was a Basotho young lad. I was not ill-treating him as other boss boys did. I was very nice to him, did everything for him, and he was very polite.

'I did that, firstly, because miners were not allowed to go and visit women in the township. Then, I felt very lonely for the long period without meeting a woman. I was bored, I needed someone to be with me. I didn't do it in public, not in the room where all the miners lived together. I did it in the old section of the mine, underground, where people no longer worked.

'I proposed love to him in the compound, called on him in our spare time. I promised to give him some of my pay, but not all of it as the other miners did. And he agreed. I warned him that everything was our secret. I didn't want my homeboys to know I was doing this, because they may have told people at home, or girlfriends on the farm. But I loved that boy very much. He had quick feelings, but he had to control himself because he was my girlfriend. Also, I loved him because he was a very quiet person. Other miners didn't notice at all. They were proposing love to him in my presence. If they knew they would never do that, because there would be trouble.

'With my boy we parted as we left for our homes. And after that we didn't write to each other. It was only friendship on the mines.'

'I went to Buffelsfontein, and from there to Luipaardsvlei where I was a machine boy. And then from there to Robinson Deep, where I had the same job as on other mines.

'When I was at Robinson Deep, again, I was a boss boy. There, I had an induna as my best friend, and he took me to the township. Again, at Robinson Deep, I had a boy, and my friend the induna also had one. But in the township we both had girlfriends. When we went to the township we left our boys in the compound. But we never slept in the township, we just took a few hours with our girlfriends and then went back to our boys. We loved them better.

'I went to Welkom, Number One Mine, three times more. It was better, the mine was new. There were women there, and there were inspectors who checked the food in the kitchen and the cleanliness in the compound rooms.

'After work we did our manual jobs in our rooms, work we were not paid for. Indunas and clerks had their separate quarters. They were given rations of raw meat and food. They were permitted to cook in their quarters. And that's where boys would cook for their lovers.

'Throughout all my joins I was sending money home to my family. It was safe. There were homeboys whom I trusted, although not all of them. Only one man, my uncle, did I send money home with, and he gave me his money when I left for home.'

'I now live at home with my wife and children. All those years she looked after my house, worked in the fields, made home-brew, and was helped by other clan people and next-door neighbours.

'My mates and I converse sometimes about our life in the mines, how we enjoyed ourselves with other tribes. But with other tribes with whom we were friendly.'

II. Themba

I talked to Themba near my home. He came to the isangoma's house.

He had worked at Hartbeesfontein. They called it KwaMatshetshisu in Xhosa, as they could not say the Afrikaans name. He went to the mines with two of his friends. Tribes stayed separately and so, being Pondos, they stayed together in the same room.

On the mines Themba was *layisha*. In the first week he nearly ran away. It was very difficult to load the ore and the boss boy was pushing him and told him, 'You will agree!'

At first he didn't understand what the boss boy was talking about, and he asked another old man why the boss boy was being so cruel to him. The old man laughed.

The old man told him that the boss boy was after him because he was young and fat. He said that he became very angry and decided to hit the man. On the following day he went underground, as usual. Again, the boss

1939 — Miners after-hours in a single-sex hostel.
Photograph courtesy of the Africana Museum

boy ill-treated him. He became very angry and asked him what he thought he was. But the boss boy didn't stop saying those words.

Then one day they fought. Themba took the boss boy to the white man and told him the whole story, but the white man took no notice of that. The only thing he did was to change Themba to another section, under another boss boy. Then he worked well with that man. He finished six months and went home. He didn't stay long at home and went back to KwaMatshetshisu.

He returned to the mines a second time and worked as a timber boy. He earned better wages, 30 cents a day. On his first join it had been 20 cents a day, but now he was older and had some experience.

The white staff were friendly to the workers, and as a result there were no strikes during both of his terms on the mines.

In his spare time he visited his friends from other mines. With them he had a lovely time, bought beer and meat. They talked about their homes, and their relatives on the farm. Sometimes they sent money home with a best friend or with an old man they trusted, when such people went home. But the mine managers did not like that.

During weekends they enjoyed themselves by visiting other mines, and they held dance competitions. The manager of the compound, where the competition took place, gave them beer. And then sometimes they won money to buy a goat from a white farmer nearby. Then they killed the goat, and had a good time with their friends.

Indunas and cooks had their separate quarters. They were given raw food, which was of good quality, and they cooked it themselves. But if they had young boys then these 'girlfriends' would cook for them, and would also do their washing, and the cleaning of their rooms.

'I went to Welkom, and I worked at KwaMampondo. During that time I didn't visit the township or the surrounding farms. We obeyed the law of not going out of the compound after work.

'Among the tribes-people who enjoyed visiting the township were Basothos. All Xhosa-speaking miners, especially red blanket people, didn't visit the townships at all. The Xhosas from Ciskei were not very friendly to other Xhosa-speakers like Pondos, etc. They regarded them as boys. Once a fight broke out because someone called a Nguni man a "boy". The man was insulted since only uncircumcised people are referred to as boys. But it was not a serious fight and it was stopped by indunas.

'When I finished six months of work there, I left for home. I bought some cattle, and with these cattle I got married to my lover who waited patiently all those years that I worked on the mines. And then I went back to work in Welkom.

'Once married, I sent money to my wife with another man whom I trusted, when he went home. But this man never gave my money to my family. And when I asked him where my money was, he told me he had been pick-pocketed.

'The second time I worked in Welkom I stayed for a year. I was a boss boy and I looked after people. But sometimes people didn't want to listen and one had to be very strong and had to talk to them, sometimes with cruelty, or politely to those who paid one respect.

'During the second term I worked at Welkom I saw *stabans*, men dressed like women, and miners proposed love to them. Most of these people were clerks, but I don't know which tribe they belonged to.'

Themba admitted that most of the miners agreed to be 'girls of the mines'. Some wanted to pay lobola once they had returned to their homes, so that they could marry their wives, and the money they worked for was too little. They did it to make money.

He also mentioned that boys always said, 'Why should we worry since we can't get pregnant?'

But when they went home no one talked about what had happened, because it was a disgrace for a man to do those things — what would his wife or girlfriend have said?

Mpande wa Sibuyi

Tinkoncana Etimayinini: The Wives of the Mines

Interview with 'Philemon' conducted in February 1987

When people leave their homes in Mozambique to go and work on the mines, do they leave Mozambique in groups or as individuals?
Many people would leave in small groups. For instance, two friends would walk together all the way from Mozambique. People would also leave in groups of three or four or five. It was all right as long as people knew where they were going. The one thing that people seemed not to prefer was travelling in large groups.

How did people know the way?
That was not a problem, as one would ask along the way until one arrived at one's destination.

How many days would people spend on their way to Johannesburg?
Well, some would walk to Kimberley. But anyway, people would normally walk for a week to Johannesburg.

Tell me, what were the average wages for miners in those days?
Well, there wasn't much money in those days you know. A person would earn three pounds and ten. And then they would still tell you that the money was too much. But things were not really expensive in those days. Jan Smuts's money was not as bad as that which we are having now.

Tell me about the journey?
When they left for the mines *xigugu* would be made for them.

Would the xigugu *last you until you arrived on the mine?*
Yes, and anyway it was not taken along for the sake of satisfying one like a full meal, but just to keep you going until you arrived on the mines. One would just cut a piece and then drink water.

Did you take xigugu *only?*
Yes, what else could one take except *xigugu*? You wouldn't take porridge, because then it would rot on the way. As for *tihove*, one would only keep it for two days, or sometimes even a day only.[1] So what was most preferred was *xigugu*.

Can you tell me something about TEBA (The Employment Bureau of Africa) contracts?
When they arrived in South Africa, some would get employment whereas others would not, and they would therefore have to go back home.

Those who were contracted onto the mines did so through the TEBA system. For people from Mozambique this system operated almost as if they were being sold to South Africa by the Portuguese colonists of Mozambique. This was because South Africa would pay a certain amount of money to the Portuguese for each labourer, without you even knowing how much you are worth. If you ran away you would have to come back and finish up your join.

How long would some people stay on the mines without going home?
Some would complete their joins and instead of going back home they would just stay on the compound or mine from which they got their initial join. They'd get another join, and then go back to their respective places of work. In most cases people would do this if they had not saved enough money.

Also, equally important is the fact that some of them would stay longer on the mines because of their boy on the mine.

Tell me about these relationships.
On the mines there were compounds which consisted of houses, each of which had a xibonda inside. The xibonda's job was as head of the living quarters, he had authority and was known as a counsellor.[2]

Each of these xibondas would propose a boy for himself, not only for the sake of washing his dishes, because in the evening the boy would have to go and join the xibonda on his bed. In that way he had become a wife. He, the husband, would double his join on the mines because of his boy. He would make love with him. The husband would penetrate his manhood between the boy's thighs. You would find a man buying a bicycle for his boy. He would buy him many pairs of trousers, shirts and many blankets. Eventually the young miners would go back home to their parents or wives with many things, after having been substitute wives on the mines.

The old ones did this because, by experience, they knew that they were not allowed to go and have fun outside the compounds. It was unlike today, today miners are at least independent to go where they like outside the compound. The mine managers' idea was that they were protecting us, since they were afraid that we would get killed outside the mine. And that is why some had to become wives there. But anyway, they were getting paid.

Was it possible that a man would enjoy the homosexual relationship on the mines better than that between himself and his wife at home?
Yes! For a fact I know that some men enjoyed 'penetrating the thighs' more than they did with the real thing!

What would they do to make the wife look feminine?
They would get pieces of clothing material and they would sew it together so that it appeared like real breasts. They would then attach it to other strings that made it look almost like a bra so that at the evening dancing 'she' would arrive with the husband. It would appear very real. Don't forget that guys used to play guitars there!

Wouldn't the boys feel shy?
No, no! That was a norm on the mines.

Did everyone have these kinds of friendships, or did this occur only among the xibondas?
Others who worked there would do it also. But they did it without the xibonda's knowledge, because otherwise quarrels would break out.

Even if they were not having a relationship with the xibonda's boy?
Yes, because once you have a boy for yourself it means that you expect others to respect you as well. You put yourself on the same level as the xibonda.

What else can you remember about tinkoncana*?*
When a boy decided to fall in love with a man other than his husband, especially in the same house, there would be a fight which was most likely to be taken to the seniors.[3] These were called the indunas, also known as boss boys, and they would fine the culprit for breach of contract or for

undermining so-and-so's husband. Then they would collect fines from him for two months. Even the indunas had their own boys. That was a known fact. In most cases the indunas were the first to choose the best from newcomers.

Would the men propose to the boys in just the same manner as a man proposes to a real girl? Would 'she' really behave like a girl? You know how sometimes women try to put the whole conversation of love-proposing upside-down, telling one to wait.

Yes, they would do that. But sometimes if he rejected so-and-so's proposal, he would get bewitched, mostly to the effect that he would die when working underground.

Wasn't there anything concerning tinkoncana *that sometimes sparked a conflict? Do you remember people fighting over a boy?*

Not really. But what I can remember is that the man would buy gifts, for example a bicycle, for his boy — things that he could not buy for himself. I remember that if you proposed love to someone's boy, you were liable to a fine. And that, in most cases, the man would go home at the same time with his wife.

But if they didn't come from the same place, then, when it came time to go back to the mines, one partner would inform the other through a letter. In this manner they could meet again, at a stipulated place, or again on the mines.

How would the relationship come to an end?

When the boy thought he was old enough he would tell the husband that he also wished to get himself a wife, and that would be the end. Therefore the husband would have to get himself another boy.

Was it possible that the xibonda would refuse a boy's request to end the relationship?

No, as long as you were old enough there would be no problem. That was the way of life. You would just have to explain that you are experiencing some biological problems at night.[4] You would then have to wait for newcomers, when you could choose. After choosing you would just show him which bed was yours so he could choose a bed closer to yours. But, anyway, people would not make love when others were still conversing in the evening. They would wait for everybody to sleep.

Was it not possible for the women back home to know about what was happening on the mines. Did people not say things like, 'My husband is so-and-so's wife...?'
They knew it! They knew that once a man was on the mines, he had a boy or was turned into a 'wife' himself.

So, how did they feel about it? Weren't they angry about it?
No, why should they be angry? Besides that, even if they knew, what would they do? Nothing!

What about the bosses, the whites? Did they know about it? And if they knew, what did they do about it?
The whites also used to do it, especially on the sites underground — a white man working underground would have a toolboy. Most would use these toolboys for 'boys' — and these were black boys.

I think I heard you talk about evening dances — when the boys would dance with their husbands. What type of songs would they sing?
They would come together in the evening when they had finished their supper. After their evening wash or bath they would listen to guitars being played by those who had them — jiving the *muchongolo* and participating in *makhwaya*. That was their way of entertainment — to take their minds away from their workplace issues and to help them forget about home.

Was it not possible for the women from home to visit their husbands on the mines?
Women were not allowed on the compounds. Moreover, people were not allowed to go outside the compound premises. What if you got killed out there? One's safety was also part of one's responsibility.

Can you sing for me some of the songs that were sung at gatherings?
Many work-songs were sung. These were the same that were sung when heavy things were lifted, especially underground. Some, however, were very historical. One such was 'Hey Mpisana, you are swallowed by the mountains'.

Do you know what the song is all about?
It's about a specific regiment in the past. It is sung from the point of view of a man called Thulamahashe, to another called Mpisana. Thulamahashe

left his home to go and settle near a place today referred to as Bushbuckridge. In the song Thulamahashe travels back to Mpisana to tell him to come and join him, because he has found a place where there is plenty of room for settlement.

'Swallowed by the mountain' refers to somebody's wandering. In this instance, Thulamahashe is telling Mpisana to stop his wandering.

Let's go back to the young boys. Do these relationships still exist on the mines?
Well, things have changed. In this case the basic change is that men can now go out to meet women outside.

Did the boys take pride in the fact that they were so-and-so's wife?
Yes. And if somebody attempted to propose to so-and-so's boy, then the boy warned him that he would tell his husband. And the one attempting to do so would give up, especially if he knew that the husband was very tough. Besides, he knew he would be tried and subsequently would face a fine, as I have already explained.

Was it possible that a nkoncana, *a 'wife', had a wife and children at home?*
Most cases were exactly so — especially those who had just married, the younger ones!

One thing that a *nkoncana* had to do was either to cover his beard with a cloth, or cut it off completely. He was now so-and-so's wife. How would it be if a couple looked identical? There had to be differences. And for a *nkoncana* to stay clean-shaven was one of them.

Once the *nkoncana* became a grown-up he could keep his beard to indicate his maturity, which would be demonstrated by him acquiring a boy.

Please tell me something more about tinkoncana. *It's the first time I hear about it and I think it would be important if it was written down. So please tell me everything, even what you think is not important.*
It was a bit tough then. That was not normal life. A newcomer was orientated into the mines in the most inhuman way. But I can only say this now, because I am looking at it in retrospect. But anyway, by the time a new worker arrived on the mines he had already been informed about what was going on there. He would then internalize it. He would accept it as a way of life, and even derive a sense of security from it, because he knew he wouldn't have to struggle about acquiring property — trousers, etc.

A 'husband' would rather live without anything to put on, than live without the boy. But don't forget that the boy would never make the mistake of 'breathing out' into the hubby. It was taboo. Only the hubby could 'breathe out' into the boy's legs! If the boy tried to 'breathe out', he would face a charge.

The whole system of homosexuality was known as Sokisi's Law; just like in Physics, we have Newton's Law, etc.

Who was this Sokisi?
He came from Mozambique. There was once a placard of him next to the offices of The Employment Bureau of Africa at Acornhoek, just next to the hospital. On the drawing he appeared with something that looked like tubes on his knees — they were used on the mines by underground workers to protect themselves from receiving dangerous cuts on the rocks. Sokisi was the one who brought this love to the mines. I am not sure what his name really was.[5]

Anything else?
Yes. If problems were experienced concerning 'wives' and 'husbands', they were referred to indunas. If the induna failed to resolve the problem he would take it to a compound manager. A fine would then be imposed on the culprit.

So it was accepted?
Yes. That was everybody's way of survival.

Can you tell me some of the mines in which homosexuality was practised?
All the mines, but those that I know well are Daggafontein, Springs, Benoni. On all the mines.

All the mines had the Law of Sokisi. The whole bureaucracy on the mines knew about it and they did not oppose it. Anyway, they helped to solve problems pertaining to it, especially the compound managers.

So these people behaved like they were married. That's the impression that has built up in me.
In most cases the relationship would end when they would go home for ever or, as I have explained, when the boy was old enough to start his own family. They would quarrel just as husbands and wives do. Some quarrels would also lead to divorce.

Were there prostitutes also? Were there those who would move from one husband to another for money-making purposes?
Yes, just like in conventional social situations! Prostitutes were mostly avoided. Sometimes a prostitute would be moved or expelled from one house into another. But that did not help solve the problem.

What if somebody refused to be so-and-so's wife?
Death or bewitchment would prevail. Then they would find things more problematic. As I said, they are more independent now. A man would die simply because he refused to be so-and-so's boy! It's just like what some people do to girls if they refuse to love them. Some would kill others with lightning, etc.

Was there also witchcraft on the mines?
Yes. There were also inyangas on the mines, but they were mineworkers also. Some would divine during their spare time, and people would come flocking to them in search of help.

You must understand that all the men had to stay on the compound. One had to get permission to go out to town, or any other place outside the compound situation. People were given the beer we call *mqomboti*, and other basic supplies there.

On the question of tinkoncana, *was it possible for two relatives to be husband and wife?*
No, it was impossible. It is like you cannot make love to your sister.

Regarding the fact that we Africans have long been practising polygamy, was it possible for a man to have more than one boy?
No, unless one was greedy.... Oh, yes it used to happen! It would depend on whether the 'husband' could afford to pay them both.

Would all the boys know it?
Yes, they would even boast about it.

In other words, it was possible for one to go home without money because of the 'family expenses' on the mines. Is that right?
Yes. People would turn back to the mines on the way back home, because it was embarrassing to arrive there without money. They would then have to work again, accumulate money until it was enough for them to buy things, and go back home.

Let's shift a bit now. Do you know anything about 'deserting' — people shifting from one job to another in search of greener pastures?
Yes, it was there, but it was not common. What I know well is that one could only leave a job for another after a contract expired. They would take you to jail if you ran away. One could not just escape.

I understand that all people from Mozambique had to have the 'Portuguese man's' passbook. Do you know anything concerning that?
Yes. It was used to confirm that you had been employed in South Africa. In the early days people around here would get it from Spelonker, and later from Nelspruit. There were officers there. I am not sure if the offices are still there.

Would people come from Mozambique to stay the whole five months on the compounds?
Not really, because although the boys were there, some would go out to look for females outside. But as I said, you would need permission to go out. You would meet a woman outside and 'finalize your things' with her in the bush, after which payment, to the woman, would follow. There was no other place to sleep with her because her employers would not let you onto their premises. Also, some miners would get killed by robbers outside of the mines.

Tell me some types of sport that people used for entertainment there.
Makhwaya, which was formal singing, and timbila, which was African drums and organ playing. And there were other forms of music that are no longer played these days. One song that I can remember goes like this, '*Mchocholozeni, mchocholozeni*, push the rock boys.'

This was sung when rocks or other heavy things were either pushed or lifted.

Was it not possible for one house to form a squad and play against another?
What used to happen is that people from different houses would bring money together and then buy things like tea and bread, which were considered to be luxuries, and eat together. 'Husbands' would bring along their wives. Also, when somebody was leaving the mines for ever, there were farewell parties where workers from different houses would come together. That was one way of a come-together. It was more sad when the person in whose favour it was thrown was friendly with people. Then many people

would come together, some of whom had never known each other. The boys would make the tea when the husbands were seated around the tables.

What other duties, in addition to legwork, were performed by the boys?
They would wash and iron their husbands' clothes and pack everything neatly. They did not want to be told, because it was their job.

Would the boy tell his hubby if ever he was going away, to his home or to the shops?
Yes, he had to. And if the hubby had time he would also go along. In practice, the boy would not just stand up and say it. He had to say goodbye, or any other thing, when in a kneeling position.

Would the boys have gossips, just like women?
Yes, they would perhaps discuss things like, 'My husband bought me this-and-this', or 'My husband is good for this-and-that'. And if a husband was stingy he would also come under discussion.

What about battering, was it common?
No, mine wives did not allow that. All one could do in cases of conflict was to report to the xibondas. These people were ranked. They were referred to as Xibonda No.1 and Xibonda No.2. All had boys for preventing conflicts between xibondas. Otherwise, if a xibonda did not have a boy, which was very rare, he would have to 'take care of' the other xibonda's boy when he had gone home. Even in this case, payment would still have to be effected. However, this would not be done explicitly because conflict would inevitably follow.

How do you think newcomers felt about being chosen to be wives when they had just arrived?
What could they do? At first, they must have disliked it, but then they would internalize it. It was a way of life on the mines.

We are just about to close the issue of boys, but there might be things that I have not asked you. Would you like to say anything you think is of importance?
It was possible that the husband was the first to go home. The wife would then give him things to take to 'her' home. Clothes, other equipment and messages. Upon arrival at 'her' home, he would be warmly welcomed —

chickens would be slaughtered. Especially if the wife's father knew that this very same man was 'looking after' his son on the mines. Alternatively, the same would happen to the wife if 'she' was the first to visit home. However, understanding what type of a relationship was going on, the elders would not talk about it, because it was taboo. It's just like now, son. If you had a wife, surely you would not tell me what you do with your wife behind doors. It was like that. Some of the women back home would even know what was meant by 'looking after each other'. There was no other way. One could hardly escape it. If somebody wanted you, he would go as far as sending people to come and propose to you on his behalf — until you agreed.

What about the boys? Did they wish they were so-and-so's wife?
Yes. For the sake of security, for the acquisition of property and for the fun itself. I mean, a *nkoncana* would go home with bicycles and many other things, things whose value exceeded the money that he had earned considerably. And once it was like that, the elders knew why. It's just like now, a man would rather starve himself to death, as long as his woman has all the things that she wants in the world. But it was better, because the boy would look after your things, wash your clothes, etc. It's unlike now, you spend all your money buying clothes and giving money to your wife, with whom you are not even staying.[6] That's somehow a loss of money. I mean, she does not even wash your vest. With the boys it was better because, really, what pleasure? I mean, it was just as good as one making love to oneself. But anyway, one would get the psychological relief because circumstances were bad.

Now tell me something, was it not possible for the women back home to suspect that so-and-so might be their husband's 'wife'? Especially when one would bring messages and things from the mines?
Not really. Some would, but they would never really say it out. It was taboo!

So one would not have cases of women at home quarrelling with the messengers, or the man himself, when he came back home?
Not really. What caused many quarrels at home was when a man would come back from the mines empty-handed. They would fight. It's just like myself here, I am working, and at the end of every week I'm supposed to go home or send something home. What if I don't? It's not easy to tell. If

you did not bring anything home, the suspicions of 'legs' would come up. A man would then go back to the mines for another term.

Let's shift a bit again. Tell me, what usually caused strikes on the mines?
It was possible that people would strike for food. If you went to the kitchen you would sometimes be given a bone instead of meat. It once happened to me at FOSKOR Mine.

Did you work there?
Yes. I worked there from 1953 until 1959. That's when I went to TOC (Transvaal Ore Company), where Phalaborwa Mining Company is today. I then came back for another two years. I was staying at the married quarters. We were staying with our wives and children, because there was a place for married ones and a place for the soldiers or guards.

One day they served me with a cartilage bone and, I mean, I did not go on strike but I just went to the compound manager. He then called Jackson the induna and asked why it had happened that way. I was then given a *bakoyao*, which was how we referred to a big tin of fish in Portuguese. The staff were given a warning.

People would go on strike if the food was either not good or was very little. They would also go on strike if the beer served was very little. They would strike for that, only that! People would die for that. Once somebody was arrested for brewing illegal beer called *thothotho*.[7] And the drinkers even incited the non-drinkers to go on strike! People, like myself, did not know the cause of the strike, but that did not stop us from showing solidarity.

You see, what the whites had done by then was that they made sure that people would go on strike for petty things, like food and beer. Not for money, in those days. No! They would say that the money was enough because you had crops at home.

In other words, the money that they gave you was to sustain you as an individual only, and not for your family.

Notes

1. *Tihove*, a meal that is prepared by boiling some ground grains of maize. In most cases the grains of maize are mixed with ground beans. When these have been boiled for almost four hours, ground peanuts are added. After another hour of cooking it is salted and served, usually while it is still warm.
2. The xibonda was an elected member of each house who could take the inmates' grievances to management. One must note that the xibonda system was also used by management to find out what was happening in every house.
3. This is not to suggest that if the new partner was from another house then it would be acceptable. But one must bear in mind that interaction, except in sport, was limited.
4. It was not possible for the boy to penetrate the xibonda. Only the xibonda could do the penetrating.
5. Biographical research into the life of Sokisi has been attempted, but without any success.

    [It has been suggested to me that Sokisi is adapted from the English word 'socks'. This might refer to the tubes that miners wrapped around their knees to protect themselves from the rocks. — Ed.]
6. Philemon is a migrant worker himself, but does not stay in the compounds. He has a four-roomed home in the townships where he stays alone.
7. *Thothotho* is a very strong, distilled spirit made by women in secret places in the bush. A person caught with such liquor could receive a five-year sentence.

Stephen Gray

The Building-Site

A lot has changed in my life since the builders arrived, especially as regards Dan. At the beginning of the year I paid no attention, but by Easter their activities on the building-site next door had so intruded into my routine that I'm not surprised we became acquainted.

Omar, my new neighbour, was converting the modest mining cottage he had acquired with such difficulty under the Group Areas Act into — let's call it — a Muslim pleasure palace. He was using the unregistered labour of Husein, the foreman, who packed all eight of the builders on his pick-up from the East Rand. This all takes place in my inner-city suburb of Johannesburg, which is integrating faster than the government can do anything about it. During the time I have known Dan I've also become the last white householder within these four blocks.

Husein was to build, on Omar's instructions, a common wall between our properties, in line with his general fortifications. To this I had to contribute on a fifty-fifty basis — about eighty percent of the cost, as it turns out. I wasn't used to their methods of dealing. Husein had me lined up for a sucker, and conned me as well into having a security gate built alongside the wall in his own time, on Sundays, which were not a holiday for him. He laid the bricks himself to make a bit extra. Dan brought them round on a wheelbarrow. Dan was the show-off type who enjoyed negotiating planks and trenches and muck-heaps of torn-down creeper. He'd jerk up his wrists and pile out the stolen goods.

Husein gave me no choice, really, about tightening up on security. I felt threatened because his ragged labourers were so poorly paid on the Friday, when the building-site whore and her pimp had been around and cleaned them out by the Saturday they were broke again. The petty robberies began on Sundays: washing from the line, the iron in the laundry at the back, spades and secateurs and, once when I was having a bath with the back door open, they tiptoed into the kitchen and filched the clock. I stood on the veranda, dripping, watching my kitchen-clock go down the road to be pawned at the dagga-dealers. With the corrugated-iron fence down and no wall up yet, the security gate seemed pointless, but Husein persuaded me I must think of the future; crime was always on the increase. I knew that as soon as his gang had moved on, the thefts would abate. They slept eight in one room at the back of Omar's, four yards from my office — each with his patch marked out on the concrete floor and a skimpy blanket...and me all alone in my seven-room ruin, guarding my privacy and possessions.

Husein was outrageous in his small talk. While his capacious wife sat in her embroidered smocks in the truck hooting for him, he'd tell me of the luscious mistress he'd found in neighbouring Fordsburg — 'A man's got to have some sex-life, you know; hell, I'm not over the top yet.' He looked forward to talking dirty with me, patting a few more bricks into cement.

He had me sorted out for what I was, so worked around to his early gay experiences. These took place in prison in the Cape, before his conversion and reform. During a long term he rose from ripped-apart catamite to gang-boss himself — see his tattoos — protecting his favourite slaves. For ever in his mind homosexuality meant the degradation of prison. Some grew so used to it and unable to adapt to the outside world they'd do anything stupid to be sentenced again — insult a policeman, shit on the mayor's doorstep — just to be back inside with their buddies. 'And some of them got big cocks, hey — so big. They not moffies, hey, they really men. But that's all they know, you understand.'

What was he behind bars for? Husein, who was now making my house impregnable, was in for armed robbery with assault.

'Dan, *maak gou*,' he'd complain, and Dan would trundle off for another load of larceny.

I more or less said that if ever Husein wished to come around for a service (his expression) — no charge — he was welcome, but he really preferred dressing up in his embroidered Koranic robes, skull-cap on his curly locks, and squandering a fortune in the Fordsburg harem.

One day, taking advantage of the quiet (Husein was also building a mosque out his way, so there were weeks without action — but that only protracted the ordeal), I was contemplating what to get on with in my office at the back. I suppose I was aware of a dull chopping sound and that they'd left Dan behind to guard their side of the property. In fact, when I opened my lounge curtains I'd seen the big-shouldered form of Dan and avoided looking at him, as we all agreed to ignore one another despite the enforced proximity. I knew perfectly well they knew every detail of my daily existence, as I knew theirs. With a whipping and twisting and thundering smash, the apricot-tree in Omar's yard came down in my direction, the uppermost branches scraping onto my roof. This I could not ignore — it was yet another day wiped off my schedule, without any prior consultation or my consent. I was furious actually, as it was one of the oldest trees in the suburb; it produced enough fruit to fill thousands of jars of that poor African staple — apricot jam — that had always gone to waste, and now it was weighing down my retreat in its fruity death throes.

I could not be angry with Dan; Omar was to blame. Nevertheless, I had to go out and help clear the branches off my property, if only to hurry the sad process. Dan had few verbal skills, but he did have the buzz-saw, so without any preplanning he sawed off the branches with an excruciating noise and smell of petrol while I dragged them over to Omar's dump. He had dismembered the venerable trunk before I was finished, so we jointly hauled for a while in the blazing sun. Then I gave him a rake to tidy up my garden and went inside.

When I heard he was done, I went out with two glasses of Coke, and we sat on the rockery, sweating and exhausted, and drank them. He didn't look me in the eye and I studied him obliquely. About all we said was, 'Cooldrink.' '*Koeldrank*, ja...' 'Ja.' Country boy, spoke Afrikaans. Then in the evening he guarded Omar's, playing the local black music station on the radio.

Omar and Husein fell out, which inevitably had implications for my half of the wall — still with only the foundations laid, although all the rendering and extensions Omar wanted on the walls of his house had been done. They went at each other fanatically; money grievances, I suppose, not religious ones, for they were brothers in faith. Husein shouted for his men to lay down tools; Omar said that they must continue or no pay (instant hammering). The two of them whaled into one another, grabbing up demolition hammers and taking positions in the street. Logically I was the one positioned to intervene; I wanted the whole business not to stretch to another six months. I stepped reluctantly forth to where all my new neighbours were keyed up, egging them on. They had both lost their tempers — were dangerous, hammers smashing at the glazed tiles and panes of glass. I moved forward, arms held out to separate them. As I jumped towards the breach, I felt hands clutching at my belt behind. Dan advised against this intervention and had stopped me. I glanced at his really worried face, and got out of there in disgust. Saved from a broken skull by Dan! He knew I had miscalculated, would only have lost out yet again. On his part it took a lot of guts to get a white man to change his course.

They settled their disagreement only with Husein expelled from Omar's domain and Omar taking over the men personally (since it was all illegal anyway), and good progress was made. Husein crept in at night to work on his subcontract with me for the gate, but only because I had not yet paid him for that part. When I did, he absconded, leaving the gate insecure and incompletely attached. He took the cash and tore off in his truck, which he'd had to hide blocks away. Later I learned from Dan he had gone without giving them their pay for over a month.

Now Friday was the only day I could count on for some peace because Omar was more rigorous and decreed prayer-day. So off he went to pray and the rest smoked grass, and I could actually do some work. From my clean-living, occasional domestic worker I found out how bad things were if I went out on Friday. She did her job with all the windows tightly closed against the fumes and the doors locked for fear that she would be gang-raped by the men on their highs next door. So I stayed home whenever I possibly could, now to protect my maid. The wall, when they finally got it up to ten feet, was no reassurance; they may have built it well, but not well enough to stop themselves climbing over.

On Friday when I came back from an unavoidable meeting with an editor I found Dan in my yard, doing his washing and in long conversation with my maid, who explained that Omar had cut the water off for them. I said, 'Good afternoon,' leaving them to it, knowing she knew best. She had sons of her own whom she kept strictly in Christian marching order. But there in my yard was the incredibly well-built young labourer with admirable shoulders and biceps and the skinny legs of undernourishment, wearing an old towel of mine, while his rags dried on the line. Evidently he did not smoke grass, but he had a cigarette and flicked ash into the pots. I knew enough of my maid's interests to know that in emphatic and school-sounding Xhosa they were discussing their favourite passages of the Bible. They belonged to similar sects. All this was a great relief.

One freezing winter night with a wind howling straight over the veld from the Antarctic and, if you weren't used to it, the tin roof clanking would drive your hair on end, I was trying to finish up when the front doorbell went. I thought to ignore it, but this was obviously an emergency. I was afraid to respond, frankly. But I opened the door and turned on the dim light, and nearly puked at what I saw. A black shape had been stabbed all over, blood pouring like oil down his face and it was squelching out of his boots, leaving ghastly footprints. I'm afraid I said he should go next door to the building-site where they would know how to help him. My fear accounts for my lack of charity.

In due course the bell went again and obviously next door they had elected Dan to soften me up, because they knew I was sweet on him. I had misjudged everything: the walking wounded was from next door in the first place; he had gone to the last café open, where they wouldn't let him use the phone — the ambulance would not come for any inarticulate black request, anyway. He had been stabbed ten blocks away by their old dagga-dealers for deserting them for closer and cheaper ones, and now Dan had come to me as a last resort. The victim was one of them; in fact, he was the very monster who had whipped my clock!

In the rush of desperation Dan and I were communicating perfectly. I told him to wash the man down and keep him warm; I would phone.

I phoned and the ambulance said they would come and — I'll give them that — they didn't ask if I was white or black, as in the old days. They were next door with sirens going within twenty minutes. Feeling bad about my initial hesitation, I swathed myself in gowns and scarves, and waited in the howling gale with Dan and the towering blood-wreck. He was in pain past communication. I coaxed him to sit out of the wind, as Dan did on one side of rubble and I did on the other. Such an automaton was he that he built himself a stool out of bricks first, then squatted on it. When the ambulance made its spectacular arrival, he could let go, and passed out in the drive. All stretcher-bearers are ready for that kind of thing. The commotion brought out the other neighbours. From the few houses of my once tranquil all-white suburb came no less than eighty-nine illegals, wrenched out of sleep in their bedspreads. Then when the ambulance went round the block they all streamed up to the traffic-light to get one last glimpse of the vehicle flying through. He was back at work on the Monday with forty-seven stitches.

With the Berlin Wall up between us I had little further sight of Dan. Occasionally, if I got my car out of an evening, he'd be sitting on the pile on the sidewalk, smoking. And the regular prostitute would be on Omar's veranda, suckling her baby as if she owned the place, waiting for her man to fetch her. God knows what really went on in the back of Omar's place; I no longer wished to know. Eight months had gone by and still they were not finished. I'd nod or wink at Dan, and he'd give me a smile, and I'd carry on with my life. The thought was somehow in the back of my mind that if I left my house empty while he was there, things would be all right.

Then I'd regale my white friends with the Frankenstein episode and how the snitching had become so commonplace I even put out old clothes so that they'd take them in preference to anything else. The finer points of the social mix I was experiencing were not really discussable in bourgeois South Africa, so we settled for decrying the inconvenience of neighbouring building-sites.

Omar came to having his corrugated-iron roof pulled out by the roots, and the crashing of tin sheets and rotten roof-timbers now really became unbearable. What use was it to explain yet again that as a writer I work at home and need my sanctuary? I had arranged the previous week with Omar that I would be away for their re-roofing, but no, they could never make any convenient accommodation. Try corrugated iron for a din with African enthusiasm for demolition, all a few feet from your writerly calm. With wax plugs in my ears and a towel around my head, I tried to get my so many words a day done, the chair quivering each time a piece of architectonic plate was smashed free. I was turning into a shuddering wreck.

All of a sudden the shift ended, the destruction half-way. To soothe myself I went out into my walled garden, to tidy up the new debris and maybe encourage a plant or two with the hose. The soil was warming with spring. I pulled out some runners of grass and clipped at the hydrangea, which was going to bud beautifully. I knew I was being studied at my old-womanish tasks, being inexplicably finicky. Dan on the roof-tree, up in the clouds in his rags, surveying the neighbourhood.

I gazed up at him, shaking with relief from the quiet. I said: 'Do you want a beer?'

He said edgily, no...no way, he didn't drink beer.

Wine, a glass of?

He didn't drink.

Coffee?

He drank coffee.

I said he could come round later on if he wanted for coffee, but he must have misunderstood, for within seconds the doorbell was going.

I made him coffee with lots of milk and lots of sugar, and we settled at opposite ends of the kitchen table. He was hunched in terror, never having shared a social occasion with a white before. Where he came from, if he ordered and paid for coffee in a white establishment, a plastic throw-away cup came out and the hatch slammed down. I emptied six biscuits onto a plate and shoved it across to him. When I eventually thought to have one myself, the whole lot had gone. No pay again; he was actually starving.

I offered him a cigarette, but he declined, although I knew he smoked and the sight of me exhaling must have made him desperate. So on an impulse I grabbed a plastic bag and opened the fridge. I emptied into the bag the half-eaten steak and other delectables I was saving for myself, and handed it to him. He took it respectfully. As I wished to continue gardening while the quiet endured, I showed him out. At the front door the TV very obviously came into view and, as I closed the door on him, I said he was welcome to watch it in the evenings if he had nothing better to do. I went back to my budding plants and he to eat his spoils across the wall.

That evening when I had the news on he came to watch with me. He perched on a corner of the bed as if he didn't mean to dirty anything. I tried to gauge how much he took in, because language was a great problem between us. Gorbachev swooping into Malta and Bush braving the swell for a summit important to us all, even to backwater South Africa, I thought might be proving inexplicable to Dan. Anyway, I showed him how to use the remote control and once it had got to the soccer which he loved, I went off to have a bath. I was no longer interested, so he could choose what he liked.

Once I'd bathed and, instead of getting into night garb, re-dressed in honour of my guest, I saw he had lost interest in the box and smoked out the end of his pack. I offered him a cigarette and this time he took it. His monosyllables of defence were giving way to more confident sentences of ordinary chat. My pink, waterlogged hands closed over his damaged workman's ones to shield the flame.

After a thoughtful smoke he clearly wasn't ready to go, and had fixed up a way of explaining his absence next door. So I dared to ask the usual giveaway question — wouldn't he now like to have a bath? He would, so I stacked up all the bath oils and towels I could find and turned on the gushing hot and left him to it. All that prevented me from going any further (rubbing his back, insisting he try on new clothes for old, etc.) was the thought of some unforeseeable reaction at the building-site. If he returned there in new garb, sweet-smelling, they would know. Their revenge would be against him, not me. Besides, I was not sure I was ready to admit an illiterate black worker into my life just then, no matter how great the temptation. The gap was too great, or so I thought.

But Dan thought differently. When he was not at work next door he never had anything better to do than take a bath and watch TV with me. These were his special privileges in the neighbourhood. Omar's gang were finishing up and the place was transformed: inlaid brick yard with not a piece of greenery to make a mess, sunken, walk-in bath, venetian blinds, wrought-iron burglar bars, Italian tiles. But it was still not too late for Dan to get a screwdriver through him out of sheer jealousy for being someone's pet. I could hear complaints over their pot of stewing chicken gizzards that someone among them was getting the whole mixed grill with the moffie white boss next door. It also occurred to me that they might have set me up with Dan. I'd come back one night to find everything of value in the house, that he had marked out, gone. These were mean thoughts on my part, but since Omar was never likely to pay them any more than Husein had, and they had all run up debts at hire-purchase stores on what anywhere else in the world would be considered workmen's basic essentials, provided by the employer (overalls, tools, footwear), and they had now stripped my outside of everything movable, what else could I think?

I was going out one evening to post off an article at the quickest box in the city and I had forgotten Dan was in the bathroom, performing his toilette. The thought did occur: can I leave him alone inside? I mumbled that I would be back soon and left him to it. I posted the article and did a few things I had to do at the late-night bookshop, and returned. The TV was going, but Dan was not before it.... Instead, he was before the mirror in the bathroom — door now open — studying the spectacle of himself — stark naked — wiping his skin to a gloss with Vaseline. Obviously I could trust him with all my valuables, and probably with everything else, including my life.

There was a dull strip on his back his fingers had not rubbed over, so I obliged, working the jelly in until he looked polished, agleam. Let me inspect him; I pronounced him stunningly, dazzlingly skin-preserved from scalp to toe. That we both obviously had erections by then, which he could do little to hide, was probably the decisive factor.

I asked Dan what he was going to do once the house next door was finished and he said he didn't wish to continue with Omar-Husein, as they either didn't pay or not enough. I muttered something about I'd need someone to finish the security gate. Then I lavished his shining body in what clothes I had left for him to try on; we were much the same height. When the TV reached its end, the sort of fiddling, stroking, childish glee with which he had gone about this (his incredible narcissism and my only too eager puckering and adjusting) came to an end as well, and we reluctantly agreed he'd better return to the site — for now — in his wretched rags with their built-in reek of grime, decay and sweat. For now — because we were both determined to sit this one through.

One evening Dan did not come and I was working to beat an old deadline, anyway. The crazy thought that I'd better pull in more cheques drove me on, now that the racket next door permitted, to afford Dan a new wardrobe, to prepare for a wonderful spending spree.... But an unbelievably violent uproar over there interrupted. Clearly it was reckoning-up time, as the next morning Husein would collect them at the corner, not daring to come any closer to Omar (or to me, for that matter). Their building-site whore was the cause of it, she who'd been hired out to all of them for far more than sexual favours — darning their shredded socks and treating their sores and nursing them through bouts of hangover and dagga-depression. To drive her out they threatened her baby — even that, the baby who had learned to walk holding their knees, now that it was reckoning time. She shoved the baby onto her pimp and ordered them both out while she screamingly handled this matter of eight dishonest, exploitative brutes.

She had to disunify them, pick on a vulnerable target — Dan. She had to stir up their resentments.

'Who done your washing for you?' she launched into him.

'It was not you, sisi,' he pleaded, 'for the others, yes.'

'Where you have your finger fixed when it was sore?'

'It was not you, sisi, who fix it.' He could not say it was the white man next door who plastered it over.

'Where you get clean when you only got shit?'

'Please, sisi, I was cleaning my T-shirt all by myself.'

'And where you got your stomach full when you never get pay?'

'No, sisi, no....'

'Where you get money when no one else has? Hey? From the moffie over there!'

'Hai, sisi,' from Dan.

Judging by the rumpus, the tactic didn't work. She could only stride into their circle and shove the contents of their three-legged pot on the ground. That was her last protest, apart from stomping out slamming Omar's front door.

Now their final meal together was ruined and Dan was to blame. One of them cracked him a shot, I think the sewn-up oaf, and from over the wall I heard Dan yelp. I was all for getting the ladder and climbing over to extricate him. But Dan had already shown me what little power I had to regulate the affairs of a building-site. I could not stand the thought of his delicate body becoming as smashed and dented as theirs — the scars they bore, the terrible damage they had brought only on themselves; the way they had let themselves be brutalized.

I went into my office. I put my hands over my ears and clenched my eyes and was too deeply shocked even to think if it was that wrong to offer him a glimpse of an alternative way of life. They had no one else to take their frustrations out on, other than moffies, those men.

Early the next morning they all stomped out with their tool bags and enamel mugs and scraggy blankets. Back to work on somebody else's mosque on the East Rand. I was not sorry, after close to eleven months, to see the very last of them. Omar came round with his wife, warmly inviting me over to dine — any night, every night, six o'clock — that's when they always eat, curry and special stuff I would like; always they catered for at least six people, in case anyone dropped around, they would always be honoured to have a neighbour; oh and sorry, said Omar, for all the noise.

Just for a while, I replied, I had a lot of work to catch up on and wanted to be left in peace. The very thought of their hospitality and its human cost made me physically repulsed. What I really wanted was Dan — nothing else would compensate for what they'd caused: a year of my life lost. And of course Dan had been gone for over a week.

And then a fortnight. I had done nothing to stop him being beaten to a pulp.

'Why don't you come over for dinner?' said Omar, his hairy elbows over the wall, as I was mowing the lawn.

'It's just because I've got a lot of backlog to cope with,' I said.

'You don't like Indian neighbours, that's what it is,' he said.

'I don't like Husein — look how he left that gate. Next thing the wind'll blow it out into the street,' I said.

'That Husein,' he replied. 'He's a real bastard crook. Imagine how my house'd be if I let him carry on like that! Just get yourself a boy, man — he'll fix it up if you supervise him properly.'

I switched on the mower so that I didn't have to hear more neighbourly advice.

I was mowing the lawn down to the toppling gate a month later and there, on the other side of it, behind the bars, was Dan. He had his mug and blanket with him, and I could see from the way his eyebrow drooped that the physical wounds were not yet healed.

'Come in, come in,' I hauled the gate open. 'How are you, where have you been?'

He was very afraid I would turn him away. He stepped in and put his possessions on the cut grass.

'See, it needs bricks up to here, and a firm socket — and lots of broken glass on top and plaster....'

THE BUILDING-SITE

Dan nodded; he was able to do all that.

'Go inside and put the kettle on, please. I just want to finish off. Honestly, now with summer rains it grows so fast....'

When I had done and put the mower away, Dan had two mugs of coffee made in the kitchen. He had placed them so that we would sit opposite one another, not far apart.

I washed my hands and poured out the obligatory biscuits. He took one and I took one.

We sat facing one another. He looked so emaciated.

'Can I getta job?' he said.

'Yes,' I said.

Stephen Gray

Bring Out Your Dead

He predicts no poems during plague
as the wave reaches south
by '95 and peaks at 21%
total harvest: bring 'em out
bring 'em out...mostly blacks,
women and children first...unrest causes
(read civil war) families to break
and who migrates and sleeps around most?
At all times fill the teat of this
rubber good with your burning sperm.
Employment's to be had in wards
and morgues, the low dress the lost.
An epidemic virus makes us kin
as nothing more humane has done:
the salt of tears in which we swim,
saliva as we kiss, the banks of
bottled blood may each contain
the thump and urge of level death:
bring out your dead that we may see
how each of us may risk and only lose,
figures indicate survivors positively are
an altogether sweeter people.

The Historical Moment

For once I am not in love not available
To curl your hair on an iron without burning your neck
To heave your car when it won't start in a rush-hour
To smuggle wine under my jacket up the lift to your flat
To cut a rose and pass it to you without scratching your hand

Not being in love and unavailable these days
I don't rush to the phone when it rings and hold it nervously
I don't adjust my collar ten times in case you're looking
I don't save books for you to read pictures to see
In restaurants I don't study the chair alongside

And rush home after work planning what to buy for you
When next you arrive and arrange yourself on the sofa
I breathe more easily with your ear off my heart
No more the babble of stress the hope in a calculated pause
I speak calmly and thoughtfully and forthrightly

Now that I am for once myself again
I chat to the general public in a general way
Read the newspapers through to the sports and the classifieds
Find singles are poorly catered for but persevere
Watch families with children and criticize them

All these years of toil and adrenalin and expense
I can hardly remember I've lost my memory
Of how like a mountaineer I'd scale your breath
How within you I'd reach like a serpent and coil
Through a winter inside the warmth of your sleep

Stephen Gray

Nor in my feelings damaged and scarred
Is the bleeding of that terrible pain
When the blade of an arrow dug through my back
The wound now's a trench a gutter a wrinkle
Being out of love it has healed and grown over

Meanwhile I live in a moment of history
And no telegrams come — there is news only of massacres
The red streets of this city are flushed with blood
They've blown up the powerlines poisoned the water
It's only a matter of time now since love is done.

Stephen Gray

Richard Rive:
A Memoir

One of the anecdotes Richard Rive liked to repeat, dating from the 1950s when that old racist battle-axe, as she said, 'represented bulk' in South African English letters and was still a threat to her rebellious juniors, is the following. Sarah Gertrude Millin, after all, wrote an entire sub-literature on behalf of South Africa's people of colour, chronicling their 'miscegenated' origins and prophesying they would never fit into their white master-race, as exemplified by herself and General Smuts, or among the pure black underdogs packed for ever in servants' quarters and slums. In her scheme of the great South African family's bonding, she relegated 'coloureds' to a step-relationship; *God's Stepchildren* was the title of her eugenicist historical novel — and world-wide bestseller, be it said — on that subject.

So up stepped Richard Rive in his brilliant twenties, with a sheaf of short stories about 'his people', which were winning the *Drum* and the *Cape Argus* story competitions and, thanks to the much heralded rebirth of black writing in South Africa of which he was a prominent part, were being translated and republished as rapidly as he could produce them. When the colour-bar dowager encountered this upstart, evidently she was struck with genealogical confusion. All she could blurt was: 'What are you — Indian?' To which Richard suavely replied: 'No ma'am, I am your stepchild.'

This story may have been Richard's invention. But the thought of Richard confronting one of the dangerous generation of apologists for racial discrimination with his perky existence — his glossy black limbs and possibly St Helenan kinky hair, jelled down, athletically sporting a University of Cape Town cravat — freshens one's sense that literary history is a sequence of such mythical moments.

Richard saw himself as, and often enough said he was, a cultural missionary, bringing civilization to the whites of South Africa. The legacy of the British novel in Africa he wrote off as the 'scenic special', dealing with 'flora, fauna and blacks in that order' from under a sola topi or through the window of a Cape to Cairo express. In the more liberal novel up to Alan Paton he heard all too clearly the tones of 'special pleading' and the messages that blacks like him were to expect no more than hand-outs with passive recipiency.

Paton and he did meet, in Durban in 1962. Richard was there to ask the legend in his lifetime for an endorsement and, I suppose, blessing for *Quartet*, the anthology of short stories Richard had compiled from the new school and was taking to London:

> This was an important meeting for me as we represented different directions. He represented the high point of Liberal Writing in South Africa. I was representative of the nascent Protest School. Liberal writing may be loosely defined as writing mostly by Whites about Blacks to move Whites out of their socio-political complacency. It ranges from Olive Schreiner's *Trooper Peter Halket of Mashonaland* to Paton's *Cry, the Beloved Country*. Protest writing on the other hand is writing mostly by Blacks articulating their position to a White readership they feel can effect change. Sol Plaatje and Peter Abrahams were among its progenitors, forcing South African writing into a new, protest, direction.

Stickily, Paton lent his patronage to this youngster outpacing him in his demands for a changed dispensation.

But most of Richard's cultural missionizing was devoted to a further direction in the development of South African teaching — the re-education of black people in terms of their own literature, rapidly ceasing to exist under the Bantu Education Act. Thus, a life of detoxicating the way white texts of the past were to be read, dealing with their submerged loads of bigotry and spelling out the grounds for a democratic, non-colour future. He was not to see this future achieved before his horrific death. Thus, also, a life lived interstitially in the loopholes of apartheid, holding a place for himself that was getting smaller — ducking frequently, emerging only when he knew he could strike a telling, solitary literary blow.

In a no-choice situation he had made the hardest choice of all. While virtually every other black writer of the 60s in Verwoerd's South Africa went voluntarily or was forced into exile, Richard remained at home. For this he has been held endlessly suspect — collaborator? quisling? But for at least fifteen years he was to have his published work banned; as he said, 'I was now part of a small elite of South African writers not allowed to read their own works in case they became influenced by them.' When I first met Richard, he was immobilized, depressed, going through the motions of a literary career without writing at all, unable legally to reach an audience — except occasionally for a small and loyal one overseas, notably through that life-saver, the BBC Africa Service.

Richard Rive was born of 'mixed parentage' in 1931, and never knew his father. In his autobiography, *Writing Black*, published when he was fifty, he said he was genuinely unsure about his ancestry.

> I remember a mounted print which had pride of place on our dining-room wall; it showed a man I later learnt was my maternal grandfather. He sported a cheesecutter and a droopy Dr Crippen moustache and stood next to a racehorse he owned which had won the Metropolitan handicap. He was unmistakably White. Blacks did not at that time own horses that won races. I must therefore conclude that my maternal grandmother must have been Black or Brown, as my mother was beautifully bronze.

With his mother and siblings Richard grew up in a decayed Edwardian apartment in District Six, the slum known to white Capetonians somewhat romantically as the Tavern of the Seven Seas. Now much celebrated retrospectively for its melting-pot culture — besides Richard it bred Alex la Guma and James Matthews in the writing world — District Six, like Sophiatown in Johannesburg, was condemned for clearance, its inhabitants dispersed to white-supervised and remote township ghettos, so that a long-standing and pell-mell tradition of freehold rights and urban-minded independence was dismantled and demolished by government decree.

'Mrs Rive's Boy' climbed out of District Six faster. The family, he recorded, was always destined to upward social mobility anyway: 'Our hankering after respectability became obsessive. We always felt we were intended for better things.' At twelve he made the switch from Afrikaans to English in his reading and found his potential self in black Americans — the influence of Richard Wright and Langston Hughes remained his mainstay. During World War II a municipal scholarship got him to high school, where Latin and English paved the way to a life of teaching them in turn. 'I endured a harrowing childhood in District Six, where drunkenness, debauchery and police raids were the order of the day,' he noted, adding: 'No

White authority had ever bothered to ask me whether they could take my past away. They simply brought in their bulldozers.'

The way out also opened through athletics — long-legged, gangly Richard the sprinter won a scholarship to the University of Cape Town on this account. He then trained at Hewat College, and that was his early career: teacher of Latin and English in the still-colonial syllabuses of the Cape Coloured schools and athletic coach to other aspirants.

By the time his first stories came out in book form — as *African Songs* in 1963, from Seven Seas Books in Berlin W 8, which turned out to be in East Berlin — the tug of the Cold War was underway for Richard's soul. His first grant, from the Farfield Foundation (subsequently discovered to have been a cover for the CIA), took him through Africa and to the meccas of Paris and London, where he found more African writers than on 'the continent'. In London the manuscript of his first novel was at Faber and Faber. Called *Emergency*, it recounted the Sharpeville massacre days of 1960 and the declaration of the first state of emergency as felt by a stream-of-consciousness alter ego for himself. Summoned to an editorial discussion, Richard waited...for T.S. Eliot to appear with the bulky tome and recommend changes. Richard never discussed this encounter, nor divulged the extent of the rewriting, but when *Emergency* came out it enjoyed considerable esteem as a report from the front-line. Only in 1988 did the work first appear in South Africa under the marginally more lenient censorship system and by then Richard was completing its sequel, nicknamed *Emergency II* — this time a report from the same front-line of the second state of emergency, the same characters twenty-five years on. Faber, who published all of Abrahams and Mphahlele's *Down Second Avenue* and *The African Image*, now also put out other emerging South Africans like C.J. Driver, finding exile in Britain.

The other rising London stable for South Africans was Heinemann with the African Writers Series. For this Richard compiled No.9 with the business-like title, *Modern African Prose*, the first anthology to assemble a continent-wide English selection including Chinua Achebe, Ezekiel Mphahlele, Cyprian Ekwensi, Amos Tutuola and Ngugi wa Thiong'o. In parts of independent Africa this title became the educational setwork to insert after *Julius Caesar* and the 'Immortality Ode'. Richard later refused to update and revise it, for it did have its historic position in the rise of African Literature and is still used as is today. *Modern African Prose* caught all the optimism of those heady Pan-African days — black was indeed beautiful, the African Personality as human and humane as any other; more humane, considering the centuries of exploitation by slavery and imperialism.... Heady and optimistic, assertively forward-looking, as were Richard's own stories — impressionistic slivers of the poor life, singing of dignity and scenting freedom.

It would be too glib to say the despair, darkness and disillusion that set in on Richard from the mid-60s was merely a South African variant of an Africa-wide post-colonial phenomenon. Besides, Richard was cut off from that. Nor was the downward curve of his career entirely due to the deep freeze of high apartheid, which stalled not only his own, but all black aspirations; in fact, illegalized them. But certainly when we first met in his flat in 1969 he was living like a hermit, surrounded by African works that few others knew, the struggle dating as he stared at the spines. Gagged, his books banned, proscribed, he was also washed-up. The crime against humanity in this case is as follows: Richard was an achiever; as a writer he was disallowed achievement. The fire of the brilliant young talent (warmly overpraised, uncritically adored) was utterly doused.

But this was also Rishard of Saloo Court, surely. The flat mispronunciation of his name stuck as an affectionate joke and the block was named after the great white hunter, F.C. Selous, no less. There for the middle years of his existence Richard crouched, for Selous Court was in a 'white' area, off Rosmead Avenue, near the race-track in Claremont. He did live in daily dread of a Group Areas Act bureaucrat knocking on the door. When the knock came, after all of twenty years, it did provoke a most restrained short story, 'The Man from the Board', his only one in years, and then about the suaveness of his eviction on the grounds of the colour of his skin. On principle he defied discriminatory laws, and on principle he suffered.

This matter of principle remained as intact as it could. Richard relished tea-parties for fellow writers, and once, over a bowl of cup-cakes sprinkled with hundreds-and-thousands I'd brought to cheer us, the phone interrupted. Slowly Richard's plummy tones shifted from efficient reason to heated outrage. I gathered he was negotiating a pair of sports scholarships to a select white school in the Peninsula, only just preparing to take 'coloureds' at a pinch. The one boy I'd seen — gorgeously self-assured, with green, far-seeing eyes.

'No man, they don't have courage. They take both or neither,' he said in hurt.

From me: 'Why not compromise?'

'Not on your life,' said Richard. 'They must also take the one as black as pitch and a nose all over his face; besides, he's even better at pole-vaulting.'

Between trips overseas Richard rose to the top of where he could go: head of English at his old teacher training college. Once I was due to take his in-service students through an anthology of South African texts I had compiled precisely to make the educational advance locally that *Modern African Prose* had effected elsewhere a decade before. Thanks to Richard's influence, 'coloured' schools were setting it as it was the only reader to include work by a 'non-white' South African (to whit, one of Richard's own stories — banned!). Such was the courage of educational publishers then that Richard was the only black South African writer in a heavily traditional sequence from David Livingstone through Trollope and Haggard to Kipling and Plomer. Heady, apartheid-breaking stuff in those days.

But the revolt of the black children against inferior syllabuses had overtaken us, rippling from Soweto in June, 1976, to Cape Town's Langa township and Guguletu township by August — and Crawford, where Hewat College was situated. Richard sweatingly drove through smashed barricades, all the Beirut and barbed-wire landscape of the media pictures, soon suppressed. We gathered in a decrepit class-room, stinking of burnt tyres and tear-gas, stones among broken glass between the desks. This session was now held in defiance of both police and boycotters; no electricity, none of the normal protection; a desolate, hopeless fear. We all appeared buckled, keeping out of view. My pressing question was why had these responsible adults risked coming. (Why, for that matter, had Richard and I?) In an intense workshop, during which some solemn and purposeful discussion was generated, as if in our corporate mind we could live separate from violence, ruin and squalor for a while, I managed to pose the question to Vic Wessels, banned for many years, whom I knew: they had all come because *Rishard* said they would *fail their exams* otherwise. Richard repeatedly refused comfortable job-offers at the then mostly segregated University of Cape Town, feeling its Department of English had as yet hardly acknowledged the existence of South African authors. But I now saw he had made a virtue of having been forced to work for 'his people'.

Outside countries sponsored his own further academic career: a Masters in Afro-American Literature at Columbia and a Ph.D. at Magdalen, Oxford. There his thesis was on the life and work of Olive Schreiner. Surely this is how Richard sustained himself, forming the closest professional attachment to the Cape's own liberal feminist, annotating and explicating her lost manuscripts, researching out the shape of a career then only half-admired and half-suspected. During his leaves, Richard would doggedly walk up the hill to the Jagger Library of UCT and decode her difficult handwriting. His rate was a letter a day — and in many public collections he copied several thousands of them. The first two volumes of her letters, edited by him, came out from David Philip in Cape Town and from OUP in 1987. And by that year he was able to add to his curriculum vitae: Visiting Professor, Harvard.

As the touchstone of local affairs, Richard was always visited by other writers — in fact, he collected them — or went out of his way to attend conferences and gatherings where he would meet those like himself. Too many of his early literary acquaintances died tragically (Ingrid Jonker and Nat Nakasa in 1965, Arthur Nortje in 1970), so it fell to Richard to keep alive their reputations, stressing the wastage of their aborted talents — aborted by malevolent South Africa. Not quite so expectedly he also mourned other kinds of 'death' — the slow drying up of his friends driven into exile, their twilight in the diaspora. So for many overseas he was a go-between, bringing the gritty news of his endurance. Back home he was the been-to, reminding others that at no matter what cost literary voices had to be kept audible, remembered.

By the mid-70s a new, combative and many-headed generation had arisen, and Richard was a rather token elder to them. He came up to Johannesburg for a conference organized by *New Classic*, Sipho Sepamla's literary journal called up from the ashes of Nakasa's *Classic* of the 60s. There he delivered the points summarized in the opening paragraphs here.

I organized that he should meet Christopher van Wyk and Fhazel Johennesse, if only on the drive in from the airport. Days later they were inseparable and had formed another journal, *Wietie*, No.2 of which carried a lengthy interview with Richard. There he dispensed suitable writerly advice, warning them most strongly of all not to crimp their imaginations to fit any Black Consciousness or other ideology. One of their mammoth talk sessions in my house led to more than intellectual hunger, and I am no cook. Leaving the two younger ones to recover from their rigorous debate, I drove robust, overweight Richard out for some take-aways. Absent-mindedly I kept the car going while Richard, in blazer and tie, hopped in to order. Perhaps a further thought of mine was that Richard might offer to pay. Although quite affluent by then and a noteworthy gormandizer, he was also a complete master at cadging free meals.

Whether it was a genuine case of racial discrimination and the joint was really 'Reserved for Whites Only' or Richard's meanness that caused the uproar I'll never know, but within minutes the Portuguese café-owner and Richard were abusing one another in many languages on the pavement. If he had had his mortar-board and doctoral scroll with him, I'm sure he would have waved them around too. Once the carving knife came out, Richard retreated to the car, slamming the door. His fury slowly subsided. I suggested I should buy the goods — what did he want? But Richard insisted I should show solidarity in his boycott of such a house of insult, even if I was prepared to pay — a point of principle which must have really pinched. I pointed out that local types of all grades of pigmentation were coming out of the place with soggy Sunday lunches wrapped in newspaper right before our eyes.... Richard said he'd settle for dried Marie biscuits back home. Soon Christopher and Fhazel had tucked their rand notes in their socks and were off, back to Riverlea township.

Friends may have sustained Richard with banqueting, but he gave back the inroads he made in good companionship, in unstoppable raconteuring. At the home of David and Marie Philip, our publishers, once when they were extending their cottage with an 'Alan Paton' wing, they invited us to dine with them in honour of their bestselling author. When we realized the dour old Anglican was actually due to put in an appearance, we both became morose with apprehension. Richard's impulse was to devour all of the food before he appeared...and the sheer momentum of our terror had us wolfing down everything. Only by 11.30 p.m., after an epic gorge, dead soldiers afoot, could we admit to our exhausted host and hostess the reason for our relief: the doyen himself had not pitched up.

Trips to Onrust an hour or so east of Cape Town were ritual. These were to take weekend provisions to Richard's oldest literary friends, Jack Cope, Uys Krige, Jan Rabie and his wife Marjorie Wallace, who loosely satellited around the country's oldest literary journal, *Contrast*, which Jack steered nobly. Engineering the passes of the Hottentots Holland mountains, the back seat wobbling with raw livers in plastic bags and yards of spiced sausage, is a recurring memory. Then dips off a wild stretch of coast where 'mixed' parties could enjoy their own social formations unobserved, plus mouthfuls of fatty carbonadoes, enjoyed aggressively South African style: barbecued outdoors.

After a UCT extra-mural conference on South African prose (in January, 1976), which had proved as desultory as the previous year's one on poetry had been decisive, Richard and I took Nadine Gordimer on the meat-run to Onrust. The weekend started tranquilly, adapting to the rhythms of that artists' hide-away. Jack took Nadine, Richard and I bathing, but this time conspicuously on the main public beach. There was a reason for this: the trans-Indian rollers thundering in had caught Uys earlier that morning and

Jan Rabie, Nadine Gordimer, Jack Cope and Richard Rive at Onrustrivier (Jan Rabie and Marjorie Wallace's garden), January, 1976.

Photograph by Stephen Gray

bashed his false teeth out. We were now to dredge for them in the surf with our toes. Garrulous Uys had to endure the worst punishment for him — muteness — a little longer, for we could not succeed in that churning mass. Conditions were too turbulent. For hours we sheltered from the gale in the sizzling dunes, the only shade from a 'Whites Only' notice-board. We were stranded like beachcombers.

By the Sunday the blast had strengthened. Nadine and I had to catch a plane back to Johannesburg and wondered if it could take off. On his rambling property Jack was nothing but a conservator, and right-wing neighbours had set it alight before. At the end of such a drought, he lived on acres of tinder. We picnicked out in the raging tempest, wet sacks at hand to douse any sparks blown from the coals. Some camper upwind was not as cautious; by 2.00 p.m. the mountain behind was a raging, advancing bushfire; by 2.30 we were half encircled. Jan and Marjorie broke in to help soak the homestead. With lethargic hoses we pointed into roiling clouds of yellow bush-smoke. Accustomed to threats and paranoia, wiry Jack made other practical damping manoeuvres — he was not prepared to have quite a proportion of the South African arts incinerated at one go. To Nadine and me, querulous in the roaring inferno, he just said: go. Richard I thought demented but ever wise: for some reason he was soaping our hired Beetle. With Nadine ducking beside her overnight bag in the front seat, everyone yelling and choking with encouragement along the lines of 'You can do it, now, now!', I accelerated down Jack's dirt-track drive.

Talk about sitting on a time-bomb. The tangle of wattle and Port Jackson ahead, heated to the point of ignition, just whooshed up on either side of the car. The wipers ground away at a mush of lather and firebrands, the wheels spinning in the sand. The ignition point of petrol is evidently higher than blue-gum, for the tank failed to explode. On the broader main road a wall of flame simply parted, like the Red Sea, to let us through. For miles we didn't slow down, or even look back.

At the airport we could not raise Jack, as his phone-lines were burnt. Later that night I raised Richard, back safely in Cape Town — much relieved, jesting about an 'inflammable situation' which had been 'kept under control'.

An equally unexpected occasion started innocently enough when Richard and I met up at a David Philip launch of a set of reproductions of Bushman rock art, on which he had wagered most of his resources. Always with Richard around it went without saying that we all catered for one another privately — segregated eating-places were not only off limits, but irrelevant. Richard had pointedly refused to join the local PEN Club on the grounds that they were prepared to beg for a 'permit' for him to dine with them in public. But that week, to much publicity, some prestigious restaurants had succeeded in becoming 'open' to 'international' diners of colour. Shamefacedly I mentioned the new and attractive circumstance; yes, Richard and I would now test the truth of this. Only as I write have the separate amenities — the theatres, cinemas and libraries Richard could not enter during his life — begun to go unreserved. That was also the week that in Lancaster House the 'Rhodesian' settlement was being satisfactorily concluded. Photos of Robert Mugabe and Joshua Nkomo began replacing those of Ian Smith on the front pages.

I said I would not phone the Harbour Café, the famous tourist restaurant on the Cape Town waterfront, either to make a booking or confirm if I could bring my so-called coloured friend along; we should go without fuss — surely they would have a corner table, in an alcove or behind a curtain if necessary, for two respectable-looking singles. Richard phoned them instead, and in his most toffee accent reserved a large table. As an afterthought he informed them that he was bringing his *whaat* companion along...

'White — you know, freckles and red hair — Caucasoid, Aryan.' Apparently that was unexceptional.

Richard drove, in his new air-conditioned Toyota Cressida, and what with head-rests and piped Vivaldi I suppose he did resemble some new African big-spender. At the quay he pulled up before the front of the Harbour Café, left the car idling with the doors open and threw the keys to some passing dock-hand to park. At our very central — indeed, spotlit — table, I suggested as ever we should 'go Dutch', whereupon Richard ruefully displayed his wallet — as usual he did not have a cent on him. Fearing financial overcommitment, I opted for a prawn omelette, but Richard was, for the first time in his life, to have nothing less than their world-famous Seafood Platter. Borne by three nervous Malays in tarbooshes, this trencher duly arrived for inspection: mounds of yellow rice, studded with whole abalones, red romans, bordered by mussels and a few dozen shrimps peeled to the neck for garnish. A Cape lobster on top. A fourth servitor, draped in napkins, struggled in under a warm finger-bowl in which floated bisected lemons. Behind us was a wall of Stellenbosch wines sufficient to reverse the effect of international boycotts.

Richard, I assumed, knew what he was doing. He sampled each succulent item — took huge bites out of them. By the time he was down to the shrimps, he was flipping hollow shells onto the linoleum floor. Then, if you please, he shook his head sombrely and ordered the remains of the dish back to the kitchen on the grounds that it was not properly cooked.

Before the second trencher could arrive, we were disturbed by a coachload of sightseers who filled the tables surrounding us. American tourists, obviously, in South Africa on a state-sponsored propaganda tour. The message went round in an only too audible undertone that, yes, now they did believe: why, even the most sacred historical places were admitting negroes now. Apartheid was utterly in the museum. The tour-guide beamed at us, the living proof.

This caused Richard to falter, so he took a break to think the situation through in the toilet. The Harbour Café had none of its own, so he strode purposefully down the wharf to a concrete bunker marked MALES — WHITES ONLY. Maybe this act of defiance was committed by mistake, but it certainly kindled his better spirits. He returned to relish the second platter, which naturally by this time was congealed.

During the arrival of the third trencher I availed myself of the same escape route, heading for the corresponding concrete bunker distinctly marked MALES — NON-WHITES ONLY. I wondered if defying segregated loos in reverse counted as a crime, but really premonitions of ruin at the rate of R60 per Seafood Platter were also troubling me. There another culinary ritual of a bizarre and bloody kind was about to take place. Four Taiwanese fishermen, who had absolutely nowhere else to go and were desperate, whipped open a bundle of sacking. Someone's flabby pet chow was tumbled out in front of my stall, and before it had a second to reorientate, had its throat slit. Fresh red meat for the long voyage home, one supposes, draining into the handbasin. Nor did the jerking chow go back East whence it came that readily. My trouser-cuffs were drenched in red bodily fluids.

While Richard was now not to be deterred in redressing three centuries of wrong, I tried not to convey the reasons for my queasiness. He clapped for the Special Desserts, and now six flunkeys in full regalia vied to land the embossed list before him first. He firmly believed he had at last been recognized in his own city — not as a heavy tipper, but as a writer of banned books — and why should I spoil his fun. I think he had Peach Melba, ice-cream with hot chocolate sauce and crème brûlée on the side. Coffee for me; black, without milk.

The American delegates had long tired of this messy Cape camaraderie and it came time for the tab. Credit cards were a novelty then and we had exceeded my credit limit, though in deference to their guest it was pointed out repeatedly to me that they had not charged more than once for their speciality. Richard was striding towards the door in slow motion, shaking the hand and patting the back of the head waiter and now some dozen others, cooks, bottle-washers and sundry passers-by, who were forming a guard of honour for his send-off. I slipped off my new watch, promising to clear the difference on the morrow.

And that was when it all came finally clear. The owner wished to thank me for being so discriminating as to have brought Joshua Nkomo to his humble eating-place. I never went back for the watch, nor informed Richard of the mistaken identity.

For reasons not connected to the above, Richard and I fell out. Both of us became petty and spiteful. Richard had undertaken to review my books as they came out, and often earned more on the reviews than I did for whole works. He was becoming fearfully nitpicking and I was resentful. Also I erred fatally in trying to corner him into writing fresh material of his own. I offered to anthologize his BBC radio play, *Make like Slaves*, which to his delight some students had revived as a stage play for the Grahamstown Festival in 1976 — but that was based on short-story material nearly two decades old. What I meant was: write something up-to-date. So much for chipping away at another writer's block. Vigorous correspondence was the only upshot, then silence.

But in 1979, on a lecture tour of the U.S., Richard was manoeuvred by others more conniving into a breakthrough. He was to be the keynote speaker at the closing banquet of the African Literature Association's conference at Bloomington, Indiana. Few memorable moments occur in those so efficient and routine scholarly procedures, but evidently Richard's speech was one such. He was cajoled into jettisoning his slagged-out and now outmoded position paper, and so — aged 48 — hauled forth the musty suitcase of his childhood souvenirs instead. This was the very material he had relentlessly suppressed in his thrust for respectability. This was Baldwin recovering *The Amen Corner*, or Soyinka his *Ake*. This was Richard, funny and tearful and piercing, without grudges and inspired, putting himself back on the world's literary map. So unblocked was Richard at that banquet that in the following decade no less than five books would flow from that vein.

Writing Black, the autobiography of 1981, was the first. A no-tell listing of his travels and literary encounters, it was hurried and often disproportionate: his total recall of airports, trains, ships, and increasingly of menus, crowded out the testimony of an extraordinary life of ingenuity and cheek that one hoped for. But he chose to be self-effacing, and passages at each home-coming do build up a ground-swell of threat. After London in 1963: 'I am an unenfranchised, segregated, semi-citizen.' After New York in 1966: 'If I had any illusions that coming back with a post-graduate degree from a great American university would improve my personal position these were very soon dispelled.' After Oxford in 1974: 'I was still an unenfranchised Black suffering under a policy of racial discrimination, born and nurtured in a notorious slum in a beautiful city in a bigoted country.' And in conclusion:

> I met hundreds of people of every type and nationality.... We were alike in many respects but those who were not Black South Africans differed from me in one important way. They could assert their individuality and establish their nationality.... I could not say with full conviction, that 'I am a South African.'

I wrote to him, saying how I admired his frankness. On Christmas Day, 1981, he replied: 'I'm glad you enjoyed the book. I don't think we should allow outside factors to destroy our friendship. I am certainly prepared to put the past aside.'

But old Rishard of Saloo was no longer. He was now Dr Richard M. Rive of 'Lyndall', 31 Windsor Park Avenue, Heathfield. Named after Schreiner's heroine, his high-tech custom-built villa nestled in the reeds of a bird sanctuary, a splendid fortification in Cape Town's permitted elite 'coloured' area. In the neighbourhood was also the poet-philosopher, Adam Small. There his lifestyle was conspicuously flashy. One fellow 'coloured' writer, to show scorn for Richard the sell-out, drunkenly pissed through his study window and over the word-processor.

With the Onrust set breaking up, Richard often visited Elsa Joubert and her husband, Klaas Steytler, in Oranjezicht, overlooking Cape Town city. He was passionately enthusiastic about Elsa's success with *Poppie Nongena* of 1978, the first novel in Afrikaans to carry a convincing black point of view. Much of Elsa's impetus derived from her reading of black African literature, including Richard's *Modern African Prose* so many years after the event.

Their neighbours, the artist Cecil Skotnes and his wife Thelma, entertained Richard as a regular. Their friendship led to Cecil illustrating the second selection of Richard's stories to be published in South Africa — *Advance, Retreat* — which once again ignored the law, because the bulk of them had been banned since his East German debut. As a friendly gesture Cecil also carved in relief the panels on the front doorway of Richard's villa with scenes from Schreiner's *The Story of an African Farm*. This supposed extravagance caused an exasperated visiting Belgian scholar, when Richard must have overdone the disadvantaged black man bit, to remark: 'But, Richard, in Europe only cathedrals have carved doors.'

The work everyone had been waiting for was Richard's novel of his boyhood, *'Buckingham Palace', District Six*, which got him back on the Heinemann list overseas and sold very well locally. Nostalgic, luridly funny and boisterous, the novel straight-forwardly reconstructed a vanished time and place. Its innocence and optimism, recollected during the grim uprisings of 1986, served as indictment enough, and contributed to a nation-wide upsurge in visions for an alternative South Africa. Mixed-cast musicals about District Six and Sophiatown also stomped out the news of ways of life that had been suppressed, even as the second state of emergency closed down the possibilities of reviving lost social glories. But so resistant have the arts in general in contemporary South Africa become to intimidation that they carry on nowadays; it would be unthinkable to be cowed with the scent of deliverance back in the air.

So Richard came to flourish as more than a survivor — as a participant in the new and massive mobilization of South Africans against their government. Sparking with fresh creative energy, he joined in everything. Not to miss out on the grass-roots *Staffrider* movement, he contributed a new story to the magazine. Not to miss out on theatre for liberation, he was in there, reworking *Buckingham Palace* as a stage play. He began and completed the second *Emergency* novel, which appeared from David Philip posthumously.

In a now affable routine Richard and I kept trading professional chores, like dealing with visiting scholars braving their reputations to plug into the struggle and frenzy of an emergent society. With little tolerance for the usual poseurs and opportunists here to do us favours, we linked up in an informal screening process: Richard in the Cape and I in Johannesburg would cold-shoulder one, take another to meet every other writer in each town. Occasionally, as councillors of the English Academy of Southern Africa, for our sins we'd decry the old guard and split a pizza in Braamfontein, before Richard joined his lifelong friend, Zeke Mphahlele, the first ever professor of African Literature in the country, deeply honoured by all. Or in Cape Town we'd meet at the Philips' or the Skotneses' home and update gossip.

If Richard had a sex-life, one supposed it was centred on only two women, both dead — Olive Schreiner and Ingrid Jonker. The Schreiner love was understandable enough, and all consuming. The Jonker one — fragments of chat about the two soul-siblings, charging around Cape Town on his scooter, she clutching from behind. Twenty years after her suicide, Richard's eyes would still fill. That, one guessed, was when he lost his heart, as had so many others; that confirmed his bachelorhood. If Richard was homosexual, even in the days of gay liberation he chose not to come out. Although moffiedom is a flourishing, flamboyant part of the Cape lifestyle, Richard never gave any indication he might have been attached to it. Of course, Richard had become a class of one; for him there was no logical companion.

So when he was killed on 4 June 1989, nights before the première of his new play at the Baxter Theatre, the *Cape Times* gave him all the attention it had withheld during his life:

> One of South Africa's leading literary figures, poet and author Dr Richard Rive, 59, was found murdered in his home yesterday. Dr Rive was discovered lying face down in a blood-splattered passageway.... He had been stabbed in the chest

> repeatedly.... Furniture was overturned in the study and there were bloodstains on the wall, indicating Dr Rive had struggled with his killer.... Police are investigating the possibility that Dr Rive knew his killer. There was no evidence of a forced entry.... A knife was discovered outside the house and Dr Rive's white Toyota Cressida was missing.... By late last night detectives had managed to establish that a microwave oven, a computer, computer parts and clothing were also missing from the house.... It is not known how long Dr Rive had been dead.

On 13 June, after leaving a country-wide trail, the two youthful suspected killers surrendered to the police. They are reported to have said they did not know who Richard Rive was.

At the memorial service held at Hewat Training College, Mphahlele among many other speakers said: 'He had more to give us.'

Whether Richard's terrible end is reducible to yet another instance of the attrition of South Africa's constitutional racism, or was merely the verdict of poverty delivered by two aggrieved rent-boys, is uncertain. But the former interpretation is likely to enter the mythology. Like so many others in South Africa, Richard was killed because he wished his spirit out of bondage.

Richard Rive

Riva

A cold, misty July afternoon about twenty years ago. I first met Riva Lipschitz under the most unusual circumstances. At that time I was a first-year student majoring in English at University. One of the rare coloured students then enrolled at Cape Town. When I first saw her Riva's age seemed indefinable. Late thirties? Forty perhaps? Certainly more than twenty years older than I was. The place we met in was as unusual as her appearance. The rangers' hut at the top of Table Mountain near Hely Hutchinson Reservoir, three thousand feet above Cape Town.

George, Leonard and I had been climbing all day. George was talkative, an extrovert, given to clowning. Leonard was his exact opposite, shy and introspective. We had gone through high school together but after matriculating they had gone to work while I had won a scholarship which enabled me to proceed to university. We had been climbing without rest all afternoon, scrambling over rugged rocks damp with bracken and heavy with mist. Twice we were lost on the path from India Ravine through Echo Valley. Now, soaking wet and tired we were finally in the vicinity of the rangers' hut where we knew we would find shelter and warmth. Some ranger or other would be off duty and keep the fire warm and going. Someone with a sense of humour had called the hut At Last. It couldn't be the rangers for they never spoke English. On the way we passed the hut belonging to the white Mountain Club, and slightly below that was another hut reserved for members of the coloured Club. I made some remark about the white clubhouse and the fact that prejudice had permeated even to the top of Table Mountain.

'For that matter we would not even be allowed into the coloured Mountain Club hut,' George remarked, serious for once.

'And why not?'

'Because, dear brother Paul, to get in you can't only be coloured, but you must also be not too coloured. You must have the right complexion, the right sort of hair, the right address and speak the right sort of Walmer Estate English.'

'You mean I might not make it?'

'I mean exactly that.'

I made rapid mental calculations. I was rather dark, had short, curly hair, came from Caledon Street in District Six, but spoke English reasonably well. After all, I was majoring in it at a white university. What more could one want?

'I'm sure that at a pinch I could make it,' I teased George. 'I speak English beautifully and am educated well beyond my intelligence.'

'My dear Paul, it won't help. You are far too coloured, University of Cape Town and all. You are far, far too brown. And, in addition, you have a lousy address.'

I collapsed in mock horror. 'You can't hold all that against me.'

Leonard grinned. He was not one for saying much.

We trudged on, instinctively skirting both club huts as widely as possible, until we reached At Last, which was ten minutes slogging away, just over the next ridge. A large main room with a very welcome fire going in the cast-iron stove. How the hell did they get that stove up there when our haversacks felt like lead? Running off the main room were two tiny bedrooms belonging to each of the rangers. We removed damp haversacks and sleeping-bags, then took off damp boots and stockings. Both rangers were off duty and made room for us at the fire. They were small, wiry plattelanders; a hard breed of men with wide-eyed, yellow faces, short hair and high cheekbones. They spoke a pleasant, soft, guttural Afrikaans with a distinct Malmesbury brogue, and broke into easy laughter especially when they tried to speak English. The smell of warming bodies filled the room and steam rose out from our wet shirts and shorts. It became uncomfortably hot and I felt sleepy, so decided to retire to one of the bedrooms, crawl into my bag and read myself to sleep. I lit a lantern and quietly left the group. George was teasing the rangers and insisting that they speak English. I was reading a novel about the massacre in the ravines of Babi Yar, gripping and revolting; a bit out of place in the unnatural calm at the top of a cold, wet mountain. I was beginning to doze off comfortably when the main door of the hut burst open and a blast of cold air swept through the entire place, almost extinguishing the lantern. Before I could shout anything there were loud protests from the main room. The door slammed shut again and then followed what sounded like a muffled apology. A long pause, then I made out George saying something. There was a short snort which was followed by peals of loud, uncontrolled laughter. I felt it was uncanny. The snort, then the rumbling laughter growing in intensity, then stopping abruptly.

By now I was wide awake and curious to know to whom the laugh belonged, though far too self-conscious to join the group immediately. I strained to hear scraps of conversation. Now and then I could make out George's voice and the low, soft Afrikaans of the rangers. There was also another voice which sounded feminine, but nevertheless harsh and screechy. My curiosity was getting the better of me. I climbed out of the sleeping-bag and as unobtrusively as possible joined the group around the fire. The newcomer was a gaunt, angular white woman, extremely unattractive, looking incongruous in heavy, ill-fitting mountaineering clothes. She was in the centre of the discussion and enjoying it. She was in the middle of making a point when she spotted me. Her finger remained poised in mid-air.

'And who may I ask is that?' She stared at me. I looked back into her hard, expressionless grey eyes.

'Will someone answer me?'

'Who?' George laughed. 'He's Paul. He's the greatest literary genius the coloured people have produced this decade. He's written a poem.'

'How exciting,' she dismissed me. The others laughed. They were obviously under her spell.

'Let me introduce you. This is Professor Paul. First year B.A., University of Cape Town.'

'Cut it out,' I said, very annoyed at him. George ignored my remark.

'And you are? I have already forgotten.'

She made a mock, ludicrous bow. 'Riva Lipschitz. Madame Riva Lipschitz. The greatest Jewish watch-repairer and mountaineer in Cape Town. Display shop, 352 Long Street.'

'All right, you've made your point. Professor Paul — Madame Riva Lipschitz.'

I mumbled a greeting, keeping well in the background. I was determined not to participate in any conversation. I found George's flattering her loathsome. The bantering continued to the amusement of the two rangers. Leonard smiled sympathetically at me. I remained poker-faced, waiting for an opportunity when I could slip away. George made some amusing remark (I was not listening) and Riva snorted and started to laugh. So that was where it came from. She saw the look of surprise on my face and stopped abruptly.

'What's wrong, Professor? Don't you like the way I laugh?'

'I'm sorry, I wasn't even thinking of it.'

'It makes no difference whether you were or not. Nevertheless I hate being ignored. If the others can treat me with the respect due to me, why can't you? I'm like a queen, am I not George?' I wasn't sure whether she was serious or not.

'You certainly are like a queen.'

'Everyone loves me except the Professor. Maybe he thinks too much.'

'Maybe he thinks too much of himself,' George added.

She snorted and started to laugh at his witticism. George glowed with pride. I took in her ridiculous figure and dress. She was wearing a little knitted skull-cap, far too small for her, from which wisps of mousy hair were sticking. A thin face, hard around the mouth and grey eyes, with a large nose I had seen in caricatures of Jews. She seemed flat-chested under her thick jersey, which ran down to incredible stick-thin legs stuck into heavy woollen stockings and heavily studded climbing boots.

'Come on, Paul, be nice to Riva,' George encouraged.

'Madame Riva Lipschitz, thank you. Don't you think I look like a queen, Professor?'

I maintained my frigid silence.

'Your Professor obviously does not seem over-friendly. Don't you like whites, Professor? I like everyone. I came over specially to be friendly with you people.'

'Whom are you referring to as you people?' I was getting angry. She seemed temporarily thrown off her guard at my reaction, but immediately controlled herself and broke into a snort.

'The Professor is extremely sensitive. You should have warned me. He doesn't like me but we shall remain friends all the same; won't we, Professor?'

She shot out her hand for me to kiss. I ignored it. She turned back to George and for the rest of her stay pretended I was not present. When everyone was busy talking I slipped out quietly and returned to the bedroom.

Although falling asleep, I could pick up scraps of conversation. George seemed to be explaining away my reaction, playing the clown to her queen. Then they forgot all about me. I must have dozed off for I awoke suddenly to find someone shaking my shoulder. It was Leonard.

'Would you like to come with us?'

'Where to?'

'Riva's Mountain Club hut. She's invited us over for coffee, and to meet Simon, whoever he is.'

'No, I don't think I'll go.'

'You mustn't take her too seriously.'

'I don't. Only I don't like her type and the way George is playing up to her. Who the hell does she think she is, after all? What does she want with us?'

'I really don't know. You heard she said she was a watch-repairer somewhere in Long Street. Be reasonable, Paul. She's just trying to be friendly.'

'While playing the bloody queen? Who does she think she is because she's white?'

'Don't be like that. Come along with us. She's just another person.'

George appeared grinning widely. He attempted an imitation of Riva's snort.

'You coming or not?' he asked laughing. For that moment I disliked him intensely.

'I'm certainly not.' I rolled over in my bag to sleep.

'All right, if that's how you feel.'

I heard Riva calling for him, then after a time she shouted, 'Goodbye, Professor, see you again sometime.' Then she snorted and they went laughing out at the door. The rangers were speaking softly and I joined them around the fire, then fell asleep there. I dreamt of Riva striding with heavy, impatient boots and thin-stick legs over mountains of dead bodies in the ravines of Babi Yar. She was snorting and laughing while pushing bodies aside, climbing ever upwards over dead arms and legs.

It must have been much later when I awoke to the door's opening and a stream of cold air rushing into the room. The fire had died down and the rangers were sleeping in their rooms. George and Leonard were stomping and beating the cold out of their bodies.

'You awake, Paul?' George shouted. Leonard shook me gently.

'What scared you?' George asked. 'Why didn't you come and have coffee with the queen of Table Mountain?'

'I can't stand her type. I wonder how you can.'

'Come off it, Paul. She's great fun.' George attempted a snort and then collapsed with laughter.

'Shut up, you fool. You'll wake up the rangers. What the hell did she want here?'

George sat up, tears running down his cheeks. He spluttered and it produced more laughter. 'She was just being friendly, dear brother Paul, just being friendly. Fraternal greetings from her Mountain Club.'

'Her white Mountain Club?'

'Well yes, if you put it that way, her white Mountain Club. She could hardly join the coloured one, now, could she? Wrong hair, wrong address, wrong laugh.'

'I don't care where she goes as long as you keep her away from me. I have no need to play up to Jews and whites.'

'Now really, Paul,' George seemed hurt. 'Are you anti-Semitic as well as being anti-white?' My remark must have hit home.

'No, I'm only anti-Riva Lipschitz.'

'Well anyhow, I like the way she laughs.' He attempted another imitation, but when he started to snort he choked and collapsed to the floor, coughing and spluttering. I rolled over in my bag to sleep.

Three months later I was in the vicinity of Upper Long Street. George worked as a clerk at a furniture store in Bree Street. I had been busy with an assignment in the Hiddingh Hall library and had finished earlier than expected. I had not seen him since we had last gone mountaineering, so strolled across to the place where he worked. I wanted to ask about himself, what he had been doing since last we met, about Riva. A senior clerk told me that he had not come in that day. I wandered around aimlessly, at a loss what to do next. I peered into second-hand shops without any real interest. It was late afternoon on a dull, overcast day and it was rapidly getting darker with the promise of rain in the air. Upper Long Street and its surrounding lanes seemed more depressing, more beaten up than the rest of the city. Even more so than District Six. Victorian double-storied buildings containing mean shops on the ground floors spilled over into mean side-streets and lanes. To catch a bus home meant walking all the way back. Caledon Street, the noise, dirt and squalor. My mood was as depressing as my immediate surroundings. I did not wish to stay where I was and at the same time did not wish to go home immediately. What was the number she had said? Was it 352 or 325? I peered through the windows of second-hand bookshops without any wish to go inside and browse. Number 352, yes that was it. Or 325? In any case I had no money to buy books even if I had the inclination to do so. Had George been at work he might have been able to shake me out of this mood, raise my spirits.

I was now past the swimming-baths. A dirty fly-spotted delicatessen store. There was no number on the door, but the name was boldly displayed. Madeira Fruiterer. Must be owned by some homesick Portuguese. Next to it what seemed like a dark and dingy watchmakers. Lipschitz — Master Jewellers. This must be it. I decided to enter. A shabby, squat, balding man adjusted an eyepiece he was wearing and looked up from a work-bench cluttered with assorted broken watches.

'Excuse me, are you Mr Lipschitz?' I wondered whether I should add 'Master Jeweller'.

'What exactly do you want?' He had not answered my question. 'What can I do for you?' His accent was guttural and foreign. I thought of Babi Yar. I was about to apologize and say that I had made some mistake when from the far side of the shop came an unmistakable snort.

'My goodness, if it isn't the Professor!' and then the familiar laugh. Riva came from behind a counter. My eyes had become accustomed to the gloomy interior. The squat man was working from the light filtering in through a dirty window. Rickety show-cases and counters cluttered with watches and cheap trinkets. A cat-bin, still wet and smelling pungently, stood against the far counter.

'What brings the Professor here? Coming to visit me?' She nodded to the squat man indicating that all was in order. He had already shoved back his eyepiece and was immersed in his work.

'Come to visit the queen?'

This was absurd. I could not imagine anything less regal, more incongruous. Riva, a queen. As gaunt as she had looked in the rangers' hut. Now wearing an unattractive blouse and old-fashioned skirt. Her face as narrow, strained and unattractive as ever. I had to say something, explain my presence.

'I was just passing.'

'That's what they all say. George said so last time.'

What the hell did that mean? I started to feel uncomfortable. She looked at me almost coyly. Then she turned to the squat man.

'Simon, I think I'll pack up now. I have a visitor.' He showed no sign that he had heard her. She took a shabby coat from a hook.

'Will you be late tonight?' she asked him. Simon grumbled some unintelligible reply. Was this Simon whom George and Leonard had met? Simon the mountaineer? He looked most unlike a mountaineer. Who the hell was he then? Her boss? Husband? Lover? Lipschitz — the Master Jeweller? Or was she Lipschitz, the Master Jeweller? That seemed most unlikely. Riva nodded to me to follow. I did so as there was no alternative. Outside it was dark already.

'I live two blocks down. Come along and have some tea.' She did not wait for a reply but began walking briskly, taking long strides. I followed as best I could half a pace behind.

'Walk next to me,' she almost commanded. I did so. Why was I going with her? The last thing I wanted was tea.

'Nasty weather,' she said, 'bad for climbing.' Table Mountain was wrapped in a dark mist. It was obviously ridiculous for anyone to climb at five o'clock on a weekday afternoon in heavy weather like this. Nobody would be crazy enough. Except George perhaps.

'George,' she said as if reading my thoughts. 'George. What was the other one's name?'

'Leonard.'

'Oh yes, Leonard, I haven't seen him since the mountain. How is he getting on?'

I was panting to keep up with her. 'I don't see much of them except when we go climbing together. Leonard works in Epping and George is in Bree Street.'

'I know about George.' How the hell did she?

'I've come from his work. I wanted to see him but he hasn't come in today.'

'Yes, I knew he wouldn't be in. So you came to see me instead? I somehow knew that one day you would put in an appearance.'

How the hell did she know? Was she in contact with George? I remained quiet, out of breath with the effort of keeping up with her. What on earth made me go to the shop of Lipschitz — Master Jeweller? Who the hell was Lipschitz — Master Jeweller?

The conversation had stopped. She continued the brisk pace, taking her fast, incongruous strides. Like stepping from rock to rock up Blinkwater Ravine, or Babi Yar.

'Here we are.' She stopped abruptly in front of an old triple-storied Victorian building with brown paint peeling off its walls. On the upper floors were wide balconies ringed with wrought-iron gates. The main entrance was cluttered with spilling refuse bins.

'I'm on the first floor.'

We mounted a rickety staircase, then a landing and a long, dark passage lit at intervals by a solitary electric bulb. All the doors, where these could be made out, looked alike. Riva stopped before one and rummaged in her bag for a key. Next to the door was a tray of cat-litter smelling sharply. The same cat?

'Here we are.' She unlocked the door, entered and switched on a light. I was hesitant about following her inside.

'It's quite safe, I won't rape you,' she snorted. This was a coarse remark.

I waited for her to laugh but she did not. I entered, blinking my eyes. Large, high-ceilinged, cavernous bed-sitter with a kitchen and toilet running off it. The room was gloomy and dusty. A double bed, round table, two uncomfortable-looking chairs and a dressing-table covered with bric-a-brac. There was a heavy smell of mildew permeating everything. The whole building smelt of mildew. Why a double bed? For her alone or Simon and herself?

'You live here?' It was a silly question and I knew it. I wanted to ask, 'You live here alone or does Simon live here also?' Why should I bother about Simon?

'Yes, I live here. Have a seat. The bed's more comfortable to sit on.' I chose one of the chairs. It creaked as I settled into it. All the furniture must have been bought from second-hand junk shops. Or maybe it came with the room. Nothing was modern. Jewish, Victorian, or what I imagined Jewish Victorian to be. Dickensian in a sort of decaying nineteenth century way. Riva took off her coat. She was all bustle.

'Let's have some tea. I'll put on the water.' Before I could refuse she disappeared into the kitchen. I must leave now. The surroundings were far too depressing. Riva was far too depressing. I remained as if glued to my seat. She reappeared. Now to make my apologies. I spoke as delicately as I could, but it came out all wrongly.

'I'm very sorry, but I won't be able to stay for tea. You see, I really can't stay. I must get home. I have lots of work to do. An exam tomorrow. Social Anthropology.'

'The trouble with you, Professor, is that you are far too clever, but not clever enough.' She sounded annoyed. 'Maybe you work too hard, far too hard. Have some tea before you go.' There was a twinkle in her eye again. 'Or are you afraid of me?'

I held my breath, expecting her to laugh but she did not. A long pause.

'No,' I said at last. 'No, I'm not afraid of you. I really do have an exam tomorrow. You must believe me. I was on my way home. I was hoping to see George.'

'Yes, I know, and he wasn't at work. You've said so before.'

'I really must leave now.'

'Without first having tea? That would be anti-social. An intellectual like you should know that.'

'But I don't want any tea, thanks.' The conversation was going around in meaningless circles. Why the hell could I not go if I wished to?

'You really are afraid of me. I can see that.'

'I must go.'

'And not have tea with the queen? Is it because I'm white? Or Jewish? Or because I live in a room like this?'

I wanted to say, 'It's because you're you. Why can't you leave me alone?' I got up determined to leave.

'Why did you come with me in the first place?'

This was an unfair question. I had not asked to come along. There was a hiss from the kitchen where the water was boiling over onto the plate.

'I don't know why I came. Maybe it was because you asked me.'

'You could have refused.'

'I tried to.'

'But not hard enough.'

'Look, I'm going now. I have overstayed my time.'

'Just a second.' She disappeared into the kitchen. I could hear her switching off the stove, then the clinking of cups. I stood at the door waiting for her to appear before leaving.

She entered with a tray containing the tea things and a plate with some assorted biscuits.

'No thank you,' I said, determined that nothing would keep me, 'I said I was leaving and I am.'

She put the tray on the table. 'All right then, Professor. If you must then you must. Don't let me keep you any longer.' She looked almost pathetic that moment, staring dejectedly at the tray. This was not the Riva I knew. She was straining to control herself. I felt dirty, sordid, sorry for her.

'Goodbye,' I said hastily and hurried out into the passage. I bumped into someone. Simon looked up surprised, then mumbled some excuse. He looked at me puzzled and then entered the room.

As I swiftly ran down the stairs I heard her snorting. Short pause and then peals of uncontrolled laughter. I stumbled out into Long Street.

Gerry Davidson

Knife

I live on the knife-edge
woman and white
and my black sister lives
on the dark side of the knife

Was it my sister's hand
so small, so sure
that bombed the bus-stop
yesterday?

I'll never know

but my heart knows
the dark side of the knife

Blood

I saw a heelprint
in blood
outside Edgar's Store today
I wondered
a sudden rush of menstrual blood
unchecked?
Stab wounds
left/right, left/right
or just a nosebleed in the city?

I'll never know

but on those hard
hot streets
who needs to know?

Joaquim & Bester

Two Sex-Workers
Accounts of the lives of two male sex-workers recorded by Matthew Krouse in Johannesburg, November 1991.

In a Dark Corner
The Story of Joaquim

My name is Joaquim, I was born in Mozambique. I lived there until I was eight years old, when my father bought a house in Umlazi, near Durban, the black location where I grew up. So we moved from Maputo when I was young and I forgot how to speak Portuguese. Now I only speak Shangaan, that's my home language.

Umlazi was fine, quite interesting, we had shebeens and a few clubs. Sometimes you get violent people, it's the same as Soweto, there's no difference. But nothing was really wrong with Umlazi because we had a big house. I've got four brothers, three sisters and my parents. My mother works in a hospital, and my father works for Lion Matches.

I always knew that I was a gay because I used to like the young guys in school. I used to like looking at them; I'd get an erection and I'd feel like fucking them. Then I used to take them out, we'd go to the bushes, all of us, we'd smoke some dope and then we'd fuck. I was about fourteen years old.

I was lucky because I once met a guy in school, his name was Bongani. He was quite young and he was very good-looking, so I told him I liked him. And he was my very first person I slept with. We slept in the sugar-cane. It was nice. Oh, we had a nice love. I kissed him in the sugar-cane. Then I asked him, 'Take your pants off,' which he did. Then I asked him, 'Take your underpants off,' and he did that. Then I played with his cock, and he did get an erection. I was already randy. And I asked him to open his arse, which he did open, and then I fucked him. That was nice and very fantastic. Oh, I was lucky to get him because I think he was also gay, otherwise he wouldn't have done it.

Then from there I had the rest. But I didn't tell my parents because it is my secret, I don't think they will accept it and they won't like me anymore.

I left Durban when I finished my matric, when I was twenty-one years old. I decided to come to Johannesburg to look for a job, but I couldn't find one. And so I decided to become a male hooker.

I arrived in Johannesburg in 1984, I got here by train. On the train I met a guy, he was going half-way between Johannesburg and Durban. He was gonna climb off in Newcastle. So I had a drink with him, we had some talks, and we had a dance because he had a radio. Everything was quite nice. Then we took a walk, to the toilets. We smoked some marijuana, it was quite lovely. But the guy jumped off in Newcastle. And then I was lonely on the train, so I fell asleep and just woke up in Johannesburg, thank you.

When I got off the train it was strange to me, Johannesburg was something I hadn't been to. I hadn't seen Johannesburg since I was born. I was looking around. Fortunately I had enough money, something like five hundred rand my father gave me.

I asked somebody where I could find a hotel, and I got one in Hillbrow. At the hotel I asked somebody where I could find the gay bar. I knew there was a gay bar somewhere in Hillbrow, because I used to meet people in Durban who came from Johannesburg and they would tell me of it. So I thought that if I couldn't get a job it would be the way of making money, from the gay guys in the bar.

At the bar I met a white guy and he liked me, but I told him I wanted money and he said, 'No, I won't pay for a fuck, but I can show you a place where you can go and stand, and then you can make money there.'

He took me to the street where the hookers all hang around. And that is where I started.

Now I live with a brother in Hillbrow. He stays with his wife and doesn't know I'm a hooker. What he knows, I guess, is that I go out and do gambling. It's quite nice there, but at the same time I don't have good friends who like to keep me. I am looking for one though. I wish to find a nice guy who will like me, who will like to keep me. That's what I'm into at the moment. I had this once — I was living with a guy in a flat in Hillbrow, a white guy, a dancer. But his parents didn't accept it. They know he is gay but they didn't accept that he had a black lover. They wanted he must have a white lover. So it created a problem and we had to broke up because of that.

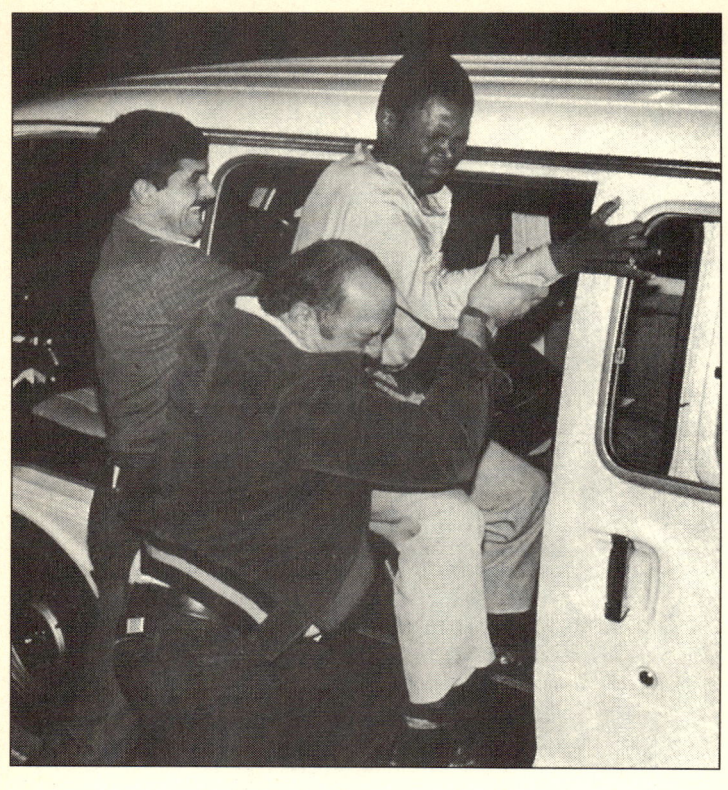

A prostitute is arrested by Vice Squad police, Johannesburg, 1984.

Photograph by Juhan Kuus

Really, that white guy I stayed with was the guy I like, but because of his parents it couldn't work. But I'm still worried about him because I still remember him. He used to do nice things for me, treat me nicely. We'd go out together, have supper, go to clubs, have drinks, have a joint together — we were like family, me and him. So I still remember him; and I would be happy if I can have a lover again. Love means something important, it's something great, to have someone who you can think of wherever you are, even when the guy is not around....

It's nice to be gay. But for the black people, it's something funny to them, if you don't sleep with women. They don't understand what kind of a person you are. They call you a moffie, *stabane*. In Africa, people don't accept you if you are a gay, they don't like you. So I don't tell them, because they mustn't know. If they know they must be gay themselves as well. And then they're not really friends but just people I meet in the bar — somebody to talk to for that night, to keep you company whenever you're having a drink. Whenever I feel lonely, then I talk to one of the black gays in the bar, this is it.

It's nice to have sex with a black guy, but as I'm black they don't really turn me on. I prefer the white men because they got soft skin, nice hairs, nice faces, nice eyes. And a nice body. So I like white guys more than I love black guys. To go with them into bed, I mean.

Being a hooker is a risk, you win or you lose.

Sometimes a policeman drives around the street and stops his car. He calls you over and asks how much you charge. You tell him your price, and he asks you to get into his car. Then from there he will take you away, maybe in a dark corner somewhere. He'll wank with you and then finally tell you, 'I'm a policeman, I won't pay you.' One policeman did this to me. The rest were okay.

You know, if you don't go with somebody and you need money, and you're hungry, it's terrible because it seems like you're losing the business, that's how it is. It's quite tough — no money, tough time. You cannot have what you want, for the next day. And that's the point.

So if a guy wants to pay me, he can be anything, but I will go with him. I've been with the white guys. Some they like to look at my body. Some they ask me I must suck them. Some they ask me I must fuck them. And some they ask me I must dance for them. I charge eighty rand. But it depends, if the guy's got fifty or sixty bucks I still take it. But I won't do more sex. I can only do everything when the guy pays me eighty rands.

The nicest thing to me, mostly, is that I prefer to go to the guy's house, then I feel more comfortable. That's the best way for me.

This is how I meet different people every night. They're quite nice, very friendly. But some they can be terrible.

Last year in September I was in the Diplomat Hotel and I met a big white guy, tall, he was wearing a cap. He came to me when I was sitting alone having my beer. Then he asked me can I join his company; and I did. And then he told me I must come with him to his house, and promised to

Joaquim

pay me something like a hundred rands. I agreed with that, and when I got to his flat, he asked me if I wanted something to eat, and I said yes. Then he gave me something to eat and he asked me if I wanted a drink, and I said, 'Yes, I want a drink.' Then afterwards, unexpected, the guy just punched me with a punch, and told me to turn around. I didn't have a chance because he was bigger than me. And he fucked me up. He told me to open my arse because he wants to fuck me, very badly, which he did, all the styles that he wanted to, for the whole night. I couldn't even sleep. It was very sore.

In the morning I was feeling very sick. And then he gave me the money. But he saw, when I was walking, that I wasn't in a good way. Well, at least he took me to hospital. Then he paid for the hospital as well. I was in hospital for about three weeks. There they asked me what happened and I said that I was just raped by the guys. I didn't want to point him out, because he gave me the money.

Afterwards, I was feeling bad about that day. But I forget about it at the moment because I get the nice guys now. Nice clients for me.

The other rents are very terrible, especially the Afrikaans guys who are standing in the street. Most of the time, whenever they get a score they rob the guy, they take his money, or they take whatever they can take from him. And people know, and are scared of them. Because of this, people prefer to go with the black guys. And so the white rents have become jealous of the blacks and whenever they see you there, as a black man in the street, they will try their best to fuck you up as much as they can. So I can say that they are very bad people and I don't like them.

I've been fucked up by them about three times. Once I was standing in the street and a score came over to speak with me and they jumped us. They fucked me up, and the guy ran away.

The second time I was just walking past them. They thought that maybe I was returning from a score, and they tried to rob me. But I got away that time.

The third time, a guy arrived at the street and saw me standing there. He drove around, decided he liked me, stopped his car, and called me over. I was sitting inside his car when two Afrikaans guys came over. They asked him, 'You are a white man, why do you sleep with the black guys?'

And he said that he only wanted business and could go with whoever he wanted. He said that it doesn't matter about the skin, if one is black or Indian, or coloured or white. He said that he would go with whoever he liked. Then they started to pull him out of his car, and they fucked him up, and did the same to me.

These days I go to the club, have a drink, have a dance, talk to people. Sometimes I get picked up, sometimes I don't. Then I go home, I sleep, I wake up in the morning, I have some breakfast, I take a shower. I dress, I walk around in the street looking at people when they're walking around, looking at cars when they're driving around, doing window-shopping, for the day. Then in the afternoon I go in the street, trying to get picked up again.

In a couple of years time I would love to be a modeller, that's what I'd like to do. But at the moment I've got a problem, I got no money to pay for the agency and I'm looking for a guy who can help with that. Then I'll be happy. I need eight hundred rand. Then I would like to have my own business.

I can make money in modelling, plus, maybe I will be a hooker now and again, but with the rich guys who can pay me big money. Then I will try to keep that money in the bank so that when I'm old, about forty years old, I can buy myself a car, a nice house, then I can open a business.

In politics I support nobody because I think those people are working for their families — they can't help me with nothing. I'm just happy about my life, if I've got something to eat, I've got a roof over my head, I've got some money in my pocket, I can go out if I want to. And that's it. That's the end of the story.

Life is Hard
The Story of Bester

I was twelve years old and I ran away from home. I packed my stuff because my brother was hitting me.

Whenever I came back from school he always hit me, because he wanted to make me hard. Because he said the life is hard. I told him I don't want trouble. And every time I didn't go to school I came and cried to him, and then he hit me. That's not what I like. That's why, today, I'm a rent-piece.

I was born on a farm in South West Africa, in Tsumeb. I was born in 1970. My mother was a housekeeper and my father was a farmer. He farmed mealies and potatoes, and he was having chickens, selling eggs. The farm was about thirty morgen. The house was a little bit small and I was sleeping in the garage. It wasn't nice because it was cold in winter, and in summer the mosquitoes were biting, and it was hot.

My father and my mother died when I was five years old, then I stayed with a few guys, at my brother's. They were like my friends. I had lots of friends. Now, my friends are not my friends. These days, you can't afford to have friends, because when you have money they'll always be with you. If you haven't got money, they tell you you must just go. They kick you in the back.

The people in Namibia are very rich. And they like to speak German. If you speak to them in Afrikaans they speak back, but they battle to talk with you. So I speak Afrikaans and *ich spreche Deutsch*.

I was renting in South West Africa and lots of people stopped to pick me up. I showed my leg for them. And then they would think, 'Okay, let's take the bloke home.'

In South West Africa they like hitting and kicking a guy if he comes with them. You know, they're a little bit rough.

So I ran away from home and I was hitch-hiking, and a taxi came by and asked me where I'm going to. I said, 'I'm going to South Africa.'

He said, 'Where do you want to be?'

I said, 'I want to be in Johannesburg.'

He said, 'Hop in, have you got bucks?'

I said, 'I haven't got any money, sorry. I'll get out if you don't want me to go with you.'

He said, 'Don't worry, I'm going that way.' He was going over the *grens*.

And then I came here, in South Africa. I got a South African passport and I became a S.A. burgher.

Before I left home I thought that Johannesburg's a nice place, very busy in the nights. There's plenty places to go. I thought I'd survive. Because you have to.

So I came to Johannesburg and I saw the big buildings, I saw the people, how they move, how they talk, how they eat, how they look, everything. I was thinking it's a good thing — people are very nice.

I was going with this one guy. I met him one night. He just got out of his car, and he tuned me. He said, 'I want to take a few photos of you, like six, how much do you want?'

I asked him, 'Why you want six photos?'

But he said he'd give me three hundred rand — fifty rand a photo. Plus, he booked me into a room for the night and bought me some food. He asked me if I smoke, I said yes. Then he bought me a few packets of smokes, and he gave me money for buttons. And I'm beginning to became a drug addict. I'm using drugs.

With him, I went to Durban, I went to Cape Town, Thabazimbi, and Rustenburg. It was very nice. Everything I see, he said, 'Do you like it?'

I said yes, and he said, 'Okay, let me bought it for you.'

He's very big. He said that he's got his own gym in New York. That's overseas you know. So he wants to marry me. I asked him, 'Why you want to marry me? I'm a man, you're a man?'

He said that it doesn't matter. 'It's the love, I want it, you must be my lover,' he tuned me. He said I must come play with him. I must be his bodyguard and he will give me something for it.

I lived with him for three months. It was good. In the morning, when he went to work, he said, 'Listen here — here's some spending money for the day.' Then he'd give me my bike's keys. He bought me a bike, a 500 scrambler. I was having plenty chicks who wanted me.

But now, I'm living in a flat in town. In the daytime I'm smoking buttons, night-time I'm on business. How many men I go with depends on how many money I get. If I get a hundred and fifty I go home. Every night I get that money, sorry.

The black people on the corner are spoiling the whole scene. It's because they always run to the cars and the people get afraid. They think that something has happened, you know. I won't go with a black man in my whole life. Even if he wants to give me five hundred bucks I won't even go with him. Even if I'm down. I can't go with a black, really.

Aids is a very bad thing. You must always be careful on the block. You must look before you go with a bloke, you must try to get him to say that he has it. You must try to get it out of him. Then he'll think, 'This guy is clever and he knows I have Aids.'

I don't go with any guy I see. I'm not like the others on the block, running after everything.

Let me tell you about my brother.

My brother's the kind of guy who likes to always change his haircuts. You won't recognize him — he's an otherwise guy.

One night he picked me up, and I didn't recognize him. He was looking different. It was long time no see, because I come and go.

He wanted to know how much I charge. I asked him how much he could afford, and he said he would give me three hundred. He said he would give me food and a place to stay. I asked him, 'By the way, what's your name?'

He tuned me, if I knew his real name then I would get out of his car. Then he told me his name was Rasta. My brother's a merchant, you know. Rasta. I thought that I was in trouble and I tried to leave.

But he said, 'No, take the three hundred, and I'll see you when I see you.'

He told me, 'Go to Cape Agulhas, there's a room booked for you. Here's the key, go there.' Then he told me that what I am doing is not right. He told me who he was, and so I discovered that this Rasta was really my brother.

I went to Cape Agulhas and I was sleeping nicely there, alone. But I'm out of there now. I'll tell you why:

The other day I was going to visit my brother in Pretoria. When I came there I heard that they shot him. Through his head. It's because he was a bouncer and he was throwing a guy out of a club. And that's what's bothering me. That's why I now want to go to the funeral in South West Africa, Namibia.

I want to take revenge on my brother's death. I'm going to get the guy who killed him and I'm going to punish him. That's why, before I go home, I must first find this guy.

I'm feeling sorry for my brother's death. People today don't care what happens to you. And that's bothering me now. I just need a friend who can say I'm here for you, you know.

My other brothers and sisters, they threw me away because I'm a rent. I'm on the blocks and I can't get a job. I don't want to get a job, because I get more money on the blocks.

But right now, I need bucks to go to his funeral.

He's the best brother I ever met.

Young prostitutes wait to be processed at John Vorster Square police station after being arrested by the Vice Squad, 1984.

Photograph by Juhan Kuus

Alan Reynolds

Our Rent

On the southernmost end of the Marine Parade just before the breakwater at the entrance to the harbour lies a wide stretch of grass under palms, edged by a rough stone wall. 'Queen's Walk', or 'The Wall' as it is known, is a pleasant moonlit promenade popular with lovers, strollers and children.

But The Wall has another life, secret meanings. It is a kind of Masonic handshake, a secret territory in the face of the oblivious majority. Its existence is communicated as though by instinct alone, drawing men to the edge of the sea.

It is late on a balmy Monday evening; I have James Baldwin and need to read it there, on the southernmost end of the Marine Parade. I am sitting under a light so bright it is my own private sun when suddenly I am not alone. With his back to me in a red track-suit stands a teen-age boy. He is wrapped in the very atmosphere of someone on the prowl. He turns his head slightly and looks at me. I do not look away, he does. After a studied pause he casually turns to face me, but quite deliberately as if to survey some distant point beyond me, showing himself. It is Isherwood's Otto, a simian Teuton all hard voluptuous muscle and blondness. He looks at me, from under veiled eyes and, seeing me return his look, becomes bolder and looks directly at me. If I flinch he will go; I don't and he walks over, not directly but at an angle, like a wild animal approaching something unfamiliar which may be dangerous, leaving an avenue for escape. His opening line is stunning: 'What does it feel like in the police force?'

'I really don't know.'

Silence. I go on reading my book.

'Oh come on, you're a *kêrel*.'

'No I'm not.'

'Then why's your hair so short?'

'Because it makes me look like Caligula.'

He doesn't understand — a state he seems familiar with and leaves unchallenged.

'They tell me the *kêrels* are full-up here.'

'So I'm told.'

He's bolder now, but still undecided. Several questions pass behind his eyes: 'Can I ask you a really personal question?'

'Sure.'

'What do you do for a job?'

'I'm at university.'

'Well you know what my job is?'

He comes out with it in a rush, and leaves it lying there in front of us, shiny and slimy, wriggling naked: 'I'm a rent.'

He immediately regrets his frankness, prepares to bolt. I don't respond so he relaxes and, encouraged, becomes bolder, sensing a kill. 'Are you married?'

'No.'

'Are you gay?'

'Depends on who's asking.'

Once again he doesn't understand, ignores it and presses on: 'Are you looking for company?'

'Not really.'

'So what are you doing here?'

'Reading my book.'

This is not going according to routine. There is an ordered and universal procedure in which rent and john find security, through which they can ask all the important questions without committing themselves, allowing for escape, giving each other time. He gives up: 'How much will you pay me?'

'I'm not sure that I want to pay you.'

'No come on man, you must, I'm really desperate.'

Is it my social, moral and humanitarian duty to have sex with this person to save him from his predicament? I cannot just give him money, that would be an insult, a negation of the validity of the exchange value of his body, which is probably the basis upon which he has constructed his own self-image.

'Why?'

'I need money man. I've got a room, fifty bucks a day... '

'That's very expensive.'

' ... and I believe an *ou* must bath and have clean clothes.'

(His clothes are very clean, but he has the rank smell of a wild animal.)

'And do you manage to make that money?'

'Sometimes. But not here. In Jo'burg I come away with two or three hundred a night. Then I sleep at the *ou's* place. In Jo'burg the *ous* understand that you need the money.'

Silence.

'So what you into?'

'What do you do?'

'I kiss.'

'You kiss.'

'Ja, the *ous* like that. And I wank. But I can get fifteen just for talking to an *ou*. And I suck. But I don't *pomp*. I've got a cherry you know. She's coming tomorrow. I don't really like *ous*, you see, I do this for money.'

He suddenly realizes his tactical error.

'But it's not so bad going with the *ous*, you know, it's okay like.'

I don't respond, so he talks on, sustaining a conversation, consciously: 'I have to make bucks. If I don't then I have to go to the uncle, and he's only good for ten. But then I still need more for food, like bread and Coke and stuff, you know.'

Silence. He has on brown leather boots, neatly polished.

'So how's about it? You won't be sorry, I'm really big, all the *ous* say so. Look, I'll show you....'

And he does, but it is an act of friendship, as though he is bestowing on me a particular and very precious favour. The world has defined for him his value to humanity in terms of what his body has to offer, and he has accepted that definition, as though it was a great intellectual or sporting prowess, and turned it into a matter of pride.

'Why are you doing this?'

There are too many answers to this question, on too many levels.

'Look, maybe you should go a bit further down the road, most of the guys hang out by Pick 'n Chicken.'

He looks at me, about to rally one last time, but then he relaxes and smiles: 'Ah, you're hard man. It's okay, like, I check. I'll see you around some time. Maybe? We don't have to do stuff, like just hang out. Unless you want it, I mean.'

I don't know what horror he is running from, and clearly he is, but I think he means it, and that if I was nice to him only once, he would die for me with the unquestioning devotion of a faithful dog.

I do see him later, still walking up and down. He raises a hand to me as he walks over to a car, crouches down for a while, stands up as if to leave, is called back, crouches again, and then saunters to the passenger side and gets in. He looks at me as the car drives past.

I am alone again. Baldwin is talking about possession and power, and about how, with possession and power, whites lost their ability to love, and how afraid he is that that is the danger with Martin Luther King.

In this case, I'm not sure who had the power...our boy who needs to be loved, or the man who needs to give it. Probably they are equals. All victims are.

Jay Pather

Red Wine

Ah, and they were all there, queens and hunks alike. All were there, flaming bodies in Saturday night glitter.

Lights sizzling across imperfect bodies and acne skins and eyes feigning dignity and disinterest.

Ah, those eyes tearing your clothes and then putting them back on to lock you up more tightly as those eyes unveil and then coldly look away in turn, taking you in, then vomiting you out and if you're lucky an in-between smile or a nod of the head, the subtle cool, cool approval: I approve of you and your existence, he seems to say, and your knees give way in awe and prostration at this miraculous happening and...too much bitterness uh-uh....

So the lights chisel the music and vice versa and bodies in endless variations of fucking, hands in endless gestures of stroking and clutching and masturbating...whowee who needs all the new-row-sees of a ree-lay-shun-ship?

Everyone was there and I danced with all, the exuberance of seeing everybody there. Recognition. Communion — what you will. It was Saturday Night. What's so significant about Saturday night? At Tots it was pretty significant, it was *the* event, a most necessary ritual, the event of the week. No work next day, so it was until early-morning public transport, cheap trains and early Sunday minibuses; hot bright sunny mornings playing havoc with your leathers and taffeta of the night before, rubbing shoulders with the chiffon church-dress of the rotund woman with the screaming child slicing your *bablas* into tiny pieces for the easy picking of the bus-conductor who looks you over, top to toe, and smiles...ha ha ha Saturday Night.

So, sweating and slightly dizzy, I make my way to the bar to order a glass of red wine and to sit on a stool to watch the gleaming bodies, a momentary vision of an electric heaven, aggro macho side by side with soft and feminine, all in one body, one sex, one gender. And then I notice a face (in heaven), looking, not friendly, eyes penetrating mine. Familiar ones. Eyes penetrating mine indeed. Oh, for the substitute, the metaphor, the symbol! Is all this playing a worthy substitute for fucking, I ask with a tear in my eye?

But soft, he approaches, he of legendary lily-white skin, legendary and rare on this side of town. Oh, to classify, possify, fuckify, vilify! Oh, to classify!

'Do you have a cigarette?' Lights and music, lights and music, do I have a cigarette, what's your star sign, do you come here often, haven't I seen you before, can I buy you a drink, it's warm, it's cold, it's do I have a cigarette? Aw gimme a break....

'Yes,' I reply. Lights, lights and music. Laughs now, hysteria, some queen's getting bashed, or bashing more likely, on the balcony.

And then he quietly leans over me and I notice beyond the artificial light and screaming music, an attractive face with cat's eyes and a full mouth, and well-cut clothes in fashionable coal-grey and black. And all this *GQ* ease and beauty slips and slides onto the floor with the line:

'Tell me, why are you a prostitute?'

Hard lights and screaming music accompany despair into delirium and absurdity and I laugh uncontrollably and sputter: 'It's economics.'

'So why don't you go for me, I've looked at you often enough?' And given me the nod of approval, translated into, 'Yes I will suck your cock or you may suck mine', what I mean is: what is all this?

And so I reply with continued delirium:

'It's because I am a high-class prostitute.'

He's joking, he's joking surely he's joking. I've checked this out before, middle-aged white men finding me common company, seeking me out, singling me out in a room dominated by pulsating, young white bodies. A racist will also be an ageist, a sexist, etcetera etcetera etcetera, and a homophobe? I don't know how these combinations work, is there one, are these reflexive? I don't know. All I'm saying is that I, a gay black male, am often the prey to the most unlovely advances and since sex and sexual encounters are such loaded phenomena, it is such an interesting inquiry as

121

to why a white man was asking me not am I a prostitute, or whether he would have to pay for my services, or how much do I cost, no none of that even. He was asking me in full-frontal, paternal fervour, why am I a prostitute? And I was finding out, he was serious.

And I took a good look at myself, glass of red wine in hand, perched on a stool, grinning in giddy delight. But that's all, surely. I mean, you've looked like this before, at a bar, at the office party, a club, even a restaurant, surely? What are the signs with which you cut and censor, and stab and wound? What makes you think I am what you think I am? What is your context, your reference?

This shit has so clogged up my pores. I don't know whether any anger can escape through any more. It's all stuck, stuck up to here, aeons of trash.

If it wasn't so funny, if it wasn't so convenient to find it funny, I'd, well, I'd...vomit.

Lights lights lights and music.

Cape Town's 'Miss Gay Competition' finalists — Sandy, Nina Ricci and Iman.

Photograph by Sharifa

Matthew Krouse

The Barracks Are Crying

Parade

When you consider the hundreds of boys who sit, ignorantly, in the barracks crying for their girlfriends, then you will realize the great resource of loneliness that reproduces itself and stalks about here, untamed.

Just before lights out I like to look down the rows of eyes, each pair looking back at me crying for a friend. And I go home with them one by one, I go to their mothers and I say: 'Little Peter has a problem, ma'am, he gets so hard there behind the fence and he keeps coming to me kindly begging me to rescue him from all that cock hanging off all that rank. It's not enough that he has to bow before it, ma'am, it's not enough that he has to suck it. It's not even enough that he has to stick it into his pelvis until his intestines devour that power-hungry come.

'It's more than enough that he has to wake up every hopeless morning with an ache in his heart before he goes out killing those kaffirs, ma'am.'

One of the first things we had to do when we got there was have our dicks inspected. You had to lie on that green bed with your legs spread wide open and someone else with some kind of medical qualification bent over you and certified that the flesh was in a proud and healthy order for the fight. We queued for days, a queue of five thousand white boys, still in civilian clothing. Days of being processed, dressed for battle, hair cut, all those things that happen in those wild war movies you see. But this wasn't a wild war movie, no, this was war, the true story of how the rank took enough care to post a bunch of fairies to some goddamned border town, where we could manufacture our dreams without infecting the proud villains of the fighting force.

We (the new conscripts, fresh, our mothers' milk still tasting in our mouths) were standing around all innocent-like, just hanging around waiting to sign the next form. It was Day 5 or 6 of Basic Training, probably mid-morning, after tea served from mammoth silver urns in the mess, when bells started ringing. There were sirens screaming through the air. Corporals were running everywhere, and news travelled fast that the Commanding Officer was coming. So they lined us up in rows on a vast parade-ground. All five thousand of us. It was like Belsen, or Auschwitz. Every boy in a shapeless brown overall, carrying a tin plate, standing shivering in the grey winter air. Every boy peering inconspicuously from side to side with rolling eyes, trying not to move the head. People fainted everywhere, and boys were being yelled at while they cowered over each other, patting the dead face of one who had reached his limit. Already there was some kind of identification between certain blokes who liked the look of each other. It could have been one of those shabby bars downtown where men stare endlessly in fascination at other men, only it wasn't. Rather, it was a dusty playground of horror, perhaps half a kilometre squared, teeming with white skin that was goose-pimpled and afraid. Arms hung at the sides like empty jackets. And in the freezing cold, the hairs on one's legs stood on end, chafing against the rough shapeless overalls that were no different to Belsen's pyjamas.

The parade had begun. Suddenly a jeep was seen approaching on the horizon of the road that ran past the ground. When it got to the dusty square of earth, at the flag-poles, it stopped. A pink, tall, bald man dressed in camouflage jumped awkwardly out of the jeep, escorted by a Preacher, a Brigadier and various other ranks. He approached a microphone at the sides of which stood about five adoring Corporals, quite informally. They were the superstars. We out there knew nothing, we had never heard the words 'Commanding Officer' in our lives before. Anyway, the speech he delivered was like babyshit. Everyone owed their presence on earth to God. God made South Africa, and God made mommy and daddy. God had also made the South African Defence Force that would let the Jews be Jews, would let Christians be Christians. Everyone could go to whichever church they wanted to.

I watched the backs of the boys' heads, lame and disbelieving. In a way I was exhilarated, I suppose. I wasn't ready for the truth. And it was about to bare its ugly teeth.

Whenever I tell this story I get pissed off. Today, as I write it, now six years later, I'm still furious. As far as war crimes go, ours was the crime of ignorance. We knew nothing, besides the fact that we were who we were, our elders were neurotic and paranoid, they had the power and the glory, and we had to sniff their ridiculous holes. The thing is, I want you to get the full picture, I want to leave nothing out, but it's really difficult. It's almost impossible to tell you how those barracks really looked because they looked like nothing, just rows and rows of square blocks in the middle of nowhere. Just pieces of earth, shower blocks, messes, sports fields, rifle-ranges, garages of khaki vehicles, thousands of lines of males in unison, running, singing, marching, undoing equipment and reassembling it. Being howled at, assaulting each other, pissing on command, shitting on command, being shown an endless array of trashy American war films to encourage aggression. Hell on earth!

The Commanding Officer stood at the helm of his parade-ground, with stiff shoulders and an arched back. He went on for about an hour of mirthless wank. And then he promptly turned his back and drove off with his entourage. We were still out there, sizing each other up. People confronting people, with nothing to go by except height, stance and the look of the face when it comes under such bitter pressure.

We suddenly found ourselves left at the mercy of the Corporals and Captains. We stood in the freezing cold, yet our crotches and armpits were sweating. Someone urinated down his leg. The word spread. Nobody knew the boy's name, of course, but a wave of speculation was whispered from person to person that the pisser was young, really young. I imagined a thirteen-year-old, don't know why. Once the word had got out that the thirteen-year-old had pissed down his leg, everyone was doing it. I tried but I couldn't. So I held it in. I think it helped me stand straight. I shook a little.

A white-haired, rotund Captain stood before us. 'There's a problem in this camp, and I'm going to sort it out,' he said. 'Every one of you here has a problem, and I'm going to sort it out right here and now!' he said. 'I'm going to sort out every single problem right now, and then there'll be no more problems!' he said. And then he began to walk towards the five thousand men, two Corporals hugging his sides.

From a tremendous distance I saw him out of the corner of my eye. He seemed to be spending a lot of time with each boy, hovering on every word the boy said, it was a little interrogation. Speculation between the boys was growing. 'They're sending people to the border!'

'They're sending people to the Parabats!'

'They're sending people home!'

None of this was true. They weren't sending people to the border, or to the Parabats, or home. They were, in all earnestness, sniffing out queers. It was queer-sniffing going on. It was weird. 'Obviously this camp has this particular problem,' I thought to myself.

I waited my turn, feeling fatalistic, thinking that, after all, this was a spectacle of incredible theatre. And it was just that. Queer boys started to drop like flies. Truths just came out for the Captain. He heard it all. Hundreds of youths seemed to confess to luscious desires. Some wept, some fainted, many were confronted beyond speech.

To some of the more ignorant boys from the country, the Captain became father, executioner and priest.

The queers were being singled out, as I've said. Each queer being escorted by two Corporals to a newly formed squad that was in two long rows at the back of the field. It was then that I began to feel a sense of envy, and through that sense I grew to understand that many of those there must have been feeling the same way. Feeling that one wanted to be with the queers, on the periphery, on the outside of the madness looking at the madness within. Of course, rare people volunteered themselves out of a sense of solidarity, and out of a yearning for what they already began to perceive as a lack of responsibility. Young men are like that. They will opt out if things get too tough.

The Captain waded down the rows, coming closer and closer to me. I had recognized three boys I knew from television and theatre. Actors. Boys I had seen on stage and in the local magazines. All three of them were breeding the hunky look, pretty-boy hunky-types. I really was curious to see what the Captain would make of these actors. He approached the first, an Afrikaner named Marais. Marais confessed that he was an actor. The Captain asked whether he had been on television. Marais quoted a drama. The Captain hadn't seen it. He asked Marais if he was queer. Heroic Marais! Hail Marais! He told the Captain that it was none of his business!

It was a dire confrontation. Why Marais didn't just say no, I'll never know. He was strong and sturdy. He could have been anyone, but he just wouldn't budge. It was a moment of puerile dogshit. The poor old Captain sucked and sucked. 'You look like a little girl!' he screamed at Marais. 'You call yourself an actor! You stand like a kaffir-girl who hasn't had breakfast!'

Marais got sent to join the queers at the back. The other two actors got sent there too. 'Actors are queers!' screamed the Captain.

I thought, 'Ah, from now on one need not say "I'm queer"; one need only say "I'm an actor".' I decoded it quickly, and decided to do exactly that. But then I decided not to. Why? Because as the Captain neared me I heard him say quite softly to one of the Corporals at his side, 'All of the queers are going to be sent to become riflemen. They're going to Potchefstroom.' And I knew that Potchefstroom was a mean, cold place, and it was one hell of a winter.

And now the Captain drew nearer. Next would be my turn.

I told the Captain my name in a dead-pan voice that sounded to me like the flat tone of a stroke victim. The Captain asked me where I was from. Ventersdorp. It was a lie. I had moved out of Ventersdorp and had been living with some bloke in Hillbrow for some time. (A year later the army sent me back to Ventersdorp; but that's another story.) Living in Hillbrow, in the middle of the city, was trashy. I had no money and slept on the floor. I was poor, young and bewildered, and most of all, bored. That is why I obeyed the law and went to the army in the first place. I regretted it now.

The Captain didn't believe that I was from Ventersdorp. He didn't believe a word I said. Noticing that I appeared older than average, he asked me my profession. I lied again, telling him I was a teacher. Then he asked me where I taught. I went cold and just couldn't lie a moment longer. I looked into his eyes and thought, 'What kind of a man is this? Is this man a slut? Doesn't he just want to fuck every boy on the field. He's trying to fuck me right now!' And then I turned around slowly and took a long sober look at the queer platoon. And in so doing I betrayed myself. I told him where my heart was. Not between his legs, no. My heart was standing in rows, singled out and terrified, at the back of the field. I said to the Captain, 'Sir, I'm an actor.' And without waiting for my sentence I began to walk towards the queers. 'WHERE DO YOU THINK YOU'RE GOING?' he wailed. I stopped and walked back to him. The Corporals hurried over to my sides. The war was on. I was thrown to the ground and made to do the proverbial press-ups, and let me tell you, I didn't get far. But they pushed and poked and I did more and more. Eventually, when I got to the queer platoon, I was limp, asthmatic and blue. The other queers looked at me as if I were Nelson Mandela. For those fifty press-ups, I made fifty new friends.

Once all of the soldiers had been sifted and processed in this manner, those presumed to be heterosexual were dismissed by the Captain. They wiped their sweaty brows, most of them appearing to feel proud that they had passed the first test of manhood, manifested in the Captain's keen sense of who was what.

The queer platoon was left behind, and it waited for about an hour while the Captain went with the real soldiers to eat his lunch. In other words, that day the queers missed lunch. I don't think anyone really cared. But while the others ate their lunch, a loud young Corporal was posted on the queer front to see that nobody spoke. The Corporal spoke. He told us over and over, in a coarse farm Afrikaans, that we were going to Potchefstroom, a tough camp, to be broken, to be built. He told us that he had nothing against us, being what we were. But it would be for our own good. The army would do what it had to, and in the end we would be grateful to The Force. In the end, It alone would be responsible for the fact that we would graduate, from this war, with wives and children.

When the Captain returned from lunch he proceeded to march the queers around the parade-ground. Up and down we went. We walked ten paces north, then ten paces south. He tried to catch us out by slurring his commands, words we didn't understand. We went hither and thither. All of us ran and fell for our mistakes. Knees were bruised and bleeding. The palms of the hands bled. The Captain fucked us up completely. And then he posted us to some goddamned border town.

Sad was the night as we lay in our dormitory, waiting for the sun to rise, when we would fly off to queer hell.

Posted to some goddamned border town. A miserable little crew of veteran homos out to fight their first war. We were taken from our mother city and placed on the edge of a field in ten rows of tents in a fenced enclosure with one filthy toilet block, within sight of Head Quarters. In mid-winter. I said MID winter — mid-winter in ten rows of tents with one toilet block behind a barbed-wire fence in a platoon of rabbits too fluffy to be serious about this thing called Civil War. Oh the mud was thick that lay at our feet in the rain. We were issued with a metal cup and another plate and some socks and an overall, and we were lectured and inspected and made to clean the crapper six times a day.

We were made to pray for our sins of loving and had to say the lines over and over to protect us from the darkness in ourselves. We were paraded as the Captain's little success-story, and we just ambled along with his sordid plan based on the lie that improper conduct can be reformed by squeezing it out of its casing using first-degree paranoia and force.

THE BARRACKS ARE CRYING

On my third week of Basic Training I was woken at about three in the morning by some Corporal who stole into my tent brandishing a rifle complete with bayonet, and with his face hidden beneath a woollen balaclava. 'Come we go and make a blowjobbie behind the wall,' he whispered. 'Boy, I'm warning you that you'll lose your arse if you don't come to where I'm standing guard.'

He prodded me with his rifle and I jolted up in bed, my shaven scalp freezing and prickly. He prodded me with his bloody bayonet and I obediently went. I went stealthily to the looming wall, sheltering the barbed wire of a barricade. The back entrance to the camp, where the guard changed. He ushered me into the bushes behind the makeshift guardhouse, where I waited for the watch to leave. I could've run or even screamed, but I didn't. I presume I was too scared of the Corporal, armed and frustrated, watching me from the corner of his eye.

When the guard had changed, and he was left alone, he took me to the coal-shed, stuck out in the far corner of the camp, where the coal for heating the geysers was stored. And yes, I had to suck him. It was an experience of intense blindness. There was no light. My overall (quickly slipped over my pyjamas) got covered in soot, my face became smeared with black. And there I sucked him for sure. It was a long, deep, and painful suck. It was the suck we all know, that is, the particular suck you feel when you're sucking heavily on authority. When you require some kindness in return. No kindness ever came from this experience. No kindness.

I won't dwell on the months that passed. Six months of fever, exercise, bantering and labouring in the queer platoon that wiped everyone's arses, in the barracks where we were manufactured into a force fit for death. But we decorated our freezing tents with winter flowers and we hung little curtains from the gauze windows in gingham of blue and red. And then every night after physical training we would shower in a huddle of soft, unwilling flesh, preening ourselves while moaning about social injustice, our right to be equal. Yes, it was our right. But in earnest, nobody in the queer platoon that year wanted equality, not if it meant that you couldn't go straight from the shower room to that pretty khaki tent to put on your make-up and your nice pink frock before humming a sad tune to sleep.

And our singing wafted slightly above the dormitories and kitchens and guardhouses. We queens sang sad nostalgic tunes while a lad called Jenny played a melancholic guitar. And then the song we sang went high. It went with a message of reassurance to those virile quarters where the real soldiers slept before their real war, where they rose willingly and crept to our tents for strength and stories and song. The boys used to come to us, in their sleep they used to tap on the tent-flap and they used to beg us for a little comfort and warmth saying that, yes, you girls of the queer platoon sure know how to invent a genius in your song and your dance, you know how to make a guy feel that home is just a walk away. Always a word and some fine good cheer. Always a story, a true and sad story to ease those welted shoulders, to make them shrug and relax. A story to remind those that might have forgotten that we were perpetrating an essentially rotten and misguided, lonely war.

Funeral

We buried Jacob because he was dead. I know because I touched him. I touched him because I washed him, I was the only soldier there, and I saw about a hundred bullet holes, little flaccid red slits in his skin. It was the first time I had been to the cemetery at night and it was so lonely.

After supper Rabbi Mindel fetched me from the mess and we drove to the cemetery in the rain as he moaned about the limpet mine and the AK-47. The small party of men who washed Jacob's corpse was silent and afraid. All of them wore old, creased, silver suits, skull-caps and glasses; and they were all short, wrinkled, grave-looking men. They were finally seeing the war in earnest. A son had died, a son of the community — and with a short hose they sprayed and wiped at Jacob's bullet holes. As I said, it was really the first time that I was made to do this sort of thing, you know, like cleaning a corpse. I was the only Jewboy in the barracks since poor Jacob had been popped off by the enemy. Poor Jacob who in death was to be washed. I think that I began to look very pale, and so the righteous elders of Ventersdorp let me play a kind of secondary, 'honorary' role in the ritual, for after merely touching the corpse I went and stood in the shadows in the corner of the morgue for about fifteen solemn minutes. Eventually I went outside into the fresh air of the cemetery for an emergency smoke.

When Jacob had been dressed and packed in his coffin I was driven back to the barracks outside town by the Rabbi who moaned again about

THE BARRACKS ARE CRYING

the Intifada and the African National Congress until, at the camp's white-brick guardhouse, we came face to face with a blond guard who stamped my pass with a growl.

I tiptoed to my bunk, past the sleeping soldiers. And I think I tried to cry, but I couldn't because I was really too tired and pissed off at the army, and at Jacob, and at the withered community crumbling at its loss.

The next day I had to march in Jacob's burial parade. It was at the local cemetery, a small stone-paved myriad of Hebrew script on black stones. Jacob was, after all, my age — nineteen. We had grown up together and now it was his military funeral. People crowded the grounds. The collision of worlds was a shock to everyone. Afrikaans women in military uniforms stared blankly at elderly Jewish men. The brown pomp of the soldiers and officers was garish. It looked like someone had shat on the grey geometry, and on the precious stones, beneath which lay the beloved dead, a graveyard of predominantly Eastern European Jews.

I thought, 'How strange, an entire community of Russians and Poles who knew one another intimately, lying side by side, even in death, so far away from Poland, yet still together. A community imported from a place far away.'

The irony overwhelmed me. There, in their rows in the ground, lay the dead. And here on earth, stood the military funeral, also in rows. Rows stared at rows.

Oh the revelation, it jolted me! The dead are buried in communities, in a symbolic configuration representative of the roles they played on earth. The rich, influential people get big stones. Righteous elders lie beneath significant pagodas. Poor, forgotten people get numbered inside a rusty star. Children lie between parents. Marriages crumble in the soil. Stones of love stare at one another, and we stare back with love, at them, for centuries.

I realized that in death we like to lie beside the ones we loved, who loved us. So that we may decay together. This is the way we have wanted it. To be together, to reach the other side, and to greet one another. I thought of Jacob arriving in heaven, and seeing all of the people he was buried alongside, greeting him, saying, 'Welcome Jacob, Jacob, our son, whose child are you?'

'I'm the Metzinger boy,' he would reply, 'I'm the hero slain in battle, killed by Cubans beneath a dam wall. My father is Metzinger, Metzinger the builder.'

'Ah, you are Jacob the Metzinger boy!'

'Oh how terrible for the Metzinger family!'

'I knew your grandmother!' an ancient Russian fossil would croak.

And then, from the depths of heaven, Jacob's grandparents would hobble forward, and they would go on their knees before Jacob, Jacob their darling. And they would hug him and kiss him, they would love this thing that they had known as a son. Jacob, the new hero, fallen in battle, literally shot to pieces by fuck-knows-who while guarding the border some weeks before.

Jacob's funeral was a serious, orthodox occasion. We conscripts staged a crummy little parade, slouching and coughing through the whole affair.

I was stationed so close to the Colonel and the Rabbi that I just craned my neck a little bit as they shook hands and I heard Colonel 'Shooter' Malan saying to the Rabbi: 'Give me a ring in the next week and we can finalize the payment for the funeral, Rabbi.' And then when they shook hands, they shook and shook.

Oh, and then it was sad and pathetic seeing the mother and the father, the aunts, Jacob's maid (the elderly woman who had spent nineteen years cooking and cleaning so that Jacob could be strong, keen and fine), Jacob's cousins, his brother, Jacob's girlfriend, his best friend, all sheltering themselves behind total fear as various pallbearers wheeled old Jacob down the cemetery aisle amidst davening and saluting, an Afrikaans rendering of the National Anthem and Kaddish, the mourner's prayer. I spent much of the funeral standing to attention in the blistering heat staring blankly across the grave-side drama at my friend Simon who was in the military band, standing hugging his tuba. (It was awful for the band, for when they arrived at the funeral the Rabbi promptly gave the band-leader the bad news that music was forbidden on the cemetery grounds. The band members nevertheless stood throughout the ordeal at attention, instruments poised, but they never played.)

Standing there, like that, amidst all the components that made up my life, I could think only of Jacob. I saw the dark, curly hair and the intense eyes. I couldn't help seeing him naked, in the showers at school, at holiday camps, here in the army. I focused my attention on his genitals. I couldn't help myself. I thought of them in decay. How would they look after five days in the soil, after five weeks, five years? For me, I was getting to the essence of life. It was the purest vision of two round testicles, Jacob's testicles, lying side by side in the abundant earth. Like stones that could be picked up, weapons that could break windows. What I'm really talking about are the dreams, I suppose, the capacity for the genitals to remember, long after the mind has forgotten.

I felt a wild upliftment as the sand fell onto the coffin. Thud! Thud! Thud! Jacob's mother and aunt buckling under the hopelessness of this war. The men, attempting to be strong, their pale lips trembling as they said 'Amen' to every call.

Suddenly, in my mind, I was on a beach. There were people basking in the sun, laughing, playing with bats and balls. Little toddlers were swept over by waves, sometimes three times their size. I was there, somewhere, on holiday. The war was just a foggy memory of queer oppression, deprivation, of being someone else's enemy. I was on the beach. I was the baby. The waves were crashing about my head. My bonnet was lying in the sand. My father was photographing me. I was cold. I began to cry. My nanny cuddled me, took me to the picnic under the umbrella. I, the child, was no one then. I had no existence apart from the love and desire fed to me in the womb.

And what if some stranger had walked up to my parents then and said: 'This little boy of yours will one day grow up to be a shameful sinner, he will be banished in war, banished to a queer platoon.'

And what if I was Jacob, and that same stranger had walked up to my parents and said: 'This little boy will one day grow up to be a soldier, and before the war is over, he will be dead!' What then?

Would it have changed the course of this war?

Koos Prinsloo

'Border Story'

I was on the Border (90 days' ongoing military training) when she died between 18h00 and 19h00 on the evening of 1 August 1983. She was twenty-four years old. I used to tell people she's 'my closest girl-friend'.

She was the first woman whose breasts I had touched. I was nineteen at the time. For the eighteen months or so of our 'going steady', she did not want me to penetrate her. She was a virgin when I 'broke up' with her in August 1979.

The first time I went to the 'operational area' was in 1982 during a military camp of thirty days. I had to do an interview for the official South African Defence Force magazine, *Paratus*, with Lieutenant Louis Krüger, author of the novel *Die Skerpskutter*. The novel had won the Eugène Marais Prize of the South African Academy for Science and Art that year. The author was doing his two years' national service and was stationed as a chaplain at an outside base, Okalongo, in Ovambo.

'Ovambo is situated in the northern part of South West Africa. It is bordered by Angola in the north, Kavango in the east, Etosha in the south and Kaokoland in the west. Ovambo covers an area of 53 000 sq. km. lying between 14 and 18 degrees east and 17 and 18 degrees 46 minutes south,' according to a South African Defence Force information sheet.

'With the exception of a small section in the north-west, where the Kunene River forms a natural border, the northern border between Ovambo and Angola is a cartographic line which is marked on the ground by a cattle-fence. To the south of the fence a one-kilometre-wide no-man's-land has been proclaimed in an attempt to gain better control over trans-border movements. This strip of no-man's-land is known as the Jati Strip. The border between Ovambo and Angola is approximately 450 km. long.'

I travelled from Waterkloof Military Airport near Pretoria in a Lockheed C-130 Hercules to Ondangwa, from there on a Bedford to Oshakati and then in a Buffel to Okalongo.

'Ovambo is an exceptionally flat plain which forms part of the Kalahari Depression, lying between 1 090 and 1 150 metres above sea-level. The plain descends gradually in the direction of the Etosha Pan. Central Ovambo is covered with a network of shallow water-courses known as Oshanas. Hut groups and agricultural lands are situated on the higher ground between the Oshanas.'

One morning on the parade-ground Lt. Krüger read from Chapter 3 of the Gospel according to John — *Jesus speaks to Nicodemus*. He repeated the verse: 'The wind blows where it wills, and you hear the sound of it, but you do not know whence it comes or whither it goes.'

The next day I returned to Oshakati in a convoy. NO SMOKING and BUCKLE UP were painted on the side of the Buffel. On the way we stopped to look at the scene of a land-mine explosion a week earlier. The wreckage of a tractor lay in a radius of about fifty metres around a hole of about 1,5 metres deep.

'To hell and gone,' said an NCO with a scar on his cheek. 'The two locals who were on the tractor only filled up half a body-bag.'

According to a newspaper report published on the morning of 2 August 1983, she died after falling off a horse on a farm near Rustenburg.

'In an attempt to save her life, she was rushed by ambulance from the hospital in Rustenburg to the H.F. Verwoerd Hospital in Pretoria, but died on the way due to head injuries sustained in the fall,' says the report.

I never saw her corpse.

The call-up instructions ordered me to report at the parking area in front of the Pretoria Station on Thursday 7 July 1983, at 08h00, together with the other members of a citizen force unit to be sent to the Border for three months.

It was cold — the coldest day of the winter so far, according to the weather report that night on SABC-TV1. At Winterton in Natal a temperature of minus 12 degrees Celsius had been recorded.

On the other side of the station gardens, workmen in white overalls were painting the roof of the Victoria Hotel. A tramp was sleeping on one of the wooden benches at the station entrance. His dirty yellow jersey revealed a part of his back, which was full of festering sores.

The sallow-faced sergeant who had conducted roll-call was the last to say goodbye to his wife. She had two small children with her, both dressed in red crochet ponchos.

Kit-bags over our shoulders, we went to the Bedfords and then to the transit camp at Voortrekkerhoogte. No one really spoke, except for a thin man with enormous ears who told the driver he would 'fuck him up' if he gave us 'old-timers' a 'rookie-ride'.

At 1 Military Hospital they examined us, took urine samples and inoculated us against typhoid, paratyphoid and tetanus. That evening a sergeant-major with a blond moustache told us how he had scared the doctor, a woman, who had given us the tet. injections. 'I told her I've got herpes. Ha!' Three beers later he repeated the story.

After the medical we stood around outside in the sun waiting for orders. 'Hurry up and wait, that's the army's motto,' said the thin man with the big ears.

The ward next to us had a number on the outside wall: 22. The paint on its corrugated-iron roof was peeling. Some of the window-panes were broken and the doors were nailed up.

I had spent ten days in that ward as part of my national service in 1976. It had had a 'name' then: the psychiatric section housing 'junkies' (grass smokers), 'sensitive' boys with 'identity problems' and bush-mad 'straight schizophrenics' who thought they were Idi Amin, the Head of the Defence Force, the Great Instructor, Moses or Jesus Christ ('He was too pure and innocent, that's why I'm here now to be just a man, a filthy shit'), all wearing the same red, white and blue striped dressing-gowns ('technicolour dreamcoats') and heavy brown boots. On one of the walls there had been a poster of a girl, back-lit by a sunset, holding a flower in her hand, with four lines from a poem by William Blake printed in the lower right-hand corner:

> To see a World in a Grain of Sand
> And a Heaven in a Wild Flower,
> Hold Infinity in the palm of your hand
> And Eternity in an hour.

That afternoon in the transit camp, having been issued with R1 rifles and sleeping-bags, we lay in the barracks 'baking our balls' on naked foam-rubber mattresses covered in single 'piss-sheets'.

'This camp is P.W. Botha's fault, the black-bitch-fucker,' said a man with frizzy blond hair and pimples.

'How come?' asked the thin man with the ears.

'Well, he wants us to marry the kaffirs now.' The frizzy-haired man took out a photograph of a woman and showed it around. 'My wife,' he said.

'Christ, she's ugly,' said big ears.

'Maybe on the outside, but inside she's beautiful.'

A truck loaded with beer drove past outside. Someone took a ghetto-blaster from his kit-bag, turned the volume up high, then switched it off. At the far end of the barracks the thin man was telling the redhead next to him about *Deep Throat*, which he'd seen on a pirate video: '...Yes, man, that's where her clit was all the time, in her throat.'

'That's fuck-all,' answered the redhead. 'One of the appies in our shop says he's poked a cow. In the nose.'

The thin man started laughing hysterically.

'He tunes me, when the cow gives his balls the second lick with that nice rough tongue, he shoots like a rocket.'

The thin man fell off his bed.

That evening the commander of the citizen force unit — a grey-haired man with a sagging throat — addressed the men in the barracks. There was a chaplain with him.

'You are not allowed to talk religion or politics, or to say kaffir,' he said. 'And please be careful, I don't want the painful task of having to tell your grieving parents one of my boys has died.'

The chaplain sang Psalm 100. The men joined in raggedly. Some of them did not know the words.

'I've been on the Border a long time,' the chaplain said, 'but recently, since I've been back in the States, I've only been dealing with clergymen. That is why it's such a pleasure tonight to speak to people again.' He smiled and asked if there were any Jews among us. A man with black curly hair put up his hand. He was wearing a modern green and pink tracksuit.

'Acorn dick,' mumbled a man with LOVE tattooed on the knuckles of his left hand, next to me.

'I'll stay kosher and read from the Old Testament,' said the chaplain, as he took off his purple beret and read the new Afrikaans translation of Psalm 23.

'If you haven't been Up There yet, you can't talk,' said the chaplain. 'In three months' time you'll know what it's all about. Just remember it's a privilege. And the responsibility is yours. Up There, some guys get very strong after six beers...' He gripped the Bible in his hand so tightly that the muscles stood out on his hairy arm. The man with the tattoo grinned.

'...And before you know where you are, you get shot by a guard — your own buddy, yes — or your truck sets off a cracker,' he continued. 'Be responsible. Remember, the Lord is your Shepherd who will lead you and always be with you.'

Then he prayed.

Before our departure, we signed form DD 1112. Sections 118 and 119 of the South African Defence Act (Act No. 44 of 1957 as amended) and Section 3 of the Official Secrets Act, 1956, were printed as Annexure A of the form.

The beginning of Section 118 reads as follows: '(1) No person shall publish in any newspaper, magazine, book or pamphlet or by radio or any other means — (a) any information relating to the composition, movements or dispositions of — (i) The South African Defence Force or any auxiliary or voluntary nursing service established under this Act, or any force of a country which is allied to the Republic; or (ii) Any South African or allied ships or aircraft used for naval or military purposes; or (iii) Any engines, rolling stock, vehicles, vessels or aircraft of any railway, road, inland water or sea transport system or air service over which an officer of the South African Defence Force has assumed control in terms of Section 102 (1), or anything which has been supplied on requisition by the Minister in terms of Section 102 (2), or any statement, comment or rumour calculated directly or indirectly to convey such information, except where the information has been furnished or the publication thereof has been authorized by the Minister or under his authority; or (b) any statement, comment or rumour relating to any member of the South African Defence Force or any activity of the South African Defence Force or any force of a foreign country, calculated to prejudice or embarrass the Government in its foreign relations or to alarm or depress members of the public, except where publication thereof has been authorized by the Minister or under his authority.'

Three weeks after her death a letter she wrote on 30 July 1983 reached me via Ondangwa.

I sat down at a window in my flat with a view of the garden. There were poppies in the flower-beds. I opened the envelope and read the letter. The room was light and warm.

The memorial service was held at 11h00 on Friday 5 August 1983, after which she was cremated. It was a clear, windy day. From the church on a ridge in Melville, Johannesburg, one could see the city shining above the roof of the hearse. 'Like an ancient temple,' said the man who was the last to have spoken to her before she died. He also said that after falling off the horse she immediately lost consciousness and that blood poured from her mouth and ears.

The minister read from Romans 8. He repeated verse 31: 'What then shall we say of this? If God is for us, who is against us?'

That afternoon after the funeral I went to a Turkish steam-bath and health clinic in the city centre where I picked up a man. He had prominent eye-teeth, acne and a short chin.

When he penetrated me, with my knees bent over his shoulders, I cried for the first time. The afternoon sun shone through the Sunfilter curtains on the damp white sheets.

The chaplain at Ondangwa sent for me on a Wednesday morning after parade. On the way to his office I walked past the HQ, a corrugated-iron building, and the volleyball-court, where two pied crows stood pecking. One of the chaplain's office walls sported a poster with a drawing of a cartoon character, The Conquering Soldier. He has a long forefinger and says with a crooked smile: 'Say hello to a Vambo today, tomorrow it could save your life.' The chaplain informed me of the accident about thirty-six hours earlier in which my 'fiancée' had been killed. He also told me of the newspaper report.

'I'm glad you didn't see the paper yesterday, or you might have cracked,' he said and then prayed.

I went to Oshakati on the back of a Bedford to go and sign out. Inside my service and pay book in my shirt pocket was a photograph of me and her. I am twenty and she is eighteen. On the wall behind us is a Persian carpet.

Next to the road between Ondangwa and Oshakati, orange, purple and yellow blankets hung over the barbed-wire fences. Under the trees, goats stood on their hind legs, stretched their necks, and ate the lower ends of the branches flush. People, Vambos, sat in the shade, and among the trees, suspended from cross-beams, carcasses dangled in the wind.

The man said he liked my 'bush cut' and wrapped a towel around his waist.

I got up and opened the window. The smell of the jasmine in the hedge entered the room. On the pavement a poodle was trying to cover an Alsatian. He could not reach. With a forepaw he scratched at the firm red flesh of his penis, sticking out far, into the air.

I turned to my NAD hi-fi set and put a Mendelssohn string octet on the turntable. He composed it in 1825 when he was sixteen. According to his sister, Fanny, the scherzo was inspired by the last four lines from Part 1 of Goethe's *Faust*:

> Wolkenzug und Nebelflor
> Erhellen sich von oben.

Luft im Laub und Wind im Rohr.
Und alles ist zerstoben.

The Viennese Octet plays the scherzo on this recording (Decca Jubilee JB 128) in 4 minutes and 41 seconds.

Translated by Laurens Seliye

David Lan

Above the Bridge

Above the bridge where jazz bands play
the crowds pass by, some sad, some gay.
The moon revolves.

Turned on by a sexy trombone
four soldiers feel themselves alone.
The crowd dissolves.

Eyes skitter, flicker, dart and hop.
The pianist, cursing — he can't stop
till after nine —

observes one soldier trail his gaze
past girls who've not been screwed for days
and onto mine.

I hardly breathe, just soak him in:
unbuttoned shirt, pale secret skin,
lean jaunty hip,

hard creamy thighs, strawberry hair.
I blow a kiss. It skims the air
and bites his lip.

Beneath the bridge the dark is deep
but I can see an insect creep
across the grass

and climb up soldier boy's left knee
as he folds like a coat around me
and feels my arse.

The band is playing 'Mack the Knife'.
I'm bursting with his joy, his life.
He sighs: 'Baby ...'

and, like a planet, rolls away.
One down. I stand. 'As you were,' I say
the other three.

Above the bridge the band has gone.
The pianist, past all rage, hangs on,
wretched, forlorn.

Beneath his feet five soldiers fight
to keep the flame of love alight
until the dawn.

The Siege

The town's besieged. As night falls
from each other's beds our soldiers rise
to guard each other's bodies. The bush crawls
with enemy platoons, fire in their eyes.

At dawn strangers like us stroll into our sight.
Our men interrogate them, feed, strip, lay them down.
By noon we're dead. Under cover of light
the enemy has taken the town.

Brent Meersman

A Fear Comes to the Door

Perhaps it was not unusual that it should happen when the phones were left dead and the power cut off by a thunderstorm. For we all know that is when fears choose to act. They become a lump in the darkness. Or something formless with unseen eyes. In my half-sleep just such a thing trampled the gravel path. Then it rattled the kitchen door. My hand groped for the bedside table, knocked over an empty glass. This is nothing unusual, I said to myself, a fear has come to the door, that is all. It often does when you're completely alone and in a deserted place. It comes to pull you out of your sleep. It's only the wind, I told myself, only the wind banging at the door. Or a cow that has wandered in. Ridiculous to take the revolver. You can't live like that — taking a gun with you every time a window shudders. I refuse to. And so, I shut the drawer, taking only the flashlight.

Victor had assured me I needn't even lock the doors. No white man had ever been attacked in the Winterberg. Besides, I was only to look after the guest-house for a month, the worst month. Nobody in their right minds would be out here in these mountains at this time of year, at this time of night! No, it was only the wind trying to open the shutters. Or one of the wild cats scratching at the blinds.

But I stood absolutely motionless. Listening, listening. The fear was at my throat. Victor had said, 'Just take a deep breath every now and again.' The nearest neighbour is eight kilometres away. I strained to hear. But this was no stricken animal. This was no confused beast bumping into things. No, it was not the wind that had flung the kitchen door open. The wind drew itself in. My teeth took hold of my upper lip. For there — in the pregnant silence — was the fear. It stood panting where darkness clotted. I darted my flashlight at it. The beam illuminated an enormous, unshaven head. The head of a man, an intruder. He didn't flinch or avert his gaze. He didn't even put his hand up to guard his eyes. He just stared steadily, fixedly into the light. I kept the beam trained on him, full in his face. But it was I who was caught, caught beneath the giant, grisly shadow of the fear. It spread up the wall and across the ceiling, as if it were stooping. Something of the panic of being trapped in a room with some giant insect beating its wings gripped me. I couldn't speak. Until the dressing-gown cord cut into my thumb.

'Who are you? What do you want? What are you doing here?'

But the questions were ludicrous. As if such words could dissolve the scent of fear, could return the air to my chest! I felt powerless, at his mercy. But he just stood, breathing, long jets of cold white air at his nostrils. I felt as if he were about to charge, to fall upon me and rip me to pieces. But it was the thought that he would bring with him that massive, manned shadow on the wall that paralyzed me.

Then the wind gave a protracted howl. The shutter was ripped open and moonlight swam in. He turned calmly and drew the shutter closed. He rammed the bolt home. This struck me as such a concerned, domestic gesture. The fear seemed to be withdrawing slowly into the dark recesses. I smelt the pungent odour of the *buchu* bush clinging to him. I put the flashlight down and fumbled some matches out of my pocket. I pulled at a drawer, but it stuck. It wouldn't budge. My eyes pricked. I felt embarrassed, helpless. But the stranger gently pushed his frame forward. I noticed that his huge hands were covered in scratches and small cuts. The hands of a man on the run. He eased open the drawer for me. Again, the gesture of a guest, not an intruder. Almost apologetic, I switched the harsh flashlight off. Then, in the moonlight, I removed a candle from the drawer and lit it. In that moment of darkness, before the match was struck, without a word, we established an unholy communion. I felt we had accepted each other. What else was to be done? The comfort of a house, warmth, food — it was impossible to turn him out into the night, even if he never explained himself. Yes, we had made a pact to follow this meeting through to the end. There was nothing else to be done.

In the warm light his lips were full, voluptuous but well defined. His dark brown tan had not smoothed the features of his face. Rather, they appeared exaggerated and rough. His nose, Arabic. His hair and eyebrows curly, luscious, black. His eyes black. But there was so much white in those eyes too. It was alarming. He folded his hands and rested them on the old mahogany table. I thought him passive, and yet his bull-like head seemed to be thrust forward. He was not the kind of man to run, I would have thought.

'My name is Brent,' I volunteered.

'You may call me Mark.'

His voice was no surprise — deep and perfectly modulated — but his accent spoke of a good school and wealth. Certainly, he had not been born of some struggling, poor-white family.

'Should I make some honey-bush tea? And would you like something to eat?'

Even to this suggestion his response was controlled. 'Please,' is all he said. Though I knew he could not have had food for some time, or nothing cooked, at least.

This young man — he looked to me about twenty-seven — I could tell had spent much time by himself. I lit the gas.

'There is some bobotie left over. I'll heat it up for you. It's difficult to cook single portions.' And I put some water on to boil, too.

'You live out here completely by yourself then?'

'Yes, I live alone.' And he didn't ask me if I got lonely.

'Were you in that storm this afternoon?' I asked.

'Yes, I was,' he replied stonily.

'It must have been dreadful. A veritable mountain deluge. And it's freezing tonight. I think the lightning must have struck a pylon. The power has been off ever since.'

'And the telephone? Is your phone working?'

I hesitated. Should I tell him? Had his car broken down, or had he been a hiker or climber who had lost his way, had he, in short, wanted to make a call, he would have asked about the phone as soon as he arrived. This young man was a fugitive. And he was making no attempt to hide it. Furthermore, I did not have the impression that he was asking because he was concerned about his own safety from the law. No, he wished to learn whether I was cut off from the world. And something compelled me to tell him, I wanted him to know.

'It's not dead, but I can't get a line out.'

Yes, I wanted him to be completely, acutely aware of my vulnerability. The spoon scraped the enamel teapot. I stirred the stalks and leaves of the bush tea and put some sticks of cinnamon into the boiling water.

'You haven't explained yourself. So I presume the worst.' The bobotie spluttered and breathed. 'The rice is cold, I'm afraid.' I was standing just behind him with the cast-iron pot in my hands.

And then he said: 'People are always getting murdered on lonely, remote farms in this country. Aren't you afraid?'

So, he was a game-player. 'Sometimes.' And I put the plate of food in front of him. He didn't hesitate. The poor man was starving. Some of it spilt over his lip and he went after it with his tongue. After the first frenetic spoonfuls he seemed satiated. He paused. Then he asked: 'Don't you keep a shotgun or a revolver?'

'Yes.'

'But you didn't come to the door with it.'

'There was no need to,' I said firmly. And I poured some of the strong, aromatic tea into the mug before him.

A slight smile crossed his face. There is something beautiful and cruel about a faint smile on a face of those dimensions.

'So, you mistook me for the wind. I rather like that idea,' he said. How clever of him to insist that I had left the gun behind by mistake.

He removed his coat. The hot food had made him sweat. It was a torn, soiled army jacket. At first I had thought nothing of it, for vestiges of military clothing are not uncommonly worn by civilians in South Africa. But when I glanced down at the worn, brutal boots, it became obvious.

'AWOL?'

His head jerked up. He swallowed. He didn't blink. There was so much white in those eyes.

'Worse,' is all he said. Then he wiped his mouth and grinned.

'You can trust me, you know,' I said, looking straight at him.

'Of course I can, Brent. You're in your dressing-gown. You're alone. And you're in the middle of nowhere.' He grinned again, only this time showing some teeth. Then he gulped his tea down, his head tossed back, firm yet careless. But his eyes slanted down at me. I refilled the mug. We had already fallen into a little routine, I observed. How quickly he had established control! The mug, the teapot, the plate, myself, all grouped around him, waiting.

'Are you a convict then?'

'Sort of.'

'Are you or aren't you?'

'I escaped from military detention barracks.'

He seemed single-minded enough to have accomplished this. I suppose it was not particularly surprising that he should feel free to tell me. As an obviously educated, well-spoken English white South African, there was a good chance I'd be sympathetic.

'Oh God, what a mess. We've all been hoping this senseless conscription will become a thing of the past. It just doesn't have a place in the new South Africa we're trying to build.'

Mark snorted, 'It has nothing to do with politics. I hate fascists, but I'm not acting on a moral conscience. I'm not making a political statement!'

'Why were you in DB?'

'Narcotics. Just dagga. Most of the boys wouldn't survive without it.'

'You're not making life easy for yourself.'

'I'm not interested in a normal life. It doesn't matter what laws they change. Don't you see? I chose to do this. There will always be guys like me.'

Certainly he wasn't some frightened, hunted animal. He was purposefully living on the fringe. He was a deliberate criminal. The question now was to what extent he had located himself outside the law. Were his transgressions relatively common, merely against conservative laws — sex, drugs, taxes, licences, perhaps a measure of vandalism? Maybe theft? Or was he capable of some far worse act? Murder? Those eyes, with so much white in them, said anything was possible.

The fear had returned, slipped in without a warning sound, even here in the light. It occurred to me that the situation was no more dangerous than if I had picked up some stranger in a bar. And had we been in such a place, I would certainly have made a pass at him. For something of the proximity to death in him, that sadness, passing pleasure, heightened my every homosexual desire and fantasy. If it was his wish to sink deeper into the underworld, to acquire more exotic lusts for new experiences, then this was a perfect opportunity. Nobody knew he was here. My body would probably not even be discovered for a week, perhaps longer. He smacked his lips. After all this speculation on my part, perhaps murder wasn't even a new experience for him.

'Do you have a car?'

'A bakkie, yes. It's out back. I have the keys.'

'Of course you do. Who else would?' He smiled. His eyes shifted across the table. Then he pushed the mug forward with his purple knuckles.

'Could I have some more tea please?' he asked, with saccharine irony in his voice.

It suddenly became clear to me that his disconcerting questions were designed to reveal whether I thought him capable of murder, whether he could convince me that he was. And if I communicated this to him, it would either satisfy him or prompt him to strike. I felt a strange kind of pity for him, the hopelessness of his experiment, his ineffectual rebellion. Yes, he would be capable of murder. For ultimately he must destroy himself. That was the course he had set. It was then that I realized, that I knew, it could only end in one of two ways: either he would seduce me or he would kill me. He would not leave until he had accomplished at least one of these acts.

We sat in silence for a few minutes, until the fridge jolted into life and hummed.

'The power is back on,' he remarked. 'You're safe now.' And he kept smiling.

Yet I didn't switch the lights on. We sat with the candle burning. This game of his, entertaining my doubts, my fears, this game of murder, of its possibility, had joined us — as the common pursuit of sexual pleasure unites two strangers in a city park. I had not seen a soul for three weeks. Everyone was a stranger. And now there were only the two of us and not another human being for miles around. Old friends, how I wished we were old friends. Then I thought of the revolver in my bedside drawer, and the keys to the van. I had to get them before he did.

'The geyser's been off for some time, but there should still be hot water. Wouldn't you like to shower?'

'I'd love a hot shower.'

I couldn't believe he had fallen for it so easily. Perhaps the food, the tea, the candles....

'This way.' I escorted him into the passage. At the far end my bedroom light was burning. I had left the switch on to signal when the power returned. The raw light hurt.

Mark walked straight ahead. I handed him a towel.

'In there,' I prompted and motioned to the bathroom. But he did not go in. He started unbuttoning his shirt. And he didn't take his eyes off me.

I sat down on the bed and stared at my slippers. What a fool! Of course he wouldn't fall for some ridiculous, paltry suburban ritual! And what was I trying to pull on him anyway? What was I doing? Was this his game or was I inventing it all? He had not threatened me directly. Was it simply my fear? Was I not initiating the action, carrying the plot forward, encouraging him? And yet he couldn't possibly expect me to trust him, after his refusal to explain himself. Well, how could he have explained himself at the door? But he had done nothing to reassure me. He had deliberately played on my nerves, he had purposefully made me wary, he had entertained my fears, the ultimate fear. Yes, this was his game, not mine. Except. Except that I was alone. He was handsome, strong, attractive. There was a chance we'd kiss, touch, for our bodies to meet naked. It was our game, a classic game.

The sound of running water startled me. I looked up. He was in the shower. Through the glass I could see him with his arms raised, lathering his hair in shampoo. My eyes shot to the bedside table. I reached for the handle. The revolver was there all right, lying heavily in the drawer. But what was I thinking of? Good Lord, he hadn't given me enough reason to pull a gun on him. Perhaps I should leave it altogether. No — seduced into his game or not, I was not going to offer my throat to be cut. I stared at the gun, absolutely paralyzed. What to do? I couldn't throw him out at gunpoint. He'd call my bluff and then.... Hide it, then. That's what I would do, I'd hide it. I had the sleek handle in my hand. But where? My eyes flashed about the room. Every single hiding-place seemed obvious. The water stopped running. So soon! There was still time. I saw the towel slipping over the rail. Behind the books, in a coat pocket, my camera bag. But I was still sitting on the bed when I heard him say, 'So, that's where you keep it.'

I stared up at him in horror. He hadn't even dried himself. He closed the drawer with his enormous hand. It was clean and scrubbed now, and the cuts were pink and healthy. My eyes ran up his arm, the large blue vein traversing his biceps, his eyes still the same sullen black, intensified. For a long while I watched the drops of water from his wet hair flip onto his chest. They seemed to form a chain of time that held me mesmerized. The masculine nipples, like large copper coins. What beautiful, perfect skin. And the faint odour of the *buchu* still detectable. I wondered if I was dreaming this, as I watched in a trance, watched him take the revolver from my hand, watched him turn it to face me. He handled it with such complete familiarity.

Out here, alone for three weeks, now late at night, pulled out of my sleep by a stranger, almost a hallucination. Who was to say this was life, or this was a dream? Who to say this is totally impossible? I had tried to turn my fear into a lover. Incredible! Absurd!

He held the revolver in both hands, forefingers on the trigger. I had slid onto my back on the bed. He slowly lowered himself on top of me and rested the butt of the gun against my throat, the barrel at the tip of my nose. Such a weight pressing on me I could hardly move. My breathing became shallow. My arms stretched out, surrendered themselves. I whispered, the air tight and difficult to squeeze out, 'It's loaded.' He simply stared. There was so much white in those eyes. They betrayed nothing, like the innocent underbelly of a shark.

Did he have it all worked out beforehand? Had he known all along, or was he playing it out? Was he just following through the strange logic of this meeting, without intentions of his own? My lips brushed gently against the drum of the revolver.

'How did you come here?'

'I walked.'

'But how did you come to be here? How did you find this place? Out here, in the mountains, at night?'

As if with a single detail, with the discovery of a lacuna or a contradiction, I could return him, a fiction, to the world of phantoms! But he only smiled. He removed the revolver from my face, stretched his arms above my head. The copper nipples pulled up. His lips parted, then sank over my mouth. My fingers slid down his back. They passed over the lashes left by the bushes, the bruises from the beds of stone. I felt this long, hard body of a man on the run. Why, he could have crushed me, his arms ground me into a slow twist to death. His hands gripped my shoulders. I pulled his hips towards me and felt that firmness jerking up against me. I wanted to hand myself over to him, to give him complete power, this desperate, hopeless boy. To give him something in his angst, if only myself. This boy who didn't have a chance out there, who didn't have a future. To him I wanted to give the reins of my soul. This beautiful, reckless, lawless boy sucking on my neck. And somehow the revolver had disappeared, engulfed in the bedcovers.

When I awoke that morning — for I did eventually fall asleep — I found a note on the bedside table. The revolver and the keys were missing.

'Be a darling — if you have to notify the police, then give me a day's head start.

Love from Mark.'

So the game would continue.

Yes, when you're all alone in some remote part of the country, sitting on the stoep at night, or in your bed, and the hairy pedipalps of a spider appear over the edge of the table, then the shiny, blind eyes; when some ancient spirit creaks in the old wicker chair beside you; when you are all alone, completely alone, and a shadow falls across the window.

Karen Williams

They Came at Dawn

The air was rancid with tear-gas that morning. Empty bullet cartridges mingled with dust, blood, and the fog and winter rain. Shadows of what a few moments ago were living, marching people now stalked over the flats and shanty towns with the industrial smog blown by the south-easter. The Mountain was rallying her children. Propaganda pages blew ahead, paving the way for the shadows and dust to follow. Soon the pages too had to succumb to the fate of lying wet, stuck to the road, with the Casspir and Buffel tracks erasing The Word.

It was all revolution; all war.

The banging on the door that set the windows rattling was neither unfamiliar nor unexpected. Yet they were afraid. Sara and Michael looked at each other alarmed, before Michael scurried to the back door hoping to get away. There was no time for goodbyes. Petrified, Sara waited for the jackboot that would bolt out the door to shock her to her senses. She wondered whether they would use handcuffs or just beat her senseless and drag her limp body to the gaping van. Where would she wake up?

'Sara. Fuckin' hell! Open the door!' It was Kherry's hoarse, insistently urgent whisper.

It wasn't the police. She'd better go and call Michael back inside.

'Sara!'

'Coming, wait!' Sara jumped from one foot to another, unsure whether to go and get Michael first, but instead she rushed to the door. With her fingers slipping and missing the lock, she clumsily opened the door and bundled a wet and frustrated Kherry in.

'Wait,' Sara ordered and ran to the back yard to get Michael, her steps thudding over the ghastly pause that cloaked the neighbourhood. The round rattle of machine-gun fire was heard in the far distance.

Sara didn't know whether to burst out laughing at the pitifully comical picture Michael cut, stuck there in the wire fence, trying to vault out of the back yard. (When had he become so worn and haggard, so spindly?)

'Michael....' The soft whisper froze him, and his frightened, beady eyes seemed shocked in their sockets as they looked at Sara, as if to say: 'It's all right if you told. There was no chance for me to run anyway.'

'It's okay Michael — it's only Kherry.'

His body went limp and he fell to the ground as the tension snapped. 'Shot by a sniper,' thought Sara, looking at him closely. No — only nerves.

'Michael!' Kherry exclaimed in disbelief when he and Sara walked through the door. 'I thought the police had....'

'No, they haven't got me. They've got a fat chance too, I've done nothing wrong.'

'I heard that they picked up all the leaders and just about everyone they could think of, last night,' Sara said. 'Then shot like hell again this morning. Ai, this fuckin' state.' She shook her head and sighed.

'They looking for you too?' Michael asked Kherry. And then his head jerked, for somewhere there was a slight sound.

'No.' Michael and Sara stood looking at her expectantly, so she felt compelled to add: 'My mother kicked me out.'

'God, today of all days,' Sara muttered to herself.

'Politics?'

'Yes. No,' Kherry added immediately. She paused and looked at them directly. 'I'm lesbian,' she announced as boldly as she had to her mother earlier that morning. She had said it with much pride to counter the revulsion in her mother's mind. But now she closed her eyes and waited for the bullets her friends would aim at her to rain down.

'This is all we need! Jesus Kherry!' The irritability in Michael's voice couldn't disguise the minefield of nerves triggered at the mere sound of the automatic kettle switching itself off.

'Have you got other clothes and things with you?' Sara asked as if all this was nothing new to her.

Michael got up, loudly scraping the chair along the floor as he stormed out. Then he strode to the toilet, entered it and banged the door behind him. He flushed the toilet immediately, out of anger at another of Kherry's 'little problems'.

'All I have is this money,' Kherry said to Sara, digging her hands into her anorak and presenting a crumpled five-rand note between her fingers.

Marta, Kherry's grandmother, had thrust the note into her granddaughter's hand as Kherry stormed out of the house. Her eyes brimming with tears, Marta said, '*Djy's altyd in my gebede, Poplap. Kô ienige tyd dat djy iets nodig het. Ek sallie djou ma sê 'ie.*' ('You are always in my prayers, my darling. Come any time that you need something — I won't tell your mother.')

And with that she squeezed Kherry's hand as if to seal her promise. That was probably the last of her grandmother's rent money, Kherry realized as the bus stopped at the road-block to be searched by the police.

'Don't worry, you can stay here as long as you like,' Sara reassured her later that night as they all sat in the dark huddled over their coffee mugs.

'Michael,' Kherry said. She was waiting for him to comment, for he had been ignoring her all day.

'Kherry,' he spat out. 'Just pull yourself together.' His hand was sharply cutting the air in an attempt to emphasize his words. 'Just...,' he paused, now in the passageway, searching for words. 'Just — come — right.'

Kherry and Sara looked down at their coffee, embarrassed, just as they did even later when Michael suddenly jumped up in the middle of listening to Coltrane and bellowed, 'Fuck you!' at Kherry. Then he frogmarched himself back to the toilet and again flushed the toilet after banging the door behind him.

Kherry sat there, listening to Coltrane, remembering her discoveries with Michelle — love, and the denial of a truth. In the end not even the promise of togetherness could save them.

Sometimes it was easy outside, in the days when they got long, friendly stares and conspiratorial smiles from the white women in the road. The ones with short hair. But the outside also crept in, making it difficult to swallow. For it was as if they had thought all the letters of the alphabet could compensate for the not-enoughs of elsewhere. Not enough rent money; not enough to eat; not enough love to stop two young black girls from feeling so blindly, and so very alone.

Then word got around and it got around fast. Michelle was given two days to vacate her apartment. The landlady had classified her as 'funny people'.

'Perhaps it's because you're single,' Kherry tried to explain as Michelle threw the contents of her cupboard into boxes.

'They're always suspicious of young women — they think that all we do is have loud parties and bring men home!' This was Michelle, no longer able to hide the remnants of the last city she had fled from.

'Perhaps it's because you're always asking her to repair that leak in the bathroom,' Kherry said, trying to sound jovial.

'Perhaps it's because I'm a dyke,' said Michelle, her voice restrained, as she tried to control herself.

And then she was gone, to another city.

The police came at dawn all beefy and sweaty. And Michael was found and taken away. The women were beaten up and then warned.

Nobody knows what they've done with Michael — but it's rumoured, these days, that tenth floors are not the safest places to be.

Tanya Chan Sam

Coloured School Days

Tanya Chan Sam, a full-time activist, began her career as a teacher in the townships of Johannesburg. In 1991 she became the co-ordinator of GLOW (Gays and Lesbians of the Witwatersrand).

Her activism is centred around the activities of her organization, which was founded in 1988 with the purpose of raising consciousness about lesbian and gay issues.

Her task has involved speaking out, giving interviews to the media, and travelling abroad to international conferences, where she has delivered papers about conditions among the lesbians and gays of South Africa.

This account of her life experiences was recorded by Kim Berman in Johannesburg, in October 1991.

I grew up in Cape Town; we lived in an area called Maitland. The local gangster lived across the road, and his name was Jakkals, and he had a myriad of brothers and their names were Ertjie and Bier and Kat and Mainstay. They had real names too but those were their nicknames. It was a fairly rough area, but it was fine to walk around.

One day my brother got beaten up. There was a railway-line dividing two suburbs, and we went to school in the suburb next to ours. We were crossing the railway-line when he got beaten up by some boys from the other side.

And so the whole of Maitland went over to the other side to beat them up. That's how it worked.

As a woman, living in that kind of environment, one had to creep around. And we were warned, 'Don't walk around after dark. *Djy's 'n meisie, moenie laat rondloopie. Tanya, ons gaan jou kry.* (You're a girl, don't walk around when it's late. Tanya, we'll get you.) If you walk around here you're protected, but don't walk around on the other side!' This is entrenched in most women while growing up in a township environment. You be silent, and if you stick to the dark corners then you'll be safe. And it got to a point in my life where I thought, 'I don't *smaak* this any more. I can't handle this. Does this mean that, for ever, I must creep around as a woman, because you can't walk around after dark?'

When I was still in school the government formed the Coloured Representative Council. It was the start of Labour Party politics, and there were lots of demonstrations about it. Our schools were filled with progressive New Unity Movement teachers, and I was very caught up with this. And that is where my political involvement started.

My youth was a period of turmoil and uprootment. In 1976, we spent only four months at school, because there were class boycotts.

My mother's a teacher. In Cape Town she was teaching double shifts because the school was so overcrowded, with so many kids. They'd teach from seven o'clock in the morning to midday — that would be the first shift — and the second shift was from one o'clock to four o'clock. Because of this, my family decided to move to Johannesburg.

While I was growing up, there had certainly been gay people around our house. My mother's just one of those people, she attracts all and sundry, and she had a gay friend for years and years. His name was Noël. We'd come home from school in the afternoon, and my mother would be sipping wine with Noël, and they'd be reciting poetry to each other. Noël was accepted into our house. There wasn't a judgemental attitude from my mother. But my father hated Noël. My father and my brothers would say, behind his back, 'What's he doing here again?'

But my mother loved Noël, because he just paid so much attention to her, he was so wonderful for her.

After school I decided to go to the Teachers' Training College. There was no privacy at home and so I moved into the college residence for the first year. Then I moved into a house with my cousin.

Throughout all of this I'd spent a lot of the time getting involved in Black Consciousness politics, but really struggling with it. I got involved in a little reading group. It was the days of underground activity, and smuggling. I'd go off to the reading group, and then I'd come back with notes, and I'd sweat on the bus.

I was already teaching professionally when one of the people in the group was detained, at about six o'clock in the morning, and the police kept him. By seven o'clock his mother had phoned all of his friends, frantically. She knew.

Before I went off to teach at school that morning, I said to my housemate, 'Let's get rid of all the stuff.' There were books about the *Communist Manifesto* and things like that. We were really scared. These days it sounds so bloody innocent. But it wasn't innocent then.

One of my friends had just come out of detention and she was very freaked out. She would come by at twelve o'clock at night. I remember it was winter and the wind was blowing. She was wearing a flimsy little dress and she was having a bad time. And she told us horror stories about detention. She'd sit until four in the morning talking about it, about what the police would do. I was very terrified.

A conversation stuck in my head. We were discussing this situation, and someone said, 'What if they do pick us up? I'm really scared of being raped.' Certainly, sexual harassment is a big thing.

I replied, 'Yes, I'm also scared of being raped.' And then I said, 'I can't bear to think of a man touching me.' I think I'd been struggling to come to terms with it.

My friend replied, 'I know, for you it's difficult.'

I think that people knew, there were always signs. The rest of the day passed in a daze. But what was more important than worrying about being picked up was my questioning, 'What's happening to me? What is going on?' It was almost as if I'd made a huge confession, and I had, in a sense. But I wasn't aware that I was hiding anything.

When I was younger I went out to movies or dinner with boys. But I always felt anxious. I'd always try to get rid of them very quickly. One of the ploys was to engage them in discussions on socialism, and that would scare them off. At the time, in the early eighties, it was a very risky subject to talk about. Most coloured men are very unconscientized, unpoliticized. So, firstly, you're threatening him if you start talking about politics. Secondly, this is not the womanly image that they're brought up to deal with.

I wasn't very encouraging and one gains a reputation. They'd say, 'You want white. You don't like coloured boyfriends.' And then, added to that, my surname was a complete enigma to some people. They would ask me, 'Who are you? What are you? Are you half-white, are you half-black? *Waar vanaf kom djy?*' (Where do you come from?)

Tanya Chan Sam

My family's a complete mix. According to the laws of the country, some are white and are right-wingers. Others are black socialists.

Being a teacher in conservative coloured communities, one gets put on a pedestal, people are scared to approach you. There's an elite group of teachers and professionals who mix, whom I didn't enjoy, because they're very conservative. So it seemed like, on all kinds of levels, I didn't fit.

I joined a softball team in Bosmont. A friend of mine at school said, 'Come along, come and play softball, I'm sure you will like it.'

The teams were made up of coloured women only, playing the game. They're very open about their lesbianism, on the field. There's a very strong sense of camaraderie and support, but I found them to be very stereotypical, very butch and very fem stereotypes. And one needed to go through real initiation stuff. One player quite blatantly asked me, 'Are you butch or are you fem?'

I was standing in a track-suit and I had fairly short hair. I didn't quite know how to answer, so I said, 'Neither.'

She said, 'Don't be silly, you've got to be one or the other.' And we got into an argument.

Every week they would have a little get-together, after the game, with lots of alcohol. I didn't realize it at the time, but there was a test. If you drink with the boys then you're a butch. And obviously, if you can't hold your drink like a man, they reckon you're fem. I wasn't aware that the drinking was the test, and we sat down to drink. It was hot after the game. We had one beer, and then it went on and on. They're rum-and-Coke drinkers. And they just kept putting the stuff down me. I was anxious and tense. As a result, I wasn't getting drunk, I just kept slugging the stuff back. After about an hour they said, 'This is impressive! *Djy's 'n regte Kapenaar, jy kan soos 'n vis drink!*' (You're just like a person from the Cape, you can drink like a fish!)

That was my very first step into another world. I don't like the phrase 'twilight world', but it's a very different world altogether, a coloured community. But it didn't grab me. I knew that I wanted something more.

In the meanwhile I had moved away from Black Consciousness and the Action Youth. Many people had moved away. Some people had gone to university or overseas, others settled down and got married. And so that whole structure fell away.

For me, within those political structures, I found the homophobia and ignorance very frightening. The most eloquent people, and the people most concerned about human rights and social orders, all got up and sprouted homophobic rubbish. I felt quite threatened and intimidated, and I pulled out of political structures and the reading group.

We had once encountered Marx talking about sexual freedom, and they said, 'We'll just skip that part.' And they went on to the more economic issues and 'big things'. It was then that I started to think. I couldn't understand what the hassle was with discussing personal freedoms. I wanted to work through, and finally come out with, a sexual freedom and sexual orientation. For them it was okay to read it and quote it, but it wasn't okay to discuss it.

But I still hadn't told my family that I am a lesbian. And I decided to do it.

I was helping my brother move house, and I told my sister. My mother was there, and she said, 'Oh, I hear you're in love. You look very happy.'

My mind was racing. I thought, 'If my mother knows then my sister must have told her.'

And then my mother said, 'We must meet you some time.'

'You' meant plural. I was too panicky to think straight. I said, 'Ma, you do know that Gail and I....'

She said, 'GAIL!'

I didn't even mean it, it sort of popped out, I couldn't control myself. I said, 'I'm lesbian.'

She said, 'No!'

Now, we were standing in the passage. My brother was moving the furniture up and down, and my mother says, 'No!'

As she says 'No!', my brother walks past. He says, 'What you saying ma?'

And my mother says, '*Die kind sê vir my sy's 'n lesbian.*' (The child tells me she's a lesbian.)

So he says, 'Ag man, I knew, everybody knew.'

My mother looked at me in complete shock. She said, '*Ek kan dit nie glo nie, nee, jy's my oudste kind, ek kan dit nie glo nie!*' (I can't believe it, you're my oldest child!) She was going on a huge rave.

We didn't settle anything that day. And then months went by, and I'd see her occasionally. We wouldn't talk about it.

It's difficult. I've become removed from my family. I don't have the conventional Sunday lunch with them. And I can't take my lover home and present 'the lover'. It's better, on the one hand. But on the other hand, I'm completely removed from them, so they never meet my friends.

They hear vaguely when I'm on television, or on the radio. Then my granny will phone in and say, 'I saw you on television.'

My mother said, 'Don't tell your grandmother, it will kill her.' But my grandmother is like a mother to me. She brought me up. And she watches television all the time. So I had to tell her, and when I did, she was wonderful. She said, '*Ag my kind, ek het lankal geweet.*' (Oh, my child, I've known for a long time.)

The only problem I've had has been with my one brother, particularly. He is hell of a homophobic, and I think that's only because he's so threatened by women. He's quite instrumental in WOSA (Workers' Organization for Socialist Action), and I think that he's been a big part of that organization's not taking a stand, not taking a position on homosexuality and gay rights. It's outrageous, it's completely ridiculous for a socialist organization, that they still have to debate it. I don't understand how a socialist organization can debate the issue of gay rights. It's almost like they have 'It' to give out, and it infuriates me. He's been quite vociferous in his attacks, but he's cunning and insidious and he has all the socialist argument and eloquence. He says, 'It's not important, it's not on the agenda. You don't understand the political issues of the day.' He uses that kind of argument. And when one talks to him, he reverts to really low digs.

When one says, 'It is important, it is very important,' then he says, 'You're emotional,' implying that homosexual people are a bunch of emotionals. It gets reduced to that.

I got involved in GLOW (Gays and Lesbians of the Witwatersrand) and somehow I got elected onto the organization's Executive. It was then that a journalist phoned me and said, 'We want to do an article.' And he did it.

At that time I was teaching at Noordgezigt, which was a working-class school. I thought that there would be no way that the kids would read this particular article. But I was mistaken, because one or two of the kids came up and asked, 'Were you in the newspaper?' And what could I say?

I said yes, and he said, 'In that lesbian article?' And I admitted it. And then these two children asked if they could talk about it. These were really young kids, Standard Six, thirteen or so.

I said, 'Yes, I am lesbian.'

And they said, 'No, you can't be, you don't look like one.'

We had a long chat, just the three of us. They advised me what to tell the rest of the class, because there were some people in the class who didn't like homosexual people.

What happened finally was that everybody got to know about it. What was interesting was that, except for a close friend at school, not one of the other teachers brought it up. The kids were far more direct, far more open about it.

And then there was a programme on television. And that was the big one because, of course, everybody watches television. The kids were in an uproar about it, because I taught six classes. And one of the teachers said to my friend (but not to me, they're all such cowards), she said, 'Gee, I see we're going international now.' Some teachers should really be shot.

In the staff-room this guy starts chatting, a sleazeball really, and he says, 'Which of the girls do you fancy?'

Now, this is in a high school. We had matric girls there. Not girls, they're women. In the black schools they're women, they're twenty, they're twenty-five. So I said, 'Really, I'm not a child!' They all think that if you're lesbian, you're a child molester.

But at school I don't know whether they handled it admirably, because they just ignored it. The administrators just ignored it completely. But the children were wonderful. At thirteen, fourteen, fifteen years old, sex is uppermost in their minds anyway. And they wanted to know, did I have a girlfriend? How did I find a girlfriend? But what was more interesting, was that children would come to me alone. They'd start talking, and fifteen minutes later one would say, 'I think I'm lesbian.' And I would look at certain kids in the class and think, 'Oh what a dyke.' And true as God, two days later she'd be saying, 'Madam, you know, I've been thinking. There's this girl down the road.... Is it wrong to feel that? I don't want to do it, but I just feel that I want to kiss her.'

Sex education is not allowed in our schools, but it's important, particularly when you teach young school-kids who could fall pregnant. So a lot of teachers have been doing it for years. It's very important. But it was really the first time I had to speak about my own sexuality, and it was terrible. They'd say, 'We know how men and women have sex, but we don't know how lesbians have sex. Now will you tell us?'

It was fine to say, 'The penis enters the vagina and then there's the ovum, and then the sperm.' That's very clinical, one can talk about it very easily. I stood there blushing and it was terrible. On the first day I couldn't, I just couldn't talk about it. I said, 'No, you're asking me the most personal questions.' And others said, '*Hoe kan julle vir juffrou sulke vrae vra? Het*

161

julle niks respek nie? Sal jy jou ma so iets vra?' (How can you ask teacher such questions? Don't you have any respect? Would you ask your mother something like that?)

I had this huge dilemma — what to do? Do I say, 'Fine, sex is sex, and let's discuss lesbian sex, let's discuss homosexual sex.' But that would really be bringing the kids into the bedroom and under the blankets with me. 'Have a look! Have a squiz!'

Then we started talking about it. I wangled my way out by saying, 'Love-making is love-making, it's important to care.' But they weren't interested in that. They were interested in the nitty-gritty stuff. I kept saying, 'It's important to know that homosexuals are not only interested in sex. When you have a girlfriend, don't you kiss her?'

What was nice was that the kids would often tease one another, common teases. If someone's not paying attention, another would say, 'Ai, he's thinking about his girlfriend!' And then one day this boy piped up, 'He's thinking about his boyfriend!' For me, it meant so much. Because these were really young kids who could integrate it quite easily, and yet other people have such difficulty with it.

I was still at school when the demands of activism were growing in me. I felt, more and more, and I still feel, that children are the people whom we need to aim at. Because children are a lot more accepting. Once you've shown that you're not going to threaten them, that you certainly are not going to molest them, then they trust you implicitly. And they would say, 'But we don't trust Mr So-and-so, because Mr So-and-so is known for putting his hands up girls' dresses.' It is a common thing, sexual harassment of schoolchildren, it happens every day.

Shortly after I was on television, a teacher told her class, 'You must be careful of Miss Chan Sam *want sy gaan vir julle meisies vasvat.*' (She's going to grab you girls.) So some kids rushed back to me: 'Madam, madam, you know what Mrs Johnson says? Mrs Johnson says *jy gaan vir ons vasvat.*' (Mrs Johnson says you're going to grab us.)

I was furious. I marched down to her office, much to the delight of the kids. And she said to me, 'I think you are disgusting! Why did you have to do it so publicly? That's something you keep behind bedroom doors.'

I felt so disillusioned.

I'm quite lucky I suppose, I haven't met many homophobes. I haven't had someone shouting abuse at me. I haven't had anyone throwing me out of restaurants, refusing to let a flat to me or refusing to allow me on a bus. But

I'm well aware of homophobia in the society, and I'm also well aware of the kind of image one presents. What people wish to see is a kind of pseudo man-like lesbian.

I don't preface, 'I'm lesbian', when I buy a loaf of bread. So the only way to make oneself known is through gay activism.

Today in the South African public there's a new sense of bravado. I hold my girlfriend's hand. I don't French kiss her in the street. I'm not an exhibitionist.

Then people walk by, and they're people you see in a gay bar or people you've bumped into at a function. And they'll smile at you. I don't think that's the real world. I live in a very sheltered world. The only people I meet are lesbian and gay. The only people I meet are activists. The only people I meet are progressive, and quite accepting of it.

Politically, I wouldn't support a kind of middle-class reformist attitude, one of feeding us crumbs: 'You're allowed to hold hands, but we still regard you as child molesters, as criminals.' It's a kind of all-or-nothing fight.

First and foremost, we must let it be known that we are human beings. We live in this life and we must be granted certain basic rights, and one of them is the right to sexual orientation.

Gay activism has got to be a grass-roots struggle. You can't start lecturing off a platform and announcing things grandly. The only viable, possible way is to work in the townships, to integrate gay and lesbian people there, those who don't see themselves as part of the community. We must start integrating them, firstly into a broader community, so that they then feel functional, productive and worthy.

We must support the struggles of domestic workers, of commercial sex-workers, and of all other working-class people. Then we will gain support from the other sectors of the community.

And that is something I firmly believe can be achieved.

Shaun de Waal

Stalwart

'I have been a card-carrying member of the Communist Party for more than forty years.'

Something about that phrase, a cliché maybe, but there is something about the paradoxical pride of it. Do communists, even old ones, still say that kind of thing?

I was driving to Hillbrow to interview Russell Blair, just returned to South Africa after thirty or so years in exile. One of the Old Guard, the Old Old Guard, an intellectual. He was on the Executive until a year or two ago. Still writes vigorously — discussion papers, articles for *Umsebenzi* and *Marxism Today*. Blair joined the then CPSA in the late Forties; he left South Africa in 1963, after a couple of years of real Scarlet Pimpernel stuff — being on the run, hiding from the police, disguised, daring hair's-breadth escapes. Now Emeritus Professor of Political Science at a prominent British university. The (lost?) romance of being a revolutionary still hovered about Russell Blair.

There's a photo at the office, the one I'd like to use with the article (what about a before-and-after, I mean a then and now? He must be in his seventies now; but maybe that's a bit tacky) — Blair in 1950-something, round the time of the Defiance Campaign. Looking very dashing indeed, in a three-piece suit, his hair flying sideways in the wind. Certainly the most attractive man in the Communist Party at the time. But I'm being facetious.

The interview, in fact, was all but written. In my head. When I used to do theatre reviews, I'd 'write' the review in my head in the car on the way home or, occasionally, on the way back to the paper, a 'comeback' for the next morning's edition.

The interview with Russell Blair was mentally planned by the time I found parking in Hillbrow on that Wednesday afternoon; all it required was the insertion of some genuine Russell Blair quotes.

I did have a new angle, though. The connection with Blair's novel, his only novel, published in 1967, I think it was. It's about an underground cell in the first days of the armed struggle. It was banned in South Africa as soon as it appeared, but was recently unbanned and is soon to be reissued.

I got a second-hand copy last year in London. An interesting and extremely well-written book, very Graham Greeneish — one character is even a Catholic. It's clearly a roman-à-clef of some kind, despite the mandatory disclaimer: '...and the characters do not refer to the real people who held those positions in the party or any other organization.'

Like most novels, I'm sure, Blair's characters 'refer' to amalgams or composites of real people, distorted a bit by the imagination — otherwise it's not fiction, is it? There must be quite a bit of Blair himself in it, though. But which character is he?

Not the naive narrator, Paul, definitely. And not Berkman, the Catholic with a nerve-disease: Berkman is a minor character, really, though profoundly necessary in plot terms; he isn't portrayed from the inside. Somehow I suspect Norman Goldfarb, the one with all the qualms. The one who gives a lecture on Gandhi at one point. Norman's spiritual struggle parallels the physical or political struggle of the book. Then again, it could be Hodgins, of whom Blair the novelist says brusquely, 'He was a homosexual who had been unable to find love; that was why he joined the party.' For Hodgins, the 'cause' is a means towards something else; for a kind of human wholeness. On the other hand, Blair could be fictionally disguised as Moses, the black ideologue who ultimately betrays them. Or he could be in drag, pretending to be Catherine, who is certainly one of the sharpest, most committed characters in the novel; also the only one who gets away at the end.

Anyway, read it yourself. The point is that I wanted to ask Blair which character was most closely modelled on himself. That would at least give me an arresting intro. I would compare the fiction and the reality (I guessed they would come pretty close, or close enough for my purposes). That was the article, then. Nearly finished. I just had to meet the man and get something to put between inverted commas.

The young cadre at the entrance to what had been nicknamed 'the ANC hotel' scrutinized me with narrow eyes and escorted me up in the lift. He led me down a dingy corridor and knocked on one of those doors.

Blair opened it. He was very tall and thin and had a lot of white hair. He was dressed plainly in a dark suit. 'Come in,' he said. I introduced myself; he said 'I know' as we shook hands. His long face was still handsome; the high cheek-bones stuck out more obliquely than before, it seemed, and there were commodious pouches under the eyes, but the eyes themselves were almost alarmingly clear. 'Have a seat,' he said, gesturing at the single armchair in the small room. He sat on the chair that was pulled up at a small table, the Formica top of which bore several books.

'Welcome home,' I said, trying not to sound too ironic.

'Thank you,' he said. 'Though it's only been two days.'

I didn't know what to say. I couldn't be chatty and ask, 'Are things very different from when you left South Africa?'

He looked at me with cool blue eyes and said gently, 'Shall we begin?' He was sizing me up, looking me over quite openly. I prodded the tape recorder and placed it on the desk next to him. He smiled at me as I reached past him. I caught a faint whiff of pipe-tobacco. I sat down again. The armchair was low and uncomfortable, and I had to perch forward on its edge. I felt a bit like a student in the professor's office.

'I've just read your novel,' I began.

'That old thing,' he said, laughing. 'I haven't looked at it for years. I'm sure it's terribly dated.'

'I found it very interesting.'

'Thank you.'

'I'm sure you've been asked this before, but since you've been a listed person here since the Sixties, I, um, wanted to know —' (journalists often can't talk coherently), 'I mean, it's clear that the events in the novel are based on fact, and I wondered whether one of the characters was particularly autobiographical...' (that was horrible).

'You mean, who am I in the book?' He was distinctly professorial; a little, it seemed, amused at this specimen to which he was speaking.

'Yes.'

'All of them.'

I had to pause. 'They are all, um, aspects of yourself?'

'Yes. Well, Catherine is perhaps an idealization of what I, we, could have been, an example of dedication and clarity of purpose. But the others are all closer to me, really, than anyone else from those days. A rather egotistical novel, I suppose. Romantic. It was criticized for that reason by members of the party at the time.'

'Oh,' I said.

He laughed. 'Yes, I have been asked that question before. Quite a few times.'

'And how,' I asked, 'did you respond to such criticism?'

'Well....' He gazed out of the small window, which, I had seen, looked onto the blank wall of the adjacent building. 'I still believe,' he said, 'that the personal is the political; that one learns a considerable amount about the social psyche from delving into the individual psyche. The party, after all, is made up of people. But it was also as though I felt I couldn't speak for anyone else...then. A heretical view, perhaps, in some respects. I would probably attract the same criticism today.'

'You are often viewed,' I said, 'as being the devil's advocate within the party. How do you respond to that?'

He laughed again. 'I don't think I'd put it that strongly. But yes, I do think it's necessary to keep challenging things. We knew that in '68, in '79. We knew it but we didn't want to face it squarely. I think perhaps we've only just caught up.'

'You mean, the legacy of Stalinism, the....'

'Yes, yes,' he waved that away. 'Now, more than ever before, we have to interrogate our own notions. Our notions about everything. We have to keep questioning the principles of the socialist project. We have to be vigilant, intellectually vigilant.'

'Many people are saying that now,' I said, steeling myself a little, 'but where were the dissident voices within the party in '68 and '79? And why couldn't the party accommodate them?'

Blair suddenly seemed very weary. His face seemed to sink slightly, to show more openly the years that lay on it. His coolly amused glance had shifted and he looked away as if avoiding my gaze. I saw the liver-spots on his forehead. 'Some were disciplined by the party. Many left the party. For many complex reasons. Power within the party shifted, to some degree. Roles changed. For a while, we were chiefly ANC people and only marginally SACP people. There were new people, new blood that challenged us old bores. But many people stayed in the party. For many complex reasons.'

He stood up and paced across the floor, two steps, then back, and he sat down on the bed. He ran his fingers through his hair, and then he leaned back on the bed and raised his eyes once more to mine. His chin was flung out, almost defiantly. It was the same pose as in that old photograph.

'I'm sorry,' he said, 'I'm rather tired.'

'Shall I go?'

'No, no, please — carry on. If you don't mind my lying on the bed.'

'Not at all,' though I felt somewhat disconcerted. 'What, um,' I asked, 'were your reasons for staying in the party?'

He sighed. He put his arms behind his head. Weird, I thought, catching the mental image of a psychiatrist and his patient. Then he lifted his head and said, 'Will the tape recorder still reach me if I'm over here?'

'Oh,' I said, getting up. 'Thank you. I'd almost forgotten it.' I picked it up off the table and wondered where to put it.

'Here,' he said. 'I'll hold it.'

I handed it to him. He looked up at me as I leant over him and I felt as though he wanted to clasp my hand or something; his face below mine had regained a tincture of its amusement, though the wearied look was still there. But there was also something...something, perhaps, supplicatory there too.

He held the tape recorder on his chest, in both hands, rather in the attitude of the composed corpse holding the rosary. I went back to my chair.

'What,' he asked the mottled ceiling, 'were my reasons for staying in the party?'

I sat there silently, waiting for him to answer himself. I felt as though I shouldn't be intruding.

Then he said, slowly, softly, 'Do you remember the character in the novel called Hodgins?'

'Yes, I do.'

'Well, I said there that his motivation for joining the party was that he had failed in love. I suppose that applies to me, to a certain degree. And continues to apply, except that after a certain point — years and years go by — it is a permanent condition; a condition one has chosen. To fail in love is nothing unusual; but having given oneself to the party, it was as though one had given up not only the failure in love but the falling in love too. Love on the personal level. Given up for a greater love, if it exists. This is a personal foible; many people had intense and satisfying love affairs and they were still good communists.' He gave off a little laugh. Was there a taint of bitterness in it? 'For me, it was sort of either/or. One or the other.'

I felt distinctly embarrassed, and he must have sensed it. Suddenly he sat upright on the bed, swinging his legs over the edge.

He said, 'But you don't want to hear all this drivel. I'm an old man.' He smiled with what I could have sworn was rakishness, had it not been so incongruous. 'And the minds of old men wander, particularly when they've had a shock to the system like coming home after thirty years. None of this is relevant to anything.'

He took a deep breath.

'I stayed in the Communist Party because I believed and still believe in what it has the potential to do. Not because of what it has done; in South Africa it has a proud place, but I am still a communist because of what I believe the party must yet do, whether it is in the next ten years or the next hundred.'

'What,' I asked, 'do you see as the specific role of the SACP in the present transitional period?'

Again he took a deep breath. He clenched his hands together around the tape recorder. He spoke clearly and without faltering, but it was clear to me that his mind was somewhere else.

'The present role of the SACP, as I see it...in broad terms...is to preach real democracy...democracy from the ground up, grass-roots democracy... not along the lines of the Western model, the British and the American, let us take them as examples...these systems do not represent true democracy...what is democracy if the only two people you have to choose between are Michael Dukakis and George Bush?...or Neil Kinnock and John Major?...'

His voice trailed off. I wondered whether to prompt him. He was gazing out of the window again.

Abruptly he turned back to me and said, 'Have you got a car?'

'Yes,' I said.

'Would you mind,' speaking rapidly now, 'taking me on a little drive? It could be very useful for your article — Russell Blair at some of his old haunts. You have a camera?'

'Yes,' I said. 'In fact, I must take a few pictures of you. The staff photographer had to go to —'

'Well,' he stood up, and suddenly he seemed to be younger again, certainly not the weary septuagenarian of a few minutes ago, 'you certainly can't take a picture of me in this dreary little cell. Not that a dreary little cell isn't my natural habitat, as you may have gathered. I'm the monkish sort, or I have become a monkish sort — renunciation and all that.' I stood up and he handed me the tape recorder, which I switched off. He opened the door and motioned to me. Following me into the corridor, he said with a little chuckle, 'Good God, you mustn't write any of this in your article. They'll all think I'm mad.'

We went down in the lift. Blair smiled but said nothing. Well, I thought, it probably would make a good article, Russell Blair returning to his old haunts, if 'haunts' is not too spooky a word; now where was it that he was arrested before his first treason trial?

Shaun de Waal

At the entrance he told the young cadre, 'Sipho, we're just going for a little drive; tell Comrade Al if he arrives that I'll be back...well, um, I'll be back some time.' Sipho frowned and nodded.

We had to walk three blocks to my car. Blair seemed happy, taking large strides, his hands thrust in his pockets, his head up as if he were sniffing the air. 'Been cooped up ever since I got here,' he muttered. 'Meetings, meetings. Greetings. Dinners.'

We got into my car.

'This really is very good of you,' he said.

'Not at all,' I said, starting the engine. 'You're right, it would make an excellent story. I wish I had thought of it. And I wish I were a better photographer.' I swung into the road. 'Where to?'

'Parktown.'

As we drove, he looked hungrily at Braamfontein, at Wits University ('That concrete thing is new'), and he sighed as Jan Smuts Avenue rose toward Parktown. 'Right here,' he said, just as we began to plunge down in the direction of the Zoo. I turned and drove slowly between the trees that lined the street. 'One more block,' he said. 'No, it's two — it's just beyond that red car parked there.'

I stopped outside large, closed gates.

'I grew up in this house,' he said. 'Let's go and see if they'll let us look around.'

We got out of the car. I fumbled the camera out of its case and hoped it wouldn't require any special settings or tunings. Blair had pushed open the big gates. He stepped through and waited for me to catch up.

'Unusual,' I said. 'It's not locked. No intercom. People have become very paranoid. Most of these places are heavily fortified.'

We climbed the steep driveway and then the steps that led up to the high veranda. Blair looked along it, past the bare metal chairs ranged on it, smiling. 'My granny used to sit out here for hours.' He rang the doorbell.

A black domestic, in cap and apron, opened the door, though not the security gate in front of it. 'Yes?' she asked, not very loudly.

'May we come in?' asked Blair, holding onto the bars of the security gate, stooping and, I could see in profile, grinning at her. 'I used to live in this house, for many years, many years ago...as a boy....'

The domestic said, 'The master and the madam she isn't here.'

Blair frowned and looked at me. He seemed not to know what to say.

'But, um,' I said, 'we don't want to see them. We don't, um, know them. We just want to have a look around.'

'Inside?' she asked.

'Yes, please,' I said, knowing it was hopeless, showing Blair that it was hopeless.

'The master and the madam she said I mustn't let anyone in when she isn't here. Master,' she added, looking at Blair.

I was about to try again, but Blair brushed it aside. 'No matter,' he said to her and to me. 'Thank you all the same. Would you mind, though, if we sat here on the veranda,' he gestured, 'for a little while? For five minutes?'

She looked doubtful. I reiterated, 'Just five minutes.'

'Yes, master.'

'Thank you,' said Blair, and I echoed it.

She closed the door and Blair went and sat in one of the metal chairs. 'I remember it so well,' he said, looking out over the garden. 'Those trees are considerably bigger, of course.' I stood on the steps and tried to frame a decent photo of him sitting on the veranda. 'I remember it all perfectly,' he said. 'I think I even compensated for the amount the trees would grow. This is exactly as it has been in my head for thirty years.'

I clicked the shutter.

He looked at me, then away again. He closed his eyes for a moment and smiled. Then, briskly, he stood up. 'You've got your picture then,' he said. 'Let's go.'

We walked down the driveway. He glanced at a large outbuilding and said, 'That's been added on. Not the right place for it.'

Back in the car, I asked him, 'Where else do you want to go?'

'Well,' he said, putting on his seatbelt. 'I can't visit every spot, can I? I suppose a good place would be Ermelo, where I was arrested in '56. But you don't want to drive to Ermelo, do you? And, frankly, I wouldn't want to go there.' He laughed. 'God, it's strange to see that house, almost exactly as I left it.'

We had reached Jan Smuts again.

'Where now?' I asked.

'Mayfair,' he said.

As I drove, he turned to me and, with his arm hooked over the back of his seat, said, 'Tell me about yourself.'

I laughed. I gave him the basic outline; the kind of thing you say to people who ask you that question in one of its forms. It's slightly more interesting than 'So, what do you do?' But it wasn't just *politesse* on Blair's part. He kept interjecting, asking for details. At one point he even asked,

'And how did you feel about that?' And when I told him, he said, 'Yes, I felt the same in very similar circumstances.' Then he asked, 'And are you, um, romantically involved with anyone at the moment?'

'Yes,' I said, feeling a trifle odd. 'Someone I've been involved with for a few years now.'

Was there, I wondered, to be further probing in that direction?

He smiled and leant back in his seat and said, 'Good.' That seemed to bring his questioning to a close. Then he said, 'I see that, er, rights for homosexuals are now on the agenda.'

'Yes,' I said; that *someone* had been noted. 'The Winnie Mandela trial, ironically, gave gay rights something of a boost.' I wondered then whether that wasn't perhaps the wrong thing to have said. 'The ANC's bill of rights,' I said quickly, 'as I'm sure you know, has taken sexual orientation into consideration. You know, no discrimination on the grounds of.'

'Mmmm,' he said. I thought he was going into a reverie again, looking out at the Johannesburg he left so long ago, but when I looked at him I saw that he was gazing at me intently with those sharp blue eyes. 'You know,' he said slowly, 'I'm so thankful that there's a new generation to take over from our lot. Not necessarily within the party; outside the party as well. I'm glad people are still fighting. I'm glad people are fighting for things I didn't have the courage to fight for. Fighting for themselves.'

I was beginning to feel slightly uneasy again, but we were turning into Church Street, and he indicated that I turn to the left. I turned.

'No,' he said, 'not this road. It must be one down.' I turned again. 'Yes, this is it. Just over there. One before the corner.' We stopped. He leant past me in the car and peered out my window at it. 'Is that right?' he asked me. 'Is that Number 84?'

'Yes,' I said. The number, after all, stood in metre-high entangled red ciphers on the white wall.

'They've given it a new wall and a new garage,' he said. 'I barely recognize the place.'

'A lot of these houses have been done up,' I said. 'Usually by Indian owners. The whites who live here are too poor.'

'Mmmm,' he said. 'It used to be quite a dire white working-class suburb. An all-white working-class suburb. Dire.' He showed no sign of wanting to get out of the car. 'No use taking a picture of me here,' he said. 'It doesn't look anything like it did then. In those days it was a good place to hide out. This was one of the houses where I laid low when they were after me.'

'Oh?' I said, soliciting more.

But all he said was, 'It's all in the novel. This was one of the many places I and people like me hid. One house like many others....'

He looked down and I glanced at his profile. Did I see a great sadness on it? He did not speak for some time.

Then, in a muted, hoarse voice, he said, 'No, it's not all in the novel. There's nothing about what really happened here. There's nothing about the failure of love that took place here. My failure; my failure to love someone —' he swallowed after the word '— someone who loved me, wanted to love me.' Then he said, and he seemed to be quoting, 'As an individual.'

There was nothing for me to say. I pitied him, but how could I articulate it? Blair stared down at his hands, loosely clasped in his lap.

'The asceticism, the denial,' he murmured. 'I married the Communist Party. Perhaps I should have become a Catholic priest.'

I waited.

Then he said, a little too loudly, 'I must apologize to you. For being such a useless interviewee. For being such a hopeless example of a long-standing communist. And they call me a stalwart! A veteran! I've been a member of the SACP for over forty years, and this is the first time I've really felt enormous regret. As though I'd wasted my life. Isn't that stupid? When the comrades read your article, they're going to say, "Old Blair certainly has gone completely over the edge. He is clearly senile. We shall have to purge him."'

Then he laughed.

'Well, I have gone quite over the edge. Not to mention over the top. I thought coming home after all these years would be a happy occasion. Well, I suppose it is a happy occasion. But a terribly sad one too. Do you have a cigarette perhaps?'

'In the cubby-hole,' I said. 'Help yourself.'

He took out the packet and, with a manner that was strangely coy, I thought, offered me one. I took one and he lit mine and then his, with hands that were long and graceful like a pianist's, or perhaps like those of someone who worked in a laboratory. He inhaled smoke and coughed a little. He looked at me with eyes that were sad and slightly puzzled, but they were wise and were again very cool.

'We should get back to the hotel,' he said. 'They'll be wondering where the mad old bastard has wandered off to now. Sipho's such a softie. I'm badly in need of some of the party's legendary discipline.'

I started the car and headed back to Hillbrow.

'Now,' said Blair. 'Is there anything you still want to know? I've been so garbled, so self-indulgent. But you must put in what I said about grass-roots democracy. I really mean that, and it's terribly important. You've got all that on the tape, haven't you?'

'Yes,' I said. 'Let me ask you one more question. Were the years of exile very hard?'

He thought a while and said, 'No, I can't say they were, for me. Some of it was exciting, like the setting up of Solomon Mahlangu in Tanzania. A lot of it was mundane, like trying to get a decent job in England. Others suffered far, far more than I did, and they are heroes of the struggle. I'm just a romantic old bore who gets silly bees in his bonnet about all sorts of ridiculous things. The new guard, thank heavens, is taking over. I'm a dinosaur who has made too many mistakes, intellectual mistakes and all the other kinds, especially the other kinds. Luckily I am nearly extinct.'

He threw the cigarette butt out the window. We were in Hillbrow.

'Is that enough?' he asked me. 'Will you get something out of all my gibberish? I haven't been very interesting at all, have I?'

'Would you rather I didn't write the interview?' I asked, briefly imagining the editor's glower.

'No, no,' he said, almost anxiously. 'You must write your interview if you need to, as you need to. It's fine, I'll get off here — it's a one-way after the lights.' I pulled the car over and he got out. He banged the door closed and then leant through the window. 'Just don't send me up too much,' he said.

I laughed. 'Don't worry. Thank you for your time, Mr Blair.'

'No,' he said. 'Thank *you*, young man. Thank *you*, comrade.'

And then he walked off. I caught a glimpse of him in the rear-view mirror, his white hair lifted by the wind, hands in his pockets, his step raffish.

Would it be going too far, I wondered, to write of him as 'the last romantic revolutionary'? Would or wouldn't he approve?

I got back to the office. The news editor looked up from his pizza and said, 'Where the fuck have you been? Where's your story?'

'I'll do it now,' I said, lighting a cigarette. 'It's already written in my head.'

Lucas Malan

Welcoming

When you return
the cat will have been long dead,
gone like my brother, my apostate mother,
forgotten like the riots of '76
somewhere in Langa/Soweto,
like a third-party disc from that time: forgotten.

You may be a little surprised
when you return
by the slight signs of wealth since
in the flat: the carpets, the marble,
the stereophonic Mozart,
my utter consolement within;

but

you'll have to be careful now
for things have become rather brittle around here,
touchy and susceptible to rumours
about you and skeletons
in wardrobes and rooms;
what's more, you can expect the clouds
to avenge your return with lightning.

I may not even be home
— earning a living, you know —
so call at the neighbour, she has a key,
and welcome nevertheless
to my fortress, my world, your imminent fate:
this utterly fucked-up survival.

Translated by Johann de Lange

Lucas Malan

Veterans

But first a toast to us, comrade,
who survived love; and left behind

in bunkers and trenches the hate;
who talked about our scars of late,

can still take aim and shoot in skilful way
a salvo distance quite some way.

Translated by Johann de Lange

Johann de Lange

Soldier

my soldier guards my round sleep tonight
the wind in his short hair and coat   his ears
red from the June cold
he marches through my dreams and the waking hours
when sleep eludes one like a weekend pass

I search for him in the frost-covered tents
I search for him in the red Flanders
of a heroic generation
I search for him in the platoons
marching with broken eyes

but my soldier loves a gun
with the passion that once was mine

Translated by the poet

Two Sailors Pissing

after a watercolour by Charles Demuth

heavy dick-holding sailors
thicker even than those
on the walls
of Pompeii pissing
with sweet angelic faces
aiming with strong wrists
two clear flowing figures
running water or arching fire
dark blue uniforms
against the brown-of-the-wall
transparent reflections
of the noon hour
which they are part of
two foam-pissing sailors:
that so much water,
that such water-men,
can hold such fire
— the cold ashes
of Pompeii testify to this —
that they as it were piss
on smouldering ruins
a wet flame on paper

Translated by the poet

Imago

in Burger's Park the shadows
are alive   they cling
then drift away again
shyly slip across the lighted
strips   every heart
opens like a buckle
in the milky night
every coupling is death
in tree-sheltered hedges
the cocoons hatch

One midnight
(the witching hour)
your eyes gleaming like cuffs
I fleetingly longed
for a father's fire
as I guiltily slipped
from your rump

Translated by the poet

Johann de Lange

Tongue-Fuck

On your stomach, one leg pulled high,
I can see where your blond leg-hair goes,
grows darker and thicker, and the swollen ridge
of your dick disappears between hard cheeks.

Judas-eye opening wider for a rimming,
fragrant bud in a bed of brown curls,
ring clenching rhythmically as the first sharp pulses
pump the spunk deep from my heavy balls

and from the red and swollen head squirts
white wheels flying out across your back.
Your body makes me hot for randy talk
— ass and hard-on, dickhead, fuck and suck —

because in my mouth such supple words
are as thick-fleshed and acrid as you.

Translated by the poet

Shona Elder

Four Poems

Somewhere an amateur's arty attack on
God hangs blankly like a threat,
God yawns at its loudness.
The awkward airbrush folds itself around
the sheet like sickness.
Do you always bow to its garishness?
Your hands are cold and your
blood holds no possibilities.
This is the place where
pitted pallor and black crockery are
handcuffed into being serious, while
the night gapes like a bodiless
wound under congealed orange windows.

                                From a disembodied
                                obscenity or a pastless vacuum
                                of mindless subversion,
                                I worship an oversimplified
                                shudder and suck.

This Saturday
some scatological porn book
occupies my slot.
There's a sameness in our silence,
effect and life span.
We function between covers.
But we're not identical,
your book has a spine.

Shona Elder

Flaccid breasts, plastic bag of poultry innards,
squelch tepidly on a yearning pelvis.
Punish me, punish me ill.
Sordid vigil closed on the sticky slut,
tired beat trod on lifted pavement,
lifted shirt, one of the same expose the dirt.
Splendid spew splendid spew.
The virgin and the masochist Jew.

Tanya Chan Sam

Tropical Juice

Let me make love to you as I would eat a mango,
with knife-like incisions let me strip your outer skin
to reveal the fiery fruity flesh.
Proffer your soft mound covered in hairy tendrils
dripping its sweet sap.
The Venus fruit complements my palate.
How I wish to sink my teeth into your
hill of treasures,
let my hot tongue meander through the moist tunnels
into the heart of the fruit,
feel the sap course around each tooth,
filling the dark dry gaps with
the tropical taste of you.
I don't want to swallow lest I lose
the essence of you.
My mouth filled with the succulent flesh,
the juice spills down my chin.
My hands are sopping with holding the mango,
the wetness collects in the bowls of my finger webs.
I want to smear it all over,
acquainting your tropical juices
with the polar regions of your body.

Welma Odendaal

Bye Bye, Forget Me Not

1.

The balding man carries the small child loosely under his arm to the edge of the water where shallow waves collide with his ankles. He wades deeper until the water reaches his knees. She shrieks with delight, come Papa, come. He lowers her legs and kisses her on the back of her head. She wriggles and kicks, splashing both him and her. Wait, he says, wait. He takes her a little deeper, the water now up to his waist. There he rests her, stomach down on his broad hands. Like this, father and child, they await the oncoming rush of the waves.

The day she saw him strolling into the geography class, one hand in his pocket, brown satchel loosely slung over his shoulder, grinning his excuse for being late, she knew she had to have him. There was something about him and she made him her friend. Something special that everyone noticed, she thought. One day she found he was like everyone else and it broke her heart. Dear Cheeser, can I have my picture back? And a lopsided kiss under the hibiscus tree, the first taste of another's mouth under the drooping red blossoms of the hibiscus tree.

It took her by surprise when one afternoon she watched from a distance as he splashed and played in the school swimming-pool with his collection of people. His hard boy's body wet as a tongue. His side-chin dimple cracking open as he smiled, taking in their play, their touch. His bright black eyes drawing them closer, closer. He needed them so, she suddenly realized. He needed all that. You are not for me. After that day she turned away from him, something he could not understand, nobody had ever done that. He was so powerful. But she was strong.

Yet, she would not get off lightly. He would make her pay. For a while there was an uneasy state of cold war between them. And she watched her friends one by one switch their loyalty. He became bigger, better at it. His smile more enticing, his eyes hard, relentless.

The day stretches long and tiresome. Dusk draws near and with it brings the cool, even shadow. Smooth shadow of the evening. Huddled, a towel around her, she sits with her back against the stone wall, warm and comforting, and watches the four boys in the pool. She has waited for a while now for them to get out so that she can lock up and return the keys to the school janitor. She has watched through their every trick, play and manoeuvre. Their trying, mocking way. Now they are standing in a circle throwing a rubber ball from one side to the other. Waist-deep in the water he faces her. His hair matted, dark water-stains on his face, faint goose-flesh on his arms.

She shivers, gets up. Okay, I'm going to lock up now.

He has the ball in his hand. Draws his hand back and aims at her. She stares without flinching. Throw, her eyes say, come on throw. The ball crashes into the wall behind her. She turns and walks into the changing-room. Soon she hears their loud laughter in the room next to her.

The girl in the mirror has soft down on her legs, a dash of dark between and sprouts little bulbs on her chest. Her lips smile, never touching her eyes.

Outside they wait. The water in the pool moves in soft waves, gently drifting to rest. They lean against their bicycles, whispering, grinning, nudging and pointing at her. She closes the gate, locks up. Dusk comes and smells of dry tar and crushed geraniums. She pedals to the janitor's house. They follow.

The park is shaded in half-darkness. The see-saw, swings and roundabout empty. Rough gusts of wind tug at the trees. The steel bars of the roundabout are cold, dampened by nightfall. She pushes it, well-oiled it moves soon and fast. At the park entrance the whirring click-click of bicycle wheels. There are only three of them now. They saunter towards her.

Quietly she slips under the big wheel and lies on her back watching the approaching dark shadows. He catches hold of the rocking wheel, come on boys. Two of them jump on the roundabout and her stomach lurches. He runs around and around thudding in dust around her, pushes with his muscled legs, and jumps on. Spinning, spinning above her open face. He heaves himself down and lies on his stomach, flashing face-down past her again and again. The other two dig their heels into the loose sand, she tastes the dust, and slowly the roundabout comes to a standstill. He ends up right above her, looking down through the bars. He wets his mouth, she sees a small glob of spittle gather in the corner of his mouth. He bends his head down, she smells the lead smell, of him, he closes his eyes. She grabs hold of the crossbar and with all the strength she has shoves him and the wheel away from her. Her head screams in anger, hate, pain. She rolls from under the spinning roundabout, but not before she has seen the shock in his eyes.

Let's play a game. A silent game without words. Play-play and forget me not. Scared of the dark, hide from its shadow under a floppy blanket-tent. Close your eyes tightly and let no one, nothing know you're there. Hum a song to make it light. Think of something nice. Like the smell of grass after the lawn has been mowed. Smile, smile and forget me not.

2.

The day is warm and windless, the sea calm and deep indigo. Summer here is dry and hot, but beautiful.

The balding man on the beach leads the small child slowly to the water. The shallow water washes over his feet. Come on, it's nice. She smiles up at his reassuring face and tightens her hold on his hand. Together, hand in hand, they walk to meet the rushing waves.

Taking the long rocky path to the deserted beach she comes across a man lying on his back, spread-eagled, naked on the sand. He is thin and white and she wonders absent-mindedly if he will not get burnt lying so open in the hot sun. She spreads her towel a short distance away from him, opens a book but sometimes just stares at the sea. After a while she turns and watches the sleeping man.

He is smiling to himself, his hand covering his sleeping prick. He has soft fair down on his breast and his temples. She finds him beautiful. He opens his eyes, startling her, and asks: Why have you got your clothes on? As if he knew she was there all the time.

Embarrassed she shrugs, turns on her stomach and opens her book once again. He comes over, peeling an orange, sits down comfortably next to her and starts asking her about herself quite effortlessly. As if he has the right to know. What she does, where she lives, what she is doing on a nudist beach with her clothes on. She smiles at his easy manner. They share the orange. His eyes are frank, almost bland and colourless, perhaps pale green, it is hard to tell in the devious midday sun. After some easy time with him she has to go. We'll meet again, he says, sure, she knows that it is so. She trudges back along the rocky path. Her mind wanders to him, the orange, the soft down on his temples. She wonders if she has come especially just to meet him there. There's no telling.

They lived, loved, laughed well together. Travelling a lot they constantly met new people, new places, unpacking and unpicking their lives, never living in one place for longer than a year perhaps.

He had lovers from time to time, she knew because he told her. From the beginning they had decided their relationship would be 'open'. Once when he went for a week she slept with someone else, but found it didn't really mean much.

Afterwards there was always the empty space in the bed when he left for short periods, again and again. She kept watch over it, knowing he would be back always. Jealousy is a dangerous, stupid emotion, she told herself.

A game, a silent game without words. Bye bye and forget me not. Alone in a big house, hum a tune to make it better. Jeepers creepers.... Think of something nice. Laughing at a joke nobody else understands. Smile, smile forget me not.

After four years of being together he started talking of getting married.

I'm not ready, she said. Take your time.

She saw marriage as a threat to the easy spontaneity between them. Yet in some way she wanted it too. But there was something in her that was missing, something, she didn't quite know what. She tossed up the fashionable word of the moment: sexuality, that's what, kid.

Someone else was getting close to her. Closer, dearer, but not that close yet. Something had to change in her, she knew, something that only she could change. A part of her she didn't own. A part she was desperately afraid of. She had to get through to that small pebble hidden in the pit of her self. Take it in her hand and own it.

She thought she knew how. Oh, it took a long time to get there, only she knows what it took to get there. Only she can tell.

3.

There are things I have never done. Everyday things. Things lots of people do. Childhood things which grown-ups seldom learn. Things which never occurred to me before.

I have never fed a baby bird pulped bread or a seed from my mouth. But these days I often think of the pure pleasure it would give to feel the peck of a tiny beak on my mouth. I have never washed my tongue in her softest flesh and drawn from her woman's breath deep into my throat. But I've wanted to, I really did want to. But it takes more courage to drink a woman than to feed birds.

If I close my eyes I remember her as she was that first night.

It was at one of those silly so-called intimate parties artists give and artists attend. The fluffy host had spent many warm days at our beach cottage lying naked and drinking white wine with ice. He regarded us as 'special people'.

After an hour I was bored. Then she walked in. Small, tousled hair that looked as if it had only been brushed once that day, grinning, a jug of wine in her hand. I close my eyes and remember her late that night. Sitting cross-legged on the floor, gesticulating wildly, smoking, throwing her head back and laughing deep, deep from her belly. She sent a whisper up my spine, so faint, I was almost not aware of it.

We were both enchanted and invited her for a lazy weekend at the cottage. She came. We saw her again and again. Soon the three of us shared much of our lives together. Sometimes she left for a while and we missed her, but she always came back. Easy, laughingly strolling to and fro into our lives. She almost never had a lot of money, then she sold an article, a story or so, and had some again. She gave as easily as she took, oh, it was easy. So nice, so uncomplicated.

Then she went away for a year. I missed her in a faraway manner at times; I missed her to the point of distraction at times. Bye bye, but forget me not.

You're missing her, he said one day looking at me smilingly. Yeah. I think she's after you, you know. I know. What are you going to do about it? I don't know. He laughed. You will have to make up your mind, my dear. Yes...don't you mind? He looked surprised. Of course not, God, I find it exciting!

I always knew I would have to make up my own mind about you. I had to give myself time. Your going away was the time I needed, perhaps. And in the back rooms of my troubled hours I faced lonely thoughts about you. Your smile was something I had become addicted to, your warmth something I wanted to get closer to. I close my eyes and watch your body move its paces through my mixed feelings.

In September the winter wind refuses to die down. In the mornings it is dark and cold and the rain lashes against the windows. Occasionally a weak sun finds its way through the gloom, but gets driven away like an unwanted dog that has come home too soon.

There's a knock on the door. No, it's just the wind. Go and see.

She stands in my doorway grinning madly. Hi, Babes.

We hug and kiss her and rub her tousled sun-bleached hair. Her eyebrows are flaxen white, her nose peeling from the fiery sun of another world. We love you so.

Late night we sit up talking and share a joint. It is so like before, but not quite the same. The two of them start clowning on the huge mattress in the living-room. They shriek and wrestle and spill the wine. He takes his clothes off, come, let's go to bed. Cold and naked we get under the blankets. I lie on my back between him and her, feeling their warmth reaching for me. They talk lazily, soon they drift asleep. I lie awake for a while, listening to the rain mingle with the sound of the sea.

In the morning I am the first to wake up. The rain is quiet now. Traffic drones. I am curled on my side, my back to him, my arm resting on her soft brown shoulder.

The days that follow are vague and light-headed. She is with us most of the time. When she disappears down the coast for a few days, nothing makes me happier than to hear her voice in the kitchen when I get home one night. She is closer now than before. Her pale eyes and ready smile haunt me. We never talk about it, but we know, both of us know.

October is here and the first signs of summer. She moves into a friend's flat. We see less of her, my doing not theirs. They are so comfortable with each other. They laugh and rap and meet in town for lunch. They are such easy friends.

Snow on the mountains, they say, it is raining here, and cold. I wake up with a need to be with her. Phone. Hi Babe. Come over for supper, she says. I'll come. Alone? Yes, alone.

Jeepers creepers, where'd you get those peepers?

She opens the door and smiles. I had to see you today. She takes my hand and leads me inside. Quite badly, I'm not sure why. She closes the door and stands close. I wanted to talk, about us, I mean, this thing between us that we never talk about. She takes my face in her hands. There is nothing more to say.

You led and I followed gladly. Your mouth a softness, your knuckles, chin, your knee, your cheek the movement I couldn't place. The road we took was rough at the beginning, leading over narrow ledges and sluggish sand. The road we took turned and tumbled, crawled uphill and sprawled into a vast openness which had no end. We whispered we smiled we chuckled we cried out loud. And when I doubled over sobbing, you were there and never left me, not even in your sleep.

The days follow in a dreamlike haze where I seem to live in a continuous state of flux. Riding the high tides of emotion between her and him where thinking hardly comes into it and my body is the centre-pin around which everything revolves. Like a spinning ball I am flung to and fro and at times I would wake up in the early morning and wonder who was sleeping beside me.

Summer comes in full force. We become brown-skinned and tough. It is Friday afternoon, the sun hot and white, and the three of us leave for a long weekend on the West Coast. She sits at the back, her arms around both of us, and we pass a jug of cool white wine from back to front. Next to the highway the Port Jackson trees bend backwards in the path of the wind. We laugh and talk. My hand rests on his bare knee, her fingers absent-mindedly stroke the back of my neck. He lights a joint and we share it with the wine. Bitter and sweet. Near the coast the sand-dunes light-headedly rise above the shallow bush. We turn seawards and take a narrow dirt road through the nature reserve. A vapour of clouds drifts lazily above the shore. The sun moves down and when we reach the small village on the coast, rests its belly in the water.

The beach house is closed up and dusty. We open all the doors and windows and let the evening air in. She sweeps, he gathers wood and I prepare the salad and fish. Our mouths are dry from the marijuana and she slices a watermelon. We sit on the steps sucking the watery fruit and watch it grow dark over the sea. I close my eyes and hear their voices mingle with the distant calls of fishermen, the crash of waves and the shrieks of seagulls. We grill the fish. It tastes of the sea.

I am hazy and mellow sitting with my back between his legs, his arms around me. She is on her back, head on my lap, her eyes closed. As an afterthought his hands move slowly over my breasts. My nipples harden. Her eyes open. You look so funny, upside-down. She rises and kneels over me. Presses her forehead against mine. His mouth comes down in the nape of my neck. Slowly in slow-motion, every gasp a terrifying tumble, I watch in from the outside myself being taken by them.

In the morning comes the unpredictable rain. We make a fire inside. The two of them are curled on the floor, talking softly. I lie on the couch, taking turns to watch them and the fire.

Driving back I sit in the back of the car. We are quiet. Outside the city the clouds splinter apart to let the sun through.

4.

And now the days are long.

Let's play a game. A game without words. A guessing game. Pebble in the hand seed turns to plant. Jeepers.

I'll tell you a secret if you promise to keep it quiet. Of course. I'm going to have a baby. Wow. She grabs hold of me and twirls me round and round till we land in a dizzy heap on the floor. That's great.

She stops working and spends her days in the peaceful life of the commune they have moved to. The women with their open friendly faces visit her and they talk of everyday things. She enjoys their uncomplicated company. But mostly she sits alone, watches the light patterns behind the tall oaks and folds her hands over her stomach. As if to keep it warm.

Well, did you tell her? Yes. What did she say? Not much. She was silly, you know, jumping up and down. Like she is. He smiles and takes my hand.

They get married on a bright day in December. Family and friends. Women of the commune sing soft ballads. A blues musician plays the flute. There is lots of food, nice people and laughter. They watch out for her. Even try to phone. But she doesn't come. Later they hear she is somewhere in the north-western desert and will be away for a long time.

A play to end all games. Smile, smile and forget.

In the beginning everyone tells her she is getting more and more beautiful. Her cheeks glow, her skin is soft and white, her belly swells like a melon. She wears long soft dresses, woven shawls and multi-coloured scarves around her hair. Women friends visit, advise her about nursing homes, gynaecologists and baby food. She is vague and uninterested. Stares at them for hours without talking. Later they don't come any more.

He comes home at night and finds her naked in the dark, rocking in a chair by the window. Humming softly. Jeepers creepers, where'd you get those peepers? He tries to talk to her but she just smiles. A vacant lovely smile. A smile not unlike that of a newborn baby.

A game without words. Make believe and do you remember.

The balding man on the beach takes the small child by the hand and leads her to the edge of the water. She clasps his hand tightly, he looks down reassuringly. Like this, father and child, they rush towards the oncoming waves.

Dee Radcliffe

Confessions of a Failed Lesbian Separatist

In my lifetime I've tried very hard to be a good separatist, but I must admit that I can't make the grade. I had a great start though. For the first twenty-five years of my life I was a separatist by default, if not by design.

At our all-girls primary school, my friend Julie and I were inseparable friends, not to mention fairly adept sexual playmates. Together we ran the Tomboys' Club, whose members pledged lifelong aversion to boys. We laid plans to marry each other, and assured my parents that we could just 'borrow' a man if we wanted a baby.

As I headed towards puberty and an all-girls high school (bless my parents in their unknowing wisdom!), I did suffer a brief lapse. I had a flicker of interest in a boy called Angus whom I met at church. I suppose he had incomparable novelty as the first, only and last boy I ever encountered while growing up. My momentary heterosexual passion was snuffed out in its infancy by my mother's catastrophic reaction when she discovered Angus and I innocently holding hands. Happily, I went back to mutual masturbation with Julie under the bedclothes. (What do people think — that little girls together are immune to lust?)

At high school I didn't have the masochism it would have taken to seek out boys — those oddly inarticulate, macho beings with voices that suddenly fell out from under them, seen lurking on motorbikes at the school gates. Weekend exploits recounted to me by my class-mates didn't turn me on any more than the creatures themselves. And they certainly didn't seek me out — I probably had 'dyke' written all over me, worse luck that it took me so long to read it for myself. All I knew then, anyway, was that I was happy enough at school, surrounded by luscious female bodies and plenty of people on whom I could develop endlessly fascinating crushes. The mere proximity of majestic Nancy the hockey captain could give me a multiple orgasm. I floated through school on a cloud of lesbian fantasies, unsuccessfully suppressing them all the way, and entered university with my emotional space still unpenetrated by anyone in possession of a Y-chromosome.

University was something of an extension of high school. Fate seemed to push me into training for a health profession which boasts all of about six male members country-wide. My all-women class was taught by a succession of female lecturers, and my crushes continued unabated. Everyone significant in my life was replete with two X-chromosomes. I first reflected on this fact at the age of twenty-one and was flung pell-mell into a lesbian identity crisis. As if at some signal inaudible to ordinary people, friends began popping out of the closet all around me. It seemed as though I was the last person in my social circle to figure out that I was a dyke, and as soon as I had figured it out I started realizing that so were lots of other people. The crisis part didn't last too long because I was in such good company, and my sense of inhabiting a wonderful womanly world, in which males were mere passers-by, flourished.

Then my rating on the separatist scale dropped drastically when I conducted a year-long experiment in co-ed communal living. It ended, predictably, with the three women from the commune setting up a new house together, and the three men (eminently undomesticated and unsuited to communal living) going their separate ways. It also launched me into a reactive attempt to live as a separatist. Not only did I make a firm decision only to live with women (which I have stuck to over the past six years), I also tried to pretend I had no connections with men in any sphere of my life. Such an attempt was doomed to failure, because if I didn't care about men then why on earth was I working in the male ward of a psychiatric hospital? I couldn't quite manage to see my male clients as oppressors — it was too obvious that they were as oppressed for being mentally ill as I was for being a woman. Still, I declared my separatist ideals to the world at large, and developed quite a reputation as a man-hater. I came to blows with one housemate over her boyfriend, and tried to recruit others to lesbian separatism. Nevertheless, the shallowness of my commitment showed in the fact that I acquired a male kitten, and took no particular delight in his castration a few months later. A proper separatist would have tolerated neither Clifford nor his testicles for longer than a minute.

When I was given the opportunity to study in Boston, the unacknowledged dyke capital of the world, I was delighted. I still nursed dreams of a world in which I need never interact with men. Once again I found myself in an all-women class, taught mostly by women professors. This time, I was living a separatist's idea of heaven on earth. All I had to do was pop along

Dee Radcliffe

to the local women's centre to look up a female plumber, electrician, doctor, dentist, optician, therapist, landlady, hairdresser or housemover. I could find women-owned poodle parlours, guest-houses, video shops, companies, funeral homes, garages, retirement villages or savings banks, dyke bands or art classes or sex-therapy groups or hotlines on artificial insemination. 'Womyn-only space' was a holy term and there were half a dozen women's bars to choose from. In short, one could have all one's conceivable needs met without a single man befouling one's space. In the neighbourhood where I lived, local libraries and laundromats were lesbian meeting-places, and there was a crèche especially for the kids of lesbian parents. On Monday nights I went to see a lesbian rap group, on Wednesday nights there was a women's writing workshop and on Fridays women's movies were shown at the women's centre. There were monthly pot-luck suppers to welcome new women in the area, and a local theatre hosted a comedy show on lesbian safe sex attended by seven hundred women.

I lapped it up, pardon the pun, all of this women's wimmin's womyn's culture, with glee. I holidayed in Provincetown, where straight couples turned heads. I ate dinner at Different Ducks while listening to a lesbian folksinger, and jostled in the womancraft shop over Chris Williamson tapes and amethyst crystals and dildo catalogues. I camped with a dozen lesbians on the beach, spent nights in women-owned motels and in the summer I headed to the woods of New Hampshire with a group called Lesbians from Hell, who scared the pants off straight families in the camping grounds.

In short, I came as close to living a separatist life as one can without removing oneself to the wilderness. Everyone significant in my life, and a good proportion of the insignificant, was female. I had a sense of total independence from men. I noticed their presence occasionally as cashiers or bus-drivers or police officers or other functionaries, but none of them inhabited my psychic turf.

What happened next is that the fun began to wear off. When I went to work in the psychiatric hospital, I couldn't pretend that I didn't like or care for my male patients. I did like them, some of them very much. I also liked my three male colleagues (all happened to be gay), and laughed myself silly at their camp humour. They enriched my world, no matter how much I didn't want them in my kitchen or bedroom or vagina. I realized that sometimes I just wanted the uncomplicated, unemotional company of men. Sometimes I wanted to head-butt with them, to surprise them out of their complacent assumptions about our relative intellectual abilities. Sometimes I just wanted to listen to how they experienced life. And I even admit that occasionally, just occasionally, I got sick to death of women's music and wanted to hear some good old bad boys whacking their electric guitars.

So, if I'm honest with myself, I'm a failure as a lesbian separatist, for I have found that I quite enjoy men. Yet my life still continues to be dominated by important women. I have a wonderful lover, two lesbian housemates, and a social circle that consists of 98% women. I work in feminist and lesbian organizations, but I also work in mixed groups, with gay men and male clients. I come home from work feeling affectionate towards those men, and I happen to correspond with as many men as I do women.

My life feels fuller, and simpler than before. I don't have to discount half of the human race any more. I feel an ongoing greater allegiance to women than to men, but it has less of the blind, automatic quality it used to have. There is more honesty in what I like or dislike. I am also freer to get closer to men, as individuals, to let myself feel interest in them and to dare to try friendships out. I can fight patriarchy and sexism with as much energy as before, and I can enlist men to fight alongside me. I can support women-owned businesses and services and I needn't feel that I am betraying the cause when I use male-owned ones. I don't have to puritanically put up with a leaking toilet just because there's no such thing as a female plumber in the area. I can also contemplate having or adopting a boy, as well as a girl, if and when the time seems right to start a family.

Perhaps, best of all, I'm making peace with the traditionally 'male' qualities within myself, my anger and forcefulness, my courage, my drive, my need to be alone from time to time, my space.

During my attempted separatist era I disowned, and suppressed, and felt guilty about all of these. Now I am one happily fulfilled, failed lesbian separatist!

Joan Hambidge

Octet

The tiny goldfish
cannot procreate. Nature's freak
a tiny, lonely Moby Dick,
ghasps for air in plastic.

Between stones and shells
she ferrets around, and round, and round.
Yet becomes a voracious man-eater
Should a hand attempt to feed her.

Translated by Jo Nel

Departure

In every encounter
lies the end: in every arrival
the departure.

At the airport in Zurich
two females confirm La Rochefoucauld:
in their farewell the one turns
twice around after two kisses.
For the other the send-off is drawn out.

Thus after this scene
I dream in the Hotel du Théâtre
of our farewell. Constantly
I return to what was.

In this game (dreams are theatre with an unconscious
text) I wanted to prevent you
from leaving me for a new love.

A dream like a puppet show:
each character (main and not-so-important)
manipulated by the dreamer's desires.

La Rochefoucauld:
In every affaire one always feels
more.

Translated by the poet

Ernst van Heerden

Rain

The two of us went running
along the mountainside — happy
and in high spirits, but cautious all the same
for concealed holes, the hidden snake —
when the sudden rain caught us unawares
and trails of mist against the slopes
brought a drizzling refreshment
on shoulders, nose and hair.

You were fanatic on matters physical,
punctual and strict about every practice run —
so it's plain how this discipline
produced your nickname Captain.

For a quarter of an hour
we had to shelter from the gusts
below a rocky ledge,
and shake out our sodden sweaters
and laughingly take stock of each other;
the thin line of blood on your brown shoulder
in our haste scratched there by a twig,
but I only got a small blister
on a heel for your tending —
all of this
with the delightful prickling and stupor
of water's endless seeping...

So many years since make me wonder
if you ever
with your triptych-sons
— parson, lawyer, lecturer —
go running in the rain.

Translated by the poet

Dance of Death

My chest against your breast
feels like the tremors of a mouse,
against our skin's own quiver
the itching of a louse.

My arm is decimated
to a five-inch trembling stump,
but it can still caress
your cheek's pockmarked lump.

My eye has a thousand planes
and yours can equally lie;
understanding is beyond me,
for your glance is of a fly.

Our fumbling mouths will open
like on a slope the covered hole,
but my tongue has been chopped off
and yours is a little rotten pole.

My nose forms two deep caverns,
my sinuses a moulded breath,
in deepest sewers we acutely smell
the night-stench of our death.

Translated by the poet

Hennie Aucamp

On Despondency Square

The old man on Syntagma Square resembled Diaghilev. Or Somerset Maugham. Or André Gide. He possessed something of each of them: the face of a hedonist, but also that of a priest; a face that became final quickly, to quote Rilke. For pleasure consumes all one's faces until only one remains: a mask. (Even saints have final faces, wax and wood allow little nuance.)

When I arrived in Athens in the middle of that August, the old man was already there. Anastatos, a waiter on Syntagma Square, told me that the old man had, for many years, spent his summers in Athens. Sometimes he became so impatient waiting for the summer that he arrived before the first almond blossom. In previous years Athens had only been his base. From there he had travelled to Crete, Meteora, and above all to Mykonos. Since last year he had stayed only in Athens, walking from his hotel across the street to Syntagma Square. He sat on the square from shortly after breakfast, right through the day with short breaks for meals and an afternoon nap. At night he would sit until two o'clock, when service ended. If he was too drunk one of the waiters would help him home; they had an arrangement with the hotel.

Sometimes the old man looked like a dissipated saint; those were the days when he wore his cream Assam silk suit, a bow-tie, and read Robert Musil and Nietzsche. When it was particularly hot he sported a cheerful Greek-style shirt hanging over baggy shorts. On those days he would sit and drool over pornography. It was then that you saw how thin his arms and legs were — like those of a half-starved child. He would show the photographs to carefully selected waiters and they would look at them with genuine interest — the Greeks have a primordial obsession with the phallus. At any bookstall you can buy a postcard of a randy old satyr with an erection.

He aroused the interest of the beautiful young parasites less and less. The gigolos shied away from him and even the shoeshine boys avoided him.

Athens, and Syntagma Square in particular, relaxes one, there is no resisting it. Here you learn to procrastinate without feeling guilty. The little Byzantine church can wait until tomorrow, or the day after. It can even wait until your next visit. It is the people on the square with their recurring concerns that are important: the gypsy woman flogging embroidered sheets and cloths, the lottery seller, the shoeshine boys, the old man. The gypsy woman would move from table to table. She would draw out of a blue plastic bag tablecloths that she embroidered. They looked like a delicate foam, like spider webs, as she spread them over her brown arms and hands to display them to the women who called her over. The women weren't really interested. They did it because they were, as housewives, conditioned to do so. The cloth would be passed from the grandmother to the mother to the granddaughter, each examining and stroking it. No, they would decide, suddenly annoyed, go away, too expensive. After a while the gypsy woman would stuff the tablecloths back into the bag in frustration, dragging one across the paving behind her like some grubby train. Finally, defeated, she would sink into a chair — strictly against the rules of the square. Even in Greece you must pay for your place in the sun: sixty-five drachmas for a beer, a little less for a coffee or ouzo. When the waiter was humane and not too busy he'd bring her a glass of water and a few packets of sugar.

The shoeshine boys, with quick electric movements like salamanders, prey on the tables, tipping their heads right back to get the last dregs of beer or syrup from a glass. Specialists, they call themselves, as they walk among the crowds of chairs carrying their footstools, shoe polish and brushes. They are indescribably filthy, sealed with the varnish of a summer season composed of anything from dust to watermelon juice. Their chins, knees and elbows haven't been scrubbed with a corn-cob for months; if their hair were to be washed, it would leave a rim of tar in the basin.

'Why don't they clean his shoes?' I said, indicating the old man.

'They have no shoe white,' muttered Anastatos.

It was probably a valid excuse, for the old man usually wore white and brown shoes like some broken dandy. But the shoeshine boys, who show respect for nobody, were afraid of the old man, as if he could put a spell on them or was himself enchanted.

Anastatos and I decided that the old man must be a writer, because if he was not reading literature, philosophy or titillating magazines, he wrote long letters in a disciplined, old-fashioned hand.

'Have you ever seen him post a letter?' I asked one day. 'The post office is just across there.'

Anastatos pulled on his ear. 'I haven't seen him do that.'

'He writes letters to himself,' I said mysteriously and thought to myself: a reassurance that he is still alive now that all his contemporaries are dead.

It could have been so, for he was very old. The face was deathly except for his restless eyes that pleaded, or showed mistrust, or contempt. Sometimes he smiled wearily at a waiter or, when he glimpsed a handsome man, he grimaced, showing the orange-red gums of his dentures.

The old man's knees were calloused and wrinkled like those of a goat. The old folks had a saying that you should pray until you have the knees of a goat. But this old man would never have prayed, except for an erection. He would certainly kneel before any demigod of a passing night. (Then would follow the self-castigation and the doubts: What had his body really been like? If only I had not been so eager, if only I had let my eyes linger on him, caressed it for longer, smelled more avidly, something of him might have remained with me; something of his body, of his beauty.)

The old man's hands grew paler and paler by the day, in spite of the summer sun. They also grew more aged and more bejewelled.

'Isn't he afraid the pretty boys will steal his rings?'

Greek hustlers never stick to an agreement. In the end they want more than money: a ring, a watch, or a leather jacket.

'They don't go with him,' said Anastatos curtly. 'Life no longer wants him.' He threw his white napkin across his shoulder and walked away.

On a later occasion Anastatos was more forthcoming. 'The old man doesn't enjoy it,' he reported. 'He always has to say to the boys: "So you couldn't get anything else, huh?" So they stay away. What is there in it for them to enjoy?'

In an abstracted way I felt sorry for the old man. Perhaps because he reminded me of my uncle Freddie. Uncle Freddie had also been discarded by life; but when we were children his visits hit the farm like carnival time and at night we were too excited to sleep.

My uncle Freddie was a hedonist. I discovered that when I was twelve years old and the circumstances remain in my memory to this very day. It was as if a well-spring had been struck, gushing up, and I was never the same again.

My mother was busy clearing the table after breakfast and uncle Freddie was standing, his head bent over a pot of honey as if he were inhaling steam for a cold. In ecstasy and with quivering nostrils he looked up. 'If I smell this any longer,' he said, 'I'll get a hard-on.'

After forty, uncle Freddie's emotions hardened, and before he was fifty he also suffered from hardening of the arteries. His visits became trials. A penance, was my grandmother's word for them. One began to laugh at him and no longer with him: then one hated him because he betrayed one's romanticism. (The very romanticism that you had learned from him.) He became a foolish, stubborn old puppet: a public scarecrow. Towards the end he became deaf. 'There is a waterfall in my head,' he had complained incessantly. In a lucid moment he pressed a revolver to his temple and silenced the waterfall.

We are unreasonable towards old men and women. What we admire as dynamic at fifty and even at sixty, and what in a man is praised as remarkable is, suddenly, at eighty, dirty. (As was the case in Queen Victoria's reign, women get off scot-free.) Perhaps we are afraid to admit that desire shall not fade, whatever the Preacher might say, and to save our own dignity, we force an unnatural propriety upon old people.

It is too late to pay my debt to uncle Freddie, but I can dedicate a recent verse to the old man on the square:

To a Young Greek

I was seldom alone in my travels
until I met you.
Your unattainability
(even in bed),
your wholeness consumed mine
while you remain, untouched,
a bearer of Beauty,
leaving all others with loneliness.

I had wanted to include a stanza to his beauty, to give that beauty substance, to build it into a metaphor. But my description sounded like a paraphrase of that praise-song from *Raka*: 'O, beauty of the body....'

In any case the old man would have known more about beauty than I do. Its symmetry, arrogance, and those veiled eyes like ripe olives. Or does one learn no more after forty? Can it be that those who live too luxuriantly don't love life but abuse it and are, in a way, contemptuous of it so that, finally, they are punished by life? Uncle Freddie, ah, uncle Freddie.

The old man began to drink more and more. He left Nietzsche at the hotel, as well as the pornography that he usually carried in a woven Greek bag with black tassels. Frequently he fell asleep, even before the midday meal, with his head twisted oddly, as if he were a bird seeking to shelter it under a wing. One night he never woke up.

Anastatos told me about it and it was confirmed in a newspaper report; I saw the photograph. Anastatos also told me something that wasn't in the papers. It was he who found the old man early one morning as he was setting out the tables for the day's business. There, in a sheltered corner of the square, behind a tub containing a shrub and under an awning, where even the police on night duty hadn't seen him, there Anastatos found him. His fly was open. In a sense he had raised his hand against his own life, his physical posture confirmed that. Anastatos looked quickly round before he paid his last respects. He carefully zipped up the fly as if the old man could be caught in it, could still be made to feel pain.

Translated by Ian Ferguson

Glossary

ANC —	(acronym) African National Congress.
appies —	(slang) Apprentices.
bablas —	(slang) Hangover.
bakkie —	(Afrikaans and S.A. English) Open van.
Bedford —	Open military vehicle for transporting soldiers.
Bier —	(Afrikaans) Beer.
blackjacks —	(slang) Municipal police, so called because of their black uniforms.
bobotie —	(Afrikaans) Traditional Cape Malay dish of curried minced meat.
Boere —	(Afrikaans) Afrikaners. But commonly used as slang for 'policemen', or 'rightwingers'.
bottleneck —	(slang) The broken-off neck of a bottle through which marijuana is smoked.
Buffel —	(Afrikaans) Mine-proofed military vehicle.
bukhontxana —	(Tsonga) A form of physical external intercourse performed among heterosexual youths in traditional society. A similar form of loving developed among the men on the mines. Literally, a penetration between the thighs.
burger —	(Afrikaans) Citizen.
buttons —	(slang) Mandrax.
cherry —	(slang) Girlfriend.
CPSA —	(acronym) Communist Party of South Africa.
dagga —	(Afrikaans and S.A. English) Marijuana.
DB —	(acronym) Military Detention Barracks.
Ertjie —	(Afrikaans) Pea.
Fanakalo —	A pidgin language, a mixture of English, Afrikaans and Zulu. It was formulated for use on the mines.
ganja —	(slang) Marijuana.
grens —	(Afrikaans) Border.
herbs —	(slang) Marijuana.

Glossary

holnaai —	(Afrikaans) Sex: literally meaning 'arse-screwing'.
homeboy —	(slang) A person from the same rural area.
indlamu —	(Xhosa; Zulu) Traditional dancing.
induna —	(Xhosa; Zulu) In traditional tribal life, a supervisor or counsellor to the chief. The role was adopted in the mining system as an interim authority between management and workers.
ingolovane —	(Zulu) Cocopan, train-like contraption used underground to transport ore from the rock-face to the shaft.
inyanga —	(Zulu) African herbalist.
isangoma —	(Zulu) Traditional healer, sometimes called a 'witch-doctor'.
Jakkals —	(Afrikaans) Jackal.
Jo'burg —	(slang) Johannesburg.
join —	(mining slang) Term. Time-span of a worker's contract on a mine.
kaffir —	(slang) Racist slang for 'black people', equivalent of the American 'nigger'. It derives from an Arabic word meaning 'heathen'.
kaross —	(Afrikaans and S.A. English) Mantle made of animal skins.
Kat —	(Afrikaans) Cat.
kêrel —	(Afrikaans) Slang for 'policeman'. Ironically, its literal meaning is boyfriend or bloke.
koppie —	(Afrikaans and S.A. English) Hillock.
kraal —	(Afrikaans and S.A. English) Traditional enclosure for keeping cattle; also used to refer to a homestead or settlement.
laaitie —	(slang) Child, youngster — derived from 'light'.
lastige boere —	(Afrikaans slang) Troublesome policemen.
laura —	(slang) Lover.
layisha —	(Fanakalo) Loader. From the Afrikaans *laai* — to load. Loaders who use shovels to move rock underground.
lobola —	(Zulu) Bride-wealth.
maak gou —	(Afrikaans) Hurry up.
makhwaya —	(Hybrid) Formal choral singing. From the English 'choir'
Malmesbury brogue —	Accent of people from the Malmesbury area, characterized by a soft rolling of the 'r'.
mchocholozeni —	(Tsonga) Push him.
mealie —	(S.A. English) Corn.
moffie —	(slang) Queer.
morgen —	(S.A. English) An area of land, about two acres.

GLOSSARY

muchongolo —	(Tsonga) Tribal dance.
naai —	(Afrikaans) Screw, screwing.
NCO —	(acronym) Non-Commissioned Officer.
Nguni —	(Zulu) Zulu, Xhosa or Swazi people or language.
nkoncana —	(Tsonga; slang) 'Wife'. Used with specific reference to the young mineworkers. See also *tinkoncana* (plural).
ou —	(Afrikaans) Bloke.
ouens —	(Afrikaans) Blokes.
pandiete —	(Afrikaans) Convicts; properly *bandiete*.
Parabats —	Paratroopers; contraction of Parachute Battalion.
plattelanders —	(Afrikaans) Country people, yokels.
pomp —	(Afrikaans slang) Screw. Literally means 'pump'.
putu —	(Xhosa; Zulu) Meal made of maize.
rand —	The currency used in South Africa.
red blanket people —	Tribal Africans who hold traditional beliefs in the ancestors, so called because they use red clay on their bodies and blankets.
SABC —	(acronym) South African Broadcasting Corporation.
SACP —	(acronym) South African Communist party.
shebeen —	(township slang) Establishment selling liquor illicitly.
sisi —	(Zulu) Sister.
sitabane —	(township slang) See *stabane*.
skollie —	(slang) Ruffian.
smaak —	(Afrikaans) Like or enjoy.
Solomon Mahlangu —	An ANC guerilla who was captured and executed. An ANC school in Tanzania was named after him.
SPCA —	(acronym) Society for the Prevention of Cruelty to Animals.
spliff —	(slang) Marijuana cigarette or joint.
stabane —	(township slang) Queer, but literally understood to mean 'hermaphrodite'.
the States —	(army slang) Used on the border to refer to South Africa, 'home'.
stoep —	(Afrikaans and S.A. English) Veranda.
stokvel —	(slang) A syndicate or club which raises money by selling food and liquor at parties held at the homes of the members.
thothotho —	(Tsonga; slang) Illegally made brew. Euphemistic name adopted to confuse the police.
tihove —	(Tsonga) Boiled meal.
timbila —	(Tsonga) Xylophone.
tinkoncana —	(Tsonga; slang) 'The wives'. Young males adopted on the mines as concubines for older miners.

Glossary

tokoloshe —	(Zulu) An evil spirit.
tune —	(slang) Speak to, tell.
umgwaja —	(Zulu; slang) Barbarian. Yellow oilskin worn underground.
umlungu —	(Xhosa; Zulu) White man.
umsebenzi —	(Xhosa; Zulu) Workers.
umthetho —	(Xhosa; Zulu) Rule, law, norm, proper procedure.
Vaal Triangle —	Farming and mining area in the north-east of the country.
Vambo —	(army slang) The Ovambo people.
Verwoerd, Hendrik —	Prime Minister of South Africa; assassinated in 1966, at the height of his power. Commonly known as the 'Architect of Apartheid'.
Witwatersrand —	Densely populated gold-mining region around Johannesburg.
xibonda —	(Tsonga) The room representative elected by the miners themselves.
xigugu —	(Tsonga) Food made of peanuts and meal.

Notes on Contributors

WENDY ANNECKE is an educator at the University of Natal. She is currently engaged in researching and producing materials for newly literate adults. As a member of the Black Sash women's organization she has worked with people in informal settlements threatened with removal, and in particular with the women's group at Canaan, where the contribution to this book originated.

HENNIE AUCAMP, popular and prolific Afrikaans writer. Born in 1934. Best known for his short stories and cabarets. Has published over ten books including *Enkelvlug* (1978), *Volmink* (1981) and *Wat bly oor van soene?* (1986).

KIM BERMAN studied Fine Arts in Johannesburg and in Boston. She then returned to South Africa to work as a Field Officer for the Fund for a Free South Africa. She runs a printmaking studio in Johannesburg, which functions collectively to service the needs of local artists.

TANYA CHAN SAM is a qualified teacher who has taught at schools in Bosmont, Newclare, Eldorado Park and Noordgezigt. She has also been active in the teachers' union SADTU. In 1990 she joined GLOW (Gays and Lesbians of the Witwatersrand) and was elected onto its Executive. In 1991 she became GLOW Co-ordinator, and then Secretary-General in 1992.

GERRY DAVIDSON has spent some thirty years in publishing, design and related fields. She is the publisher of *Exit*, South Africa's only commercially based gay newspaper. She is presently in the process of establishing a new national lesbian magazine, *Quarterly*.

Notes on Contributors

JOHANN DE LANGE was born in 1959. Recipient of the Ingrid Jonker Prize for 1982. Has published five works: *Akwarelle van die dors* (1982); *Waterwoestyn* (1984); *snel grys fantoom* (1986); *Wordende naak* (1990) and the ground-breaking *Nagsweet* (1991).

SHAUN DE WAAL currently works as literary editor of the *Weekly Mail*. In 1989 he was co-editor of the alternative arts magazine *Blits*. His short story 'Stalwart' won second prize in the 1992 Sanlam Literary Award.

SHONA ELDER was born in 1970 and grew up in Benoni. Her poems have appeared in *Jala*, a quarterly journal of the Department of African Literature at the University of the Witwatersrand.

STEPHEN GRAY is a noted critic, literary historian, poet, editor, novelist and playwright. In 1964 he completed a Masters degree in English at Cambridge, and was a member of the Writers' Workshop at the University of Iowa. Since 1969 he has lived and worked in Johannesburg. His previous novels include *Born of Man* and *War Child*.

JOAN HAMBIDGE is a well-known Afrikaans poet. She has published *Geslote baan* (1988), *Donker labirint* (1989) and *Kriptonemie* (1989). She is currently a lecturer in Afrikaans at the University of Cape Town.

MATTHEW KROUSE has worked mostly in the theatre in Johannesburg. Plays he has co-written include *Famous Dead Man* (1986), *Sunrise City* (1988) and *Score Me the Ages* (1989). He co-wrote the feature film *Shot Down* (1986) and two short films, *De Voortrekkers* (1987) and *The Soldier* (1989). Much of his work in film and theatre has been, and remains, banned by the State censors. His articles, poems and stories have appeared in local magazines, and in the poetry anthology *Essential Things* (1992).

DAVID LAN, born in Cape Town in 1952, has lived in England since 1972. He has written a study of the liberation struggle in Zimbabwe, *Guns and Rain: Guerillas and Spirit Mediums in Zimbabwe*, a number of plays including *Flight* and *Desire*, as well as films, including *The Sunday Judge* and *Dark City*.

NOTES ON CONTRIBUTORS

LUCAS MALAN was born in 1946. He established himself as an important voice in poetry in the eighties, and has published *'n Bark vir die Ontheemdes* (1981), *Tydspoor* (1985) and *Edenboom* (1987).

MAMAKI is the pseudonym of a scholar who was born in Soweto in 1974. She is currently doing her matric at a technical college, and at the same time studying for a career as an electrical technician.

BRENT MEERSMAN was born in the Cape and lived in Belgium as a child. He returned to South Africa and later studied English and Philosophy. He currently works for the hotel industry in the Cape Province.

JOHANNES MEINTJES (1923-1980) Deceased artist and author. Published thirty five books in Afrikaans and English, including works of fiction and historical biographies. Recipient of a number of literary awards. By the time of his death, Meintjes had produced more than 1300 oil paintings, dozens of sculptures and hundreds of graphic works.

JEROME MORRISON was born in 1967 and raised in Athlone in the Cape. He has a diploma from Hotel School and works mostly in restaurants. His stories have appeared in *Vrye Weekblad* and *Staffrider* Magazine.

MARCELLUS MUTHIEN, a black South African activist, was born in 1963 in Plumstead and grew up in the Cape townships. He studied in the Western Cape and during this time was forced into exile. He studied in Italy where 'the racism was rife', and, as a British Defence and Aid Fund student, he trained as a clinical psychologist in London. He has published poems in the British gay anthology, *Take Any Train* (1990) and the *James White Review*.

VIVIENNE NDATSHE is an ex-teacher now working as a domestic servant in Durban. She grew up in the Lusikisiki district in the Transkei. Her father was a migrant who worked on the mines.

SIMON NKOLI was born in 1957 in Soweto and schooled on a farm in the Orange Free State. Nkoli is a major gay activist and currently an Aids educator. Nkoli, who was one of the defendants in the Delmas Treason Trial, was a founder-member of GLOW. He now works for TAP (Township Aids Project) as a counsellor.

Notes on Contributors

WELMA ODENDAAL published her first volume of short stories, *Getuie vir die naaktes*, in 1974. Her second volume, *Keerkring*, was published in 1977 and was banned two months later. The book was banned for eight years and all copies were pulped by the publisher. Her latest volume, *Verlate plekke*, was published in 1991. She was a founder-member of the literary magazine *Donga* in 1976. The magazine was closed down by the State in 1978. She currently works as editor and trainer for the community newspaper *Namaquanuus*, in Springbok, and is involved in freelance book design and editing.

JAY PATHER, dancer and actor, was born and schooled in Durban. He studied Theatre at Durban Westville University and Trinity College, UK. He also has an M.A. from New York University. He has lectured at the Universities of Zululand and Durban Westville. He performs for Jazz-Art Dance Group and New African Theatre Project. His articles have appeared in *Dance Journal* of the Dance Alliance and *Staffrider*.

KOOS PRINSLOO, born in 1957 in Kenya, came to South Africa with his parents in 1962. After school and military training he studied Afrikaans at the University of Pretoria. He made his debut with a collection of short stories, *Jonkmanskas* (1982), and followed it up with *Die hemel help ons* (1988) and *Slagplaas* (1993). Currently working as a journalist in Johannesburg.

DEE RADCLIFFE (pseudonym of Lee Randall) studied Occupational Therapy at the University of the Witwatersrand. Then studied for a Masters degree at Tufts University in Boston. Currently works as a researcher and facilitator for the disabled. Her articles have appeared in the journal *Critical Health* and in *Exit* newspaper.

GRAEME REID works as a human rights lawyer at PLANACT, an NGO providing technical advice and assistance to civic associations and trade unions on housing, local government restructuring and development issues. Publications he has appeared in include a report published by the Washington-based National Coalition for the Homeless on the failure of the United States to ratify the Convention on Economic, Social and Cultural Rights. More recently he co-wrote an article on political negotiations with William Cobbett, published in *Southern African Review 6*. He is Treasurer of GLOW.

ALAN REYNOLDS studied Social Science at the University of Natal. Thereafter he worked as a journalist for the Institute for Black Research based at the University of Natal. Today he works for the Natal Centre for Industrial and Labour Studies.

RICHARD RIVE (1931-1989) One of the most distinguished voices in black South African literature. He graduated from the University of Cape Town and Columbia University, and earned a doctorate from Oxford University. Richard Rive was tragically murdered in his home in Cape Town just two weeks after completing his novel *Emergency Continued*.

MPANDE WA SIBUYI was born in 1966 in Namakgale near Phalaborwa. He attended primary school in Namakgale, then boarding school in Tzaneen for matric. He went to the University of the Witwatersrand in 1984 where he studied Sociology and Politics, and then left to work as a high-school teacher in Namakgale for a year. In 1986 he attended the University of Cape Town as a Social Science student. Graduated in 1988, and went on to study Law.

ROSALEE TELELA was born in 1968. She schooled in Soweto amidst class boycotts and the political turmoils of the eighties. After a short spell at university she joined the *Weekly Mail* newspaper as a reporter. She is an active member of the GLOW Lesbian Forum.

ADRIAN VAN DEN BERG was born in 1967 in Pretoria. He is presently a student of Cultural Anthropology at Rand Afrikaans University. His writing has appeared in student newspapers and in an alternative magazine called *Absurd*.

ERNST VAN HEERDEN, noted Afrikaans critic, travel writer and autobiographer. Best known as a poet. First work published in 1942. He has published over ten volumes of poetry including *Kanse op 'n wrak* (1982), *Die swart skip* (1985), *Amulet teen die vuur* (1987) and *Najaarswys* (1993).

MIKKI VAN ZYL holds a Masters degree in Philosophy from the University of Cape Town where she has done research for the departments of Sociology and Criminology. She has also co-ordinated various surveys on violence against women. Her writing has appeared in the journals *Agenda*, *Work in Progress* and *Mayibuye*. She co-edited an issue of *Critical Arts*

Notes on Contributors

titled 'Women Represented' and was production editor of the book *Now Everyone is Afraid*. She is currently the co-ordinator of the WILD-FIRE group (Women in Law and Development for Feminist Resources and Education).

KAREN WILLIAMS is the arts editor of Cape Town's progressive weekly newspaper *South*.

A Leading Lesbian Memoir:

Pat Arrowsmith
I SHOULD HAVE BEEN A HORNBY TRAIN
A leading peace campaigner from the 1950s through to the Gulf War, and renowned for her direct action initiatives, Pat Arrowsmith has never hidden her lesbianism, which surfaces in both her poetry and fiction. In the 1980s GMP/Heretic Books published *Jericho*, her novel of the early peace camps, and *Somewhere Like This*, set in London's Holloway prison. *I Should Have Been a Hornby Train* is an original memoir, the story of a headstrong girl growing up in a seaside vicarage in the 1930s, still almost Victorian in its cocooned world. Drawing on her diaries and juvenilia, she charts a journey through boarding-school crushes to rebellion and expulsion against the background of the Second World War.

ISBN 0 85449 190 2
£7.95 US $12.95 AUS $19.95; illustrated

Discover a gay planet!

João S. Trevisan
PERVERTS IN PARADISE
A path-breaking study on the past and present of homosexuality in Brazil, from voodoo priests to guevarist revolutionaries.
"Thoughtful, informative, and highly entertaining" — *Gay Times*
ISBN 0 907040 78 0 *illustrated*
£6.95 US $9.95 AUS $17.95

Tsuneo Watanabe and Jun'ichi Iwata
THE LOVE OF THE SAMURAI
An intriguing and lavishly illustrated study that examines a thousand years of homosexuality in Japanese society, from kabuki theatre and Buddhist monasteries to the samurai philosophy of boy-love.
"An essential work for the overall picture of the history of homosexuality" — *Washington Blade*
ISBN 0 85449 115 5 *hardback*
£12.95 US $19.95 AUS $29.95

Tobias Schneebaum
KEEP THE RIVER ON YOUR RIGHT
This American artist and writer lovingly and dramatically recalls his life among the Akaramas, a primitive Peruvian tribe, their initiation ceremonies, homosexual friendships, and head-hunting expeditions.
"As a unique corner of anthropology or a kind of erotic *Jungle Book* it is gripping stuff" — *Gay Times*
ISBN 0 85449 061 2
£5.95 AUS $14.95 *not available in USA*

Gay Men's Press books can be ordered from any bookshop in the UK, and from specialised bookshops overseas.

If you prefer to order by mail, please send cheque/ postal order (payable to *Book Works*) for the full retail price plus £2.00 for postage and packing to:

Book Works (Dept. B), PO Box 3821, London N5 1UY
phone/ fax: (0171) 609 3427

For payment by Access/Eurocard/Mastercard/American Express/Visa, please give number, expiry date and signature.

Name and Address in block letters please:

Name
_____

Address
_____

_____

_____